Where Have All the Animals Gone?

Where Have All the Animals Gone?

My Travels with Karl Ammann

DALE PETERSON

Bauhan Publishing
Peterborough, New Hampshire
2015

Text ©2015 Dale Peterson
Afterword ©2015 Karl Ammann

Library of Congress Cataloging-in-Publication Data

Peterson, Dale, author.
 Where have all the animals gone? : my travels with Karl Ammann / by
Dale Peterson ; with an afterword by Karl Ammann.
    pages cm
 ISBN 978-0-87233-208-9
 1. Wildlife conservation--Africa. 2. Wildlife conservation--Asia.
 3. Wildlife as food--Africa, Central. 4. Elephants--Africa. 5. Elephants--
Asia. 6. Giraffe--Africa. I. Ammann, Karl, writer of afterword. II. Title.
 QL84.6.A1.P48 2015
 333.954096--dc23
                          2015036279

Book design by Kirsty Anderson
Typeset in Arno Pro
Cover design by Henry James
Cover photograph by Karl Ammann
Frontispiece photograph of Karl Ammann by the author
Printed by Versa Press

To contact Dale Peterson: www.dalepetersonauthor.com

BAUHAN
PUBLISHING LLC
PO BOX 117 PETERBOROUGH NEW HAMPSHIRE 03458
               603-567-4430
WWW.BAUHANPUBLISHING.COM

Manufactured in the United States of America

Contents

✳ PART I

1: TOTAL CHOKE

Kathy drops us off at the entrance to the Muthaiga Club, where Karl and I toss our bags and ourselves into the back compartment of a boxy black London taxi.

Karl is telling me about the girlie magazines he buys for their adopted son, who is on the verge of adolescence. Karl buys a variety of these magazines—Playboy, Penthouse, and the like—every time he comes to Nairobi. Their adopted son is a chimpanzee, I should mention, but as a result of living among people for most of his life, he has become attached to the human form and is now sexually obsessed by the feminine version of it.

The thing is, Karl continues, Mzee is discriminating. Not just any naked woman in any provocative twist will do. He gets specific obsessions about specific women, or at least their two-dimensional representations. What is this hormone-challenged teenager looking for? Nothing Karl can figure out. Sometimes Mzee latches on to a blonde, sometimes a redhead or a brunette. She could be dark-skinned, light, brown, pink. She might be displaying herself from the front, back, or upside down, right side up, inside out. No obvious pattern to his desire, but the ape knows it when he sees it. He rips out the pictures of his favorite nude women and carries them around with him for days.

I'm listening to Karl tell this story and looking out the window as Nairobi passes by. It's still very early in the morning, and Nairobi presents the chaotic scene of a big city waking up, of dust and people—plus honking cars and diesel-spewing trucks and overloaded matatus artistically detailed and decaled with titles and slogans—and we turn this way and that, pass through intricate streets and into slums, with garbage and rubble and shacks hammered out of spare tin.

"Over there is UNEP," Karl points out—and I glimpse a sign with the acronym extended orthographically to embrace the full concept: United Nations Environment Programme. "They're supposed to save the world. All they do is fart around and play golf."

Karl's mustache looks accidentally placed, and his face briefly twists into a squint of concentrated irritation when he says this. I laugh at the odd image: farting golfers.

But back to Mzee's nudes. They get rained on and turn to mush, Karl says. Mzee persists in keeping them around, though, even as they dissolve, and so Karl has been trying to sneak them away. But Mzee has figured this one out. He waits for Karl at the exit of his enclosure and, with a beggar's insistent, outstretched hand, implores that the pictures be returned. And now, more recently, he has taken to storing the nudes high up in his tree nest, where Karl can't get to them. It's like an art gallery up there.

It's morning rush hour now, and we join a small river of traffic that, at one point, begins slowing down and moving into a roundabout like water draining from a bathtub. Karl is still talking when, as the traffic slows at the edges of this whirlpool, I look up to see brake lights turn red ahead of us and, just beyond them, at the center of the roundabout, a car stopped, a door opened.

A woman, a South Asian dressed in a bright blue sari, is standing outside the car. It's a fight. People are getting out of the car. A man is hitting her. No. He's pulling at her purse, hung on a strap around her shoulder. He's robbing her. It's a robbery . . . and carjacking.

"Stop!" I say to the taxi driver, but he either doesn't hear or ignores me, still moving deeper into the coagulating traffic before us. Too busy driving. Not looking ahead. Now I see the AK-47. Man in a dark overcoat, his back to the stopped car. He levels his gun at the traffic circling around him as we continue to move in closer. Another man points a dark pistol at someone inside the car. Are those bodies on the ground? Yes!

"Stop!" I repeat. "Stop! Stop!"

✳

I first met Karl about ten years earlier, in the middle of what was then Zaire. Now it's the Democratic Republic of the Congo, or DRC. I had gone there with anthropologist Richard Wrangham to find some apes called bonobos. People used to call them pygmy chimpanzees. They do look rather like chimps, but their imaginative sex lives along with other habits and inclinations place bonobos in another universe from chimps.

Wrangham and I were on our way to the village of Wamba, where it was possible to find bonobos for at least two reasons. First, the people of that region, the Mongandu, maintained a cultural taboo against hunting or eating bonobos, so that, unlike in many other parts of Zaire, the apes were still alive and not completely terrified of the human ape. The second reason was that a team of Japanese primatologists, led by Takayoshi Kano of Kyoto University, had been studying the apes at Wamba for several years.

Professor Kano kept a daily watch on the bonobos, and his work made it possible for the occasional distinguished visitor such as Richard Wrangham, and sometimes an undistinguished one such as me, to see them. Karl Ammann was at Wamba, too, justifying his presence in the Japanese operation as a photographer and general resource.

The photographer part was obvious. He carried a camera. He put the camera in front of his face. He pressed a button on the camera. The general resource part will take longer to explain, but it begins with the fact that Karl, being Swiss, speaks several European languages, which is useful. Then there's the fact that, after he graduated from the School of Hotel Management at Cornell, Karl took a series of hotel managerial jobs in Africa. That career encouraged him to develop practical skills, such as dealing with difficult people, arranging travel itineraries to difficult places, fixing broken machinery under difficult circumstances, and so on. In practical ways, then, Karl was able to make himself useful at Wamba, and in return he was allowed to photograph the remarkable apes.

I started to recognize the practical side of Karl on the day Wrangham and I arrived in the middle of nowhere. A few minutes after a missionary pilot passed through a hole in the clouds and deposited us at a makeshift airstrip, our passports were confiscated and our bodies taken in custody by the airstrip troll: a tall, lean, aggressive troll with a big hat who called himself the Commissaire. After being escorted to the Commissaire's bungalow, Wrangham and I were surrounded by a dozen enforcers and onlookers, and then someone began writing down, in French, the taxes we would be required to pay in American money before we could get our passports and freedom back. The taxes—for entry, exit, processing, tourism, culture, art, flying on an airplane, and so on—had added up to several hundred dollars by the time Karl Ammann showed up, riding in a Land Rover owned by the local Catholic mission and driven by a mission worker.

Karl had flown in a few days earlier, at a moment when the troll was away somewhere, so he had not paid his taxes either. He declared that he would do just that, but since he had brought no money with him, the Commissaire would be required to travel with us back to the village of Wamba.

The distance from the airstrip and the Commissaire's place to the village of Wamba may have been only about forty miles, but the road was a sketchy track intersected by gullies, streams, and small rivers, with all the bridges washed out. The Land Rover carried its own supply of enormous planks, which at each washed-out bridge crossing were pulled out and placed over whatever remained of a supporting structure. Then slowly, with all the passengers out and watching, pushing, or pulling when necessary, the vehicle was driven over the planks until it reached the other side, at which point the planks were drawn up and the passengers climbed back in.

It was late in the evening by the time the Land Rover rolled into Wamba, where we took shelter inside Takayoshi Kano's dirt-floor, mud-brick, tin-roof house. We were welcomed, seated at a wooden table, offered something to drink. Tea, as I recall.

Having brought the four of us there, the mission driver quickly departed, returning the Land Rover to the mission, which was several miles back up the road . . . and thus began Step One in Karl's grand plan for dealing with the thieving Commissaire. Step One: How would he get back home?

Step Two was the Disputatious Negotiation. The Commissaire was adamant about the taxes owed him and the necessity of foreigners paying in American dollars—a few classical themes, really, all expressed in French and angrily repeated, with rococo variations, for the next three or four hours. The repetitiousness of his angry assertions was tiresome, but Karl kept after him, arguing point by point, responding again and again with his own rococo responses.

Meanwhile, the ingredients for Step Three were gathering. Wamba was an ordinary and therefore very impoverished Zairean village. Almost everyone was dressed in rags. No one could afford shoes. Communication with the outside world was generally limited to pounding on hollowed-out log drums. In short, the arrival of Kano's guests, along with the tall, wiry, big-hatted Commissaire, was genuine entertainment for this village of two or three hundred households. Enough entertainment to provoke a milling crowd outside Kano's house, as the epic argument between Karl and the Commissaire over the subject of imaginary "taxes" continued late into the night. The entire village was dark, except for a fire here and there, a few burning candles—and in Kano's house alone, a single electric light bulb. Kano had brought in a solar panel and some batteries, which gave his mud house the unique luxury of a dribble of electricity: sufficient to provide theatrical lighting for the argument. Step Three, in short, was the assembling of a big audience for a night's spontaneous entertainment . . . while Step Four was the subject of money.

Money! The people of Wamba lived a subsistence life. Gardening. Hunting. Some market trade with neighboring villages. Professor Kano was the principal source of cash income for Wamba, since he bought food and hired assistants and trackers from among the villages. But Kano himself lived frugally, and the Commissaire was now, as the argument continued late into the night, talking about his right to take from us sums of money beyond what anyone in the village could imagine earning in a year. Or perhaps a lifetime.

Step Five came at some time after midnight, when the two principal antagonists in this drama were forced by exhaustion to conclude their Disputatious Negotiation. The Commissaire returned the passports to Wrangham and me, while we handed to him some American dollars. Then Karl rummaged into his own pack, pulled out an enormous stack of Zaires—the nation's debased currency—worth perhaps forty dollars, and slammed it onto the table in front of the Commissaire, saying: "This is all I have! You can take it all!"

As the Commissaire gathered up this huge pile of paper money, Karl turned and said to the villagers who were still crowded tightly around: "That's your money. That was going to you, but, as you can see, your Commissaire thinks he can take it all for himself."

I'm not sure what step that was, but as the unpleasant Commissaire raised himself up from the table, placed his hat on his head, gathered all the money into his arms, and prepared to leave, I thought I detected, in his face and posture, a lurking concern about whether he would be able to summon the nerve to push his way forward. I heard an angry murmuring. I saw the restless crowd pressing in. But the Commissaire drew himself up tall, stared straight ahead, elbowed his way out of Kano's house and the villagers around it, and strode down the road and into the black night. He was followed by a dwindling gang of diehard hecklers and grumblers, who eventually gave up and returned to their own mud-brick houses, while the object of their enmity continued down the road and out of the village, furiously embracing his bundle of booty.

With great fatigue and some genuine desperation the Commissaire showed up at the Catholic mission early the next morning, still clutching his money. (This bit we later learned from Father Pierre, who ran the mission.) The Commissaire had many more miles to go, of course, and he begged for permission to rent the mission's Land Rover. Father Pierre eventually agreed to rent it, but he required the entire bundle of Zaires, while petrol sufficient to cover the trip cost at least a third of the American dollars Richard Wrangham and I had handed over.

※

Karl and I spent some minor social time together at Wamba—evenings over dinner and drinks at the Kano house, some days watching (and photographing) the bonobos or watching (and photographing) the Japanese watching the bonobos, other days being guided into the forests to find (and photograph) more bonobos or walking through the village to speak with (and photograph) people meeting, children swimming, hunters hunting, and so on.

I returned home to the United States then and, over the next few years, would hear from him occasionally—a letter, a random meeting in New York or Boston, e-mail once the Internet was working—mostly about this or that enthusiasm or project he was working on as a photographer. We briefly talked about producing a book together. His photos. My text. The life story of Takayoshi Kano, our host at Wamba: a remarkable person who, as a young man, had walked and bicycled all over Zaire searching for the bonobos, and who, as a mature man, was the first person to study them. That book project never sprouted wings, and in any case I was busy with other things.

※

One day I received an envelope in the mail, Kenyan stamps and postmark on it, containing a lock of straight, blackish or black-and-white hair and a note from Karl saying that he thought it was gorilla hair and would I please store it in a freezer until he could locate someone willing to analyze the DNA. The hair stayed in my refrigerator's freezer for some time until it wasn't there anymore. It disappeared. Did someone mistake the hair for an exotic condiment and sprinkle it over my fried potatoes? I have no idea. I don't know what happened to it.

The hair business began after Karl read a magazine article about "The Lost Gorillas of Bondo." According to this article, a European missionary or entrepreneur had, around the start of the twentieth century, found three skulls and a jawbone from four gorillas right in the middle of Africa—at a place called Djabbir (now, probably, Bondo, in the Democratic Republic of the Congo)—and mailed them off to the famous Congo Museum in Tervuren, Belgium. The skulls and jaw remained in storage for around twenty years, until in 1927 an expert named Henri Schouteden pulled them out.

They were gorilla skulls, all right, but what had they been doing in the middle of Africa? Even back in 1927, every expert on the subject was utterly convinced that no gorillas lived there. Gorillas were supposed to be separated into eastern and western subspecies (or species) by a 750-mile gorilla-less gap in the middle. Reason for the gap: an ancient drying-out period when the forests receded and the forest apes along with them. So how was it possible to find gorilla skulls in the gap where gorillas were not? More to the point, if the skulls actually came from that part of Africa, they would probably be from gorillas who had evolved separately from the eastern and western gorilla populations for a long time. A million years, maybe much longer. They would therefore belong to a new gorilla type, a new subspecies. Henri Schouteden named this possible new subspecies *Gorilla gorilla uellensis*.

The last part of that name refers to the general region where the specimens came from, which is bordered on the south by the Uélé River.

Karl persuaded a pilot to fly him and a couple of friends out to the settlement of Bondo where there was an old Catholic mission and a landing strip. Borrowing the mission's four-wheel-drive vehicle, Karl and his friends traveled north on a rutted road toward the border with the Central African Republic, stopping at villages along the way and quizzing local hunters, showing them ape photographs, trying to assess their knowledge, and asking them if they had any old ape skulls lying around. Eventually, Karl found a hunter who could correctly identify the apes in their picture collection. The hunter then declared that when he had lived near Bili, a settlement some 200 kilometers east of Bondo, he had on three occasions seen gorillas there, foraging at the edge of the forest in some savanna patches.

Karl and his friends set off for Bili, where they met other hunters who spoke of toting very large carcasses: "It took three men to carry that body!" However, when confronted with the picture material, most were unable to distinguish chimps from gorillas. Some half a dozen chimpanzee skulls were brought out for Karl to examine in Bili: none large enough to suggest gorillas. But the next day, as Karl and friends paused in the middle of a village on their return trip to Bondo, a hunter came up to the car with a skull in each hand. Both skulls looked and smelled as if they had just been excavated from a pile of garbage. One skull, however, had a gorilla-like crest, and it seemed bigger and altogether quite different from the other. Had Karl found proof that the mysterious *Gorilla gorilla uellensis* was still alive?

Karl mailed me a plaster cast of the skull in question. It was about the size of a chimpanzee skull, I thought, although it had a bony peak or crest running along the top, a so-called *sagittal crest*, which is characteristic of gorilla skulls. . . .

But then Zaire turned into the Congo and disintegrated into the chaos of a brutal civil war involving eight African nations and twenty-five separate armed groups. By the time Karl thought it was safe enough to pick up the search for gorillas again, the region was controlled by one of the rebel warlords, a man named Jean-Pierre Bemba. So Karl flew out to a town in the Central African Republic where he met up with an armed contingent of Bemba's rebels, who took him by dugout canoe across the Ubangui River into the Congo and by foot on to Bemba's headquarters.

Bemba did not believe anyone in his right mind, even a crazy white person, would want to stumble through the rain forest looking for "monkeys," and he was anxious about spies with global positioning systems. Was Karl animated by some other motive? Karl assured the rebel leader that he was not prospecting for diamonds, and he showed Bemba a copy of a photo book he had recently done on gorillas. After leafing through the book, Bemba gave permission to proceed. As a parting gift, Karl gave the rebel warlord an expensive satellite telephone.

The telephone would be useful to Bemba, obviously, but it also provided Karl with the man's phone number, so that whenever a small-plane flight into the landing strip at Bili was chartered, Karl could ring him up to make sure the plane wasn't shot down.

By the end of 1998, things had settled down enough that Karl sent Joseph Melloh, a recently retired gorilla hunter from Cameroon, out to Bili to look for signs of gorillas. Joseph the gorilla hunter—about whom more will be said later on—spent three weeks in the area following up local rumors. Perhaps his most promising find was an ape nest built on the ground, which Joseph thought had been made by a male gorilla. Chimpanzees build their sleeping nests in the trees. Gorillas construct ground nests.

In 1999, Karl hired a local tracker to search for more evidence of gorillas. The tracker was provided with a video camera to document anything he found, and he worked with several area hunters. In October of that year, Karl received a radio call from the tracker, telling of the discovery of ground nests as well as ape handprints in the soft ground that looked much bigger than ordinary chimp prints.

When Karl relayed this information to ape expert Esteban Sarmiento at the

Museum of Natural History in New York, Sarmiento responded with several suggestions about distinguishing gorillas from chimps by the size and appearance of hand and foot prints, the size and quality of dung, nest texture and size, and hair length and color. "Hairs greater than six centimeters in length are more than likely from gorillas," he wrote. "If any of these hairs are pure silver (white), or white striped with black, it is definitely a gorilla. If you are unable to find any hairs longer than five centimeters in any of the nests you have chimpanzees." Sarmiento also suggested that pigment bands—for example, alternating bands of white and brown—on the hair would very strongly suggest gorillas.

Then Karl's tracker found another set of ground nests in a river swamp. There were fresh foot and hand prints of unusually large dimensions—and from two of the nests the man retrieved gray and black hairs that measured eight to ten centimeters long. It was exciting news. Karl flew down to Bangassou in the Central African Republic, rendezvoused with the tracker, who had come up from Bili, and thus acquired several good samples of the mystery hair. He mailed samples out to a half dozen contacts in the United States and Europe.

That's where the hair in my freezer came from. Another lock of hair landed in the hands of Esteban Sarmiento at the Museum of Natural History. Karl flew to New York one day. I took a train down from Boston. And so we both talked with Esteban at the museum.

I remember long corridors and old-fashioned wooden lockers and drawers and shelves containing samples of just about every kind of creature imaginable, and we came to a room, or very large closet, holding the hairy skins taken from all the apes except humans: pelts, in other words, from orangutans, bonobos, chimpanzees, and gorillas. It was like a small but very exclusive Park Avenue fur-coat store. Esteban pulled out a large sample of gorilla skin and another of chimpanzee skin, and then he had me comb through them and look closely at the individual hairs. The hairs of the two ape types looked very different, and Esteban said he strongly suspected that the sample Karl had given him came from a gorilla.

A few days later, Karl sent me a copy of Esteban's report, in which the expert declared with a signed flourish his professional conviction that the hairs Karl sent were from a gorilla: "It is clear some of the hairs in there belong to gorillas. I will cast them, but from what I saw I doubt the cast will change my mind. So you definitely have some GORILLA hairs!! . . . MEANING GORILLA UELLENSIS EXISTS!!!!" After further tests, Esteban sent an even more compelling assessment: "On microscopic inspection two of the hairs had the diagnostic scale pattern seen in gorillas which is not seen in chimpanzees. As such I have no doubts that these are not chimpanzees and belong to a gorilla or to an animal closely allied to gorillas."

It was great news. Then there were the photographs. Karl had set up remote cameras with infrared triggers: game cameras that would take pictures of any animal walking in front of them, day or night. In that fashion, he acquired photographs of some creeping-about apes who looked very dark (like gorillas) and very big (like gorillas). But how big? It was hard to know, since nothing else in the picture provided a decent comparison for estimating size.

Karl next persuaded a handful from among the best experts in the world to fly out to this very area and determine for themselves: chimps or gorillas? Swiss TV paid for the charter flight, and along with the celebrity scientists came an American National Public Radio crew with fancy microphones to report on this expedition into the wilds of Africa. I listened to some of those ghostly, breathless, from-deep-in-the-Congo reports on NPR and found myself wishing I had been invited.

Obviously, a person can't just drop dreamily into a rain forest and find gorillas or chimps or any other kind of non-human ape. The forests are hard to get around in. For people. Not for chimps or gorillas. They hear or see or smell you before you hear or see or smell them. They know you're there, and then they've vanished, deconstructed themselves without even a leaf left fluttering, before you knew they were there. So no one in the expedition ever expected to see any of these elusive apes directly, but the experts might know who was there by other means. One way would be to look for gorilla foods. If none of the usual plants gorillas live on could be found, then it would be reasonable to conclude there were also no gorillas. That, in fact, was the conclusion of the expedition's ape foods expert. No gorilla food, *ipso facto* no gorillas.

DNA analysis of the hair took a long time because the samples Karl sent to laboratories in the United States were all confiscated by the Fish and Wildlife Service, which considered the hair, as body parts of an endangered species, contraband. Karl had gotten official permission to export the hair from Jean-Pierre Bemba, whose army actually possessed the area in question, but he wasn't able to get an equivalent permission from the government of Congo, which still claimed legal control of the area. Meanwhile, the law was complicated enough in the United States that the hair locks were illegal if they came from chimpanzees or gorillas but not if they came from, say, baboons or hyenas. And who knew the origins of that hair? Maybe it *had* come from baboons or hyenas. The source was unknown, which in Karl's opinion made it legal—or at least not illegal. Karl asked US Fish and Wildlife to use their own DNA laboratories to determine what species the hair came from. He only needed the results, not the hair. . . .

Eventually, someone made the genetic assessments, and they agreed conclusively with the opinion of the food expert. The mystery apes were chimpanzees, not gorillas.

⁂

Oddly, while the DNA identified the hair as coming from a perfectly well-known, ordinary chimp subspecies, people who observed the actual chimps thought they were not ordinary at all. Yes, Western researchers later brought in by Karl eventually began sighting them, and they agreed that the chimps were unusually big. Some people began speaking of them as Big Chimps. That could explain the large hand and foot prints, the big skulls, unusually long hairs, and why they were building their nests on the ground rather than in the trees. Maybe the chimps were just too heavy to sleep in the trees, unlike their smaller brethren elsewhere.

In that sense, they were special chimps. Karl thought they were also special because there could be a lot of them. At a time when ape habitat was being destroyed across Africa, this area, in a still remote and unexploited region of rain forest, could contain a large cache of chimps.

Two more things about the area. First, it included a large piece of forest that had been legally designated by the central government as a faunal reserve, with hunting forbidden by law, and the reserve was surrounded by other large blocks of forest designated as sport hunting reserves, with licensed hunting only for trophies. Such laws had little effect on what people actually did out in the boondocks, but—and this is the second thing—people's behavior was not too much of a concern if only because there were not so many people. The region was unusually underpopulated with people and therefore might be unusually populated with apes and other wildlife.

Why couldn't someone move in and, before it was too late, help preserve this area with its newly discovered Big Chimps? Karl spoke to some well-placed people in some big conservation organizations and concluded that no one wanted to get involved. Too far away. Too hard to get to. Too hard to survive in. Who would want to set up a conservation program in the middle of nowhere? As he was told by one prominent conservation executive, it would cost a quarter of a million dollars a year just to place a single person out there: considering salary at an American level, health insurance, retirement pay, vacation time, transportation to get there, Land Rover to get around in, decent place to live while out in the field, food, clothing, et cetera.

So Karl set up his own project. He made friends with some of the missionaries in Bili. He hired a few assistants. He brought in a couple of young scientists to study the Big Chimps, and he developed a relationship with several of the local chiefs. This region was mainly inhabited by the Azande people, and the traditional Azande chiefs, rather than the big-city suits in Kinshasa and elsewhere, had much of the real authority.

How to finance such a project? Karl developed a working relationship with someone who had made a fortune bringing an American-based fast-food hamburger franchise into a European country. A tax accountant had advised this successful businessman that his fortune could be nurtured judiciously if some portion were legally sequestered as a conservation NGO with an ongoing project in the Congo. That's how Karl got the funding to support his chimp project.

Only now it was chimps and elephants, and the deal with the local Azande chiefs was that Karl and his partner would encourage the reintroduction of coffee as a cash crop (after a long period of cash-crop neglect), then export it to Europe and market it as a green product under the promising label Elephant Coffee. That did happen. At least part of it. People in the region began growing coffee once more. Karl and his partner flew in a few hundred bicycles, which became the means of transporting the coffee along dirt tracks north, into the Central African Republic, where it would then be flown out to markets in Europe. In return for the Elephant Coffee deal, the Azande chiefs agreed that no one would hunt elephants or chimps in the region, which, after all, simply reinforced federal laws already on the books. It seemed like a good idea: community-based conservation, where everyone wins.

The rise and fall of Elephant Coffee is a story too complicated to pursue in any more detail here. In any event, the fall of it had not yet begun by the time Karl and I were riding in that taxi in Nairobi, headed to the airport but getting trapped in the gathering traffic of a roundabout and coming into the range and sights of an AK-47 in the hands of a carjacking thug.

✳

I had been in touch with Karl during the gorilla-hair-in-the-freezer years partly because he was encouraging me to write a book about *The Lost Gorillas of Bondo.* When the gorillas turned out to be Big Chimps, we talked about my writing something about them. When the Elephant Coffee project began, we tentatively discussed a book on that subject.

Those were all interesting ideas for a writer, possibly, but I was still occupied and preoccupied with other projects. In the meantime, however, Karl had become involved in yet another matter that did, at last, hoist me by my own collar and drag me back to Africa. I'm not sure exactly when this other matter actually began, although it's fair to say it started before Karl and I first met that time at Takayoshi Kano's research site in Wamba. The project developed in stages, I suppose, and I only became fully aware of it later in the decade, when Karl, in New York for some reason, began showing me some of his photographs while complaining that no one in the United States had the nerve to publish them.

The photographs were technically excellent, but they were also profoundly shocking. Once, I pulled them out to show to my own editor at a major East Coast publishing house, a wonderful man actually—who immediately refused to look at them. He actually covered his eyes with his hands, as a child might. Would not look at them. I had by then offered to help Karl find a publisher for a book of those photographs, but the fact that my editor instantly refused to expose his optic nerves to a brief excitation from the first of the series was, I thought, a strong hint that finding a publisher would be harder than I had originally hoped.

I'll have more to say about those photographs later on. For now, let me simply describe them as Karl's *bushmeat* photos. Bushmeat. Meat from the bush. Or forest. Wild animal meat. Game meat as food. There's nothing shocking about the idea, and I will hasten to add that, if you've eaten seafood, you've eaten bushmeat. Seafood is a form of wild animal meat. Anyone who has grown up around the sea has, as likely as not, grown up in a culture where seafood is a regular source of protein, where eating seafood in all its impressive variety is commonly accepted. No one I know would be shocked by photographs of seafood. Dead fish. So what? Photographs of dead mammals are a little harder for people to take, and possibly the fact that people are also mammals could have something to do with it.

Karl's photographs were shocking first of all because dead animals are not pretty, and he had treated them as fair photographic subjects. But they were also pictures of dead animals being sold in large quantities as food, and not cleverly disguised and neatly packaged as meat, thereby disconnecting animal from meat. His photographs showed dead animals that were recognizably animals but also obviously meat, and being sold that way.

More disturbing was the fact that some of those dead animals were dead apes. Chimpanzees and gorillas and bonobos. The apes look and are built a lot like humans, so seeing one in a market chopped into smaller pieces is, for many people, uncomfortably reminiscent of seeing another human butchered and up for sale. They look like people because they are, in a genetic and evolutionary sense, our closest living relatives. That's an ethical reason not to eat apes, possibly, but it's also a public health reason. You could have a successful blood transfusion with chimpanzee blood, and that means in turn that you are unusually susceptible to the viruses floating around in a chimpanzee's bloodstream and elsewhere in his body.

But Karl was now claiming, and documenting, that this hunting and eating of apes was also a major conservation problem. With the arrival of European and Asian loggers into the Congo Basin, starting in the late 1980s, opening up the vault of the great African rain forests for the first time in history—the first time ever— the African trade in ape meat had gone commercial. It was no longer a subsistence, small-time, and local activity, but rather had become a non-traditional, big-city activity involving professional hunters, professional transporters, and professional marketers. As a commercial activity, the hunting and consuming of apes was now, Karl declared, and his photographs were starting to document, a major drain on their continued existence: one very significant reason why the great apes are disappearing, going extinct—vanishing!—in our time.

Karl was right, but no one in the United States would give him a soapbox from which tell his tale. He had shown the photos and proposed the story to all the major natural history magazines. They all turned him down, claiming that his pictures were too disturbing. More about all that later. For now, I'll just say that I was moved by the problem enough that I finally told Karl I would help him find a publisher for a book featuring his photographs. As time passed, I agreed to be the author of such a book. And then, at last, we found a publisher and signed a contract to produce the book called *Eating Apes* that would feature Karl's images and my words.

I had become involved at first as a gesture of friendship and solidarity, eventually as someone who passionately believed the topic was important. I had traveled in Africa before, had already been aware of the general subject. I had also, in earlier years, visited some of the same markets and seen more or less the same scenes Karl was showing in the photographs, including the occasional gorilla or chimpanzee cut into pieces and sold as meat or for other purposes (mainly as folk medicine or symbolic magic). So I thought I knew all about the business, and I began working on the book with the fantasy that it would be easy to write and would not require further travel. Very foolish of me. At some point it became obvious that I would have to return with Karl, see what he had seen, meet some of the people he knew, and revisit the markets and the business. More African travels.

⚹

These were photographic and information-gathering expeditions for the book we did. But the actual traveling part, the diurnal ebb and flow of two awkward guys trying not to get on each other's nerves while also working to maneuver themselves across a shifting landscape and in occasionally exotic situations, has not been written about until now. Our travels and tribulations while examining the bushmeat business in parts of Central Africa is the subject of Part I, the opening five chapters of the book you're reading now.

Part II continues the story of travels through a vanishing world but is based on subsequent travels in Asia and Africa that Karl and I began later on, as we gathered images and ideas, information and inspiration for a second book with the same publisher, this one on the topic of elephants and their decline in service of the meat and ivory trade. Part III, following what had begun to look like a tradition, derives from the journeys Karl and I made as we returned to Africa yet one more time and traveled about in search of giraffes: the subject of a third book he photographed and I wrote for the same publisher.

Karl's original photographs exposing the bushmeat trade and its threat to the great apes gained currency in Europe during the 1990s and began winning attention and, on occasion, prizes. Five times he won the *BBC Wildlife* magazine's Photographer of the Year competition (in the "World in Our Hands" category). He received the Humane Society of the United States' Genesis Award for conservation journalism four times. He's addressed the European Parliament, had closed-door meetings with the World Bank president, been honored as a *Time* Magazine Hero of the Environment. And so on. OK, let me summarize his career this way: Karl makes waves. He challenges complacency. He's the mad bull in the china shop. I have disagreed with him at times about some issues, but I've still managed to get along with him over the years because I share his basic feelings about animals and much of his sense about the world he and I traveled through together: that it is a place where the great planetary wildernesses and the wild animals in them are disappearing in our historical moment. It's a dream, that world, a terrible, beautiful dream of something remarkable and infinitely precious that is coming apart, unwinding, dissolving, vanishing forever as I write these words.

Another thing we have in common, Karl and I: Neither one of us is easy to travel with. We've struggled over elbowroom on trains and planes. We've complained, argued, debated, gone through gloomy days and bad moods. He likes to talk more than I do . . . but then he can talk well in a number of languages, while I can't. His German is excellent, his Swiss German perfect. His French is far better than mine, clear and steady and easy for someone like me with only high school French to understand. He speaks some Spanish, I think, and—why not? Also Italian when Italian is called for. His English is fluent, too, although it still takes a while for the ordinary American ear to become perfectly adapted to those *j*'s that turn into *ch*'s, the *w*'s that come out as *v*'s.

✳

"Stop! Stop! Stop!"

The driver doesn't say a word. He doesn't begin to slow down. He hasn't yet figured this one out, and I now register that the traffic is sweeping us directly into the middle of this terrible crime, with the AK-47 soon to be leveled particularly at us. Karl's voice joins in, now: "Stop! Stop! Stop! Stop! STOP!"

It's too late . . . almost. But finally the driver seems to see what we see and jams a foot on the brake pedal. He looks over his shoulder, out the back window. I turn briefly and watch the slowing traffic behind us closing in—and understand that we'll soon be wedged in, with the traffic still funneling into the whirlpool. The driver throws the taxi into reverse as the whole river of traffic behind us continues to drift in ever more tightly, but he skillfully manages to escape by bursting out of a temporary hole in the traffic to his left, over a curb, and off the road. He turns around, and then proceeds onto another road. Pretty soon we're off again, back into another river of traffic, another route, continuing on our way to the airport.

It's remarkable what an impression a leveled gun can make, but the driver has said nothing. Karl merely snorts, grimaces, and says, "Total choke."

"Total choke?"

"Right: Bloody total choke."

"Total choke," I repeat. Then, as the mental rheostat slowly turns and the bulb slowly lights: "Ah, total joke."

"That's what I said."

2: BONGO'S GUESTS

At the airport, we met a tall and crusty guy named John Kavanagh, who was going to accompany us to Gabon. News to me. Kavanagh was an architect, and he and Karl were developing a proposal for the Gabon Ministry of Tourism to create a tourist operation that would make use of President Bongo's two-thousand-square-mile private hunting forest, Wonga-Wongué. Also news to me. Karl is a photographer, which was why were traveling together—to work on that book we had agreed to do—but on the strength of his past life as a hotelier and safari lodge builder, he and John had gotten this consulting job. All right! This was an unexpected digression from our original purpose of looking at the bushmeat markets and all that, but it would help pay for the trip, and maybe it would be fun, too. Or at least interesting.

We had tea and Cokes in a crowded nook off the airport's crowded hallway, waiting for our flight, and Kavanagh showed me some drawings of a fancy tourist lodge he had built in Tanzania, then described some of his recent experiences as an architect in Uganda. The World Bank had granted $29 million in loans to Uganda in order to build twenty-four regional clinics, four obstetrical units, and two hospitals. It was classic World Bank: poverty alleviation through infrastructure investment in the Third World. John was all set to become the architect for this wonderful project, and the money was disbursed. But it disappeared. The money just disappeared.

The flight, a half-day of bouncing from Nairobi on the east side of Africa to Libreville in the west, was the usual. I dozed much of the way. Passing through customs and immigration in Libreville amounted to the usual as well: slow, tedious, frustrating. Karl thought our reception at the airport showed little promise for enticing future tourists: "You can't expect tourists to come if you fuck them up at the airport like this." But we stayed overnight in a nice hotel in Libreville, meeting there a final member of the consulting party, a serious young woman named Martha Robbins, who ordinarily spent her time chasing gorillas in Uganda. And in the morning, while waiting for our flight out to Wonga-Wongué, the four of us amused ourselves by visiting some old friends of Karl's, Pierre Bruno and Emy Vernet, whom we located at the M Hotel, which Pierre managed. Pierre and Emy shared with Karl some kind of past history having to do with hotels and apes.

Emy was slender and small, with close-cropped dark hair and a curved nose. She wore a white shirt and Levi's. She spoke in French, sometimes switching to inadequate English for those of us with inadequate French, saying that when they were in Kinshasa, capital of what was then Zaire, with her husband working as a hotel director in the big city, she started a sanctuary for orphaned bonobos. These were orphans created after their mothers were shot as meat. But it wasn't so easy caring for the orphans. "We have trouble for the food. We have trouble for the medicine," she said.

They had eight new bonobos in the last four or five months they were there, animals coming on boats down the river, arriving in the company of their chopped up mothers, and since military personnel and guns had begun moving into bonobo territory, the stream of orphans had started to seem endless. Pierre and Emy were then forced by untoward political circumstances to leave Kinshasa suddenly and cross the river into Brazzaville, capital of what was then the People's Republic of the Congo. Emy's bonobos, meanwhile, went to another sanctuary in Zaire located on the outskirts of Kinshasa.

In Brazzaville, Pierre found another job in the hotel business. Meanwhile, the director of a different hotel in town had a baby chimp—another orphan—who, stupidly having been placed into a cage with some grownup monkeys, was badly bitten. So Emy offered to take care of the chimp. But (she went on), chimps are different from bonobos. "With chimps you have to say, 'It's me the chief. It's not you the chief.' You have a battle." This one was a small male, and after a few months she couldn't control him. So she took the chimp to a woman in the far western part of the country, Madame Jamart, who owned an electrical supply shop and had begun running a chimp sanctuary out of her own home. "When we left in 1990, December 21, we left very fast, to Senegal."

"We left more than fast," Pierre added, and then, referring to the moment when they gave their baby chimp to Madame Jamart, he said: "It was the first time I see a chimp crying."

Pierre was a rectangular Belgian with a round face and round glasses who smoked Gauloises and spoke bad English with good French gestures—the exaggerated puff of air and the quick shrug, meaning, *Ah, but what can you do?* Forefingers spun around the eyes meaning . . . something. Pierre told us that in Gabon, a country of one million, there were also half a million expatriates, Africans from places like Cameroon, Burkina Faso, Guinea, and elsewhere, imported to do the dirty work. The Gabonese have gotten rich on oil money, he said, and they only want a job where they can wear a suit, tie, white shirt. He pointed at his own suit, tie, and white shirt. They won't do anything with their hands. He held up his hands.

Our taxi driver out to the airfield, a very attractive woman in a colorful blue dress, was Cameroonean. "No Gabonese will drive taxis," she confirmed.

⁕

At the airfield a white sky loomed overhead, but the air was still cool and pleasant as, next to a giant helicopter, several people, one of them holding a clipboard, stood around and chattered away in French. Karl, John, and Martha were the official consultants for this important expedition, and indeed their names could be discerned in the middle of some French gibberish on the paper on a clipboard that was probably smudged with the president's official fingerprints, but the final thinking was that, with those three pens in my shirt pocket and that little notebook in my hand, I looked authentic enough to squeeze in as well. So the four of us climbed into the middle of the giant helicopter, which had a padded ceiling, four seats in the front, four in the back, and more behind that. The front seats filled up with the pilot and copilot (white crash helmets on their heads, long-zippered one-piece suits covering their bodies) along with two others: a tough guy and a not-so-tough guy.

A couple of big guns were tossed into the back at the last minute.

I had never been in a helicopter before, let alone a dark and gorgeous monster like this one, and I loved it. There was a long wait while someone towed the president's private jet out of the way. There was some staticky burping in French followed by a flickering of light, a vibration, the smell of complex hydrocarbons, and the machine started to click and whine, to shake, clatter, and roar, and soon it had lifted straight off the ground. We remained suspended that way, about ten or twelve feet off the ground, for what seemed an unnecessarily long time, and then, like the best possible magic carpet, the machine simply hopped out of place and drifted casually over to the runway, then began moving laterally forward, faster and faster along the runway before rising up and taking us up above the city and quickly out along the edges of the city where it meets the ocean. This was a fine ride in a wonderful device, and we followed the shoreline south, over the port of Libreville. The sky was gray, the sea a hammered blue with, drifting below us, four or five cargo ships, holds open, skirted with floating timber.

Within an hour or so, we were flying over burgeoning green and yellow forests with white and black hornbills gracefully swimming through the air beneath us. We passed over feather dusters of haze, a seething carpet of trees with some emerging gray stems, with greens and browns and yellows and the occasional sprinkles of red-orange flowers. We crossed over the long, straight, yellow scar of a logging road and then, after what seemed a gloriously endless stretch of more forest, onto some extended and rolling seas of savannah, which were a delicate pale green stippled with olive. We sighted a galloping herd of forest buffalo, fat and brown and urgently flexing their small legs, and then, after a time, we wheeled and chuttered over the president's hunting lodge and dropped down into a clearing right below it.

We were met by a man driving a pickup truck. The pilot and copilot stayed with the machine, while the rest of us were driven past a series of small, single-story, white-stucco, tin-roof buildings to the main building. A permanent staff lived at this place, apparently assigned to maintain it and take care of any distinguished guests, and I soon observed someone offloading boxes and cans of food, and bottles of wine and beer, and I smelled the wood smoke of a cooking fire. But, I concluded, the president must have lately lost enthusiasm for the place, since I now saw that the living room of the lodge was not really in presidential condition: musty smell, collapsing ceiling, holes in the three big orange and brown couches— each substantial enough, nonetheless, to hold about twenty people, and stuffed in a way that made them look like inverted lion's paws. The floor was covered with old tile, and the walls were decorated with bad nature paintings, a couple of framed jigsaw puzzles of animals, some impala horns poking out, and one completely tasteless red and gold plastic Chinese clock. Some tassel decorations hung down from the ceiling for no clear reason, and someone had left an elephant skull in one corner, complete with jaw and small tusks, and, in another corner, a gold-painted elephant jaw.

Karl discreetly reported what he had overhead on the flight out: "They're saying that there are poachers' camps all over." And out back, behind the house, he added, were the empty tiger cages. Someone had once given President Bongo Siberian tigers, and where had the big cats gotten to now? The president, Karl went on to say, was a short man: about five feet tall. But he made up for the minimal stature with elevator shoes and maximal proliferation—more than thirty acknowledged children—and he always liked a good romp. Whenever he invited his VIP friends out to Wonga-Wongué on hunting parties, so Karl asserted, they imported fresh European prostitutes for invigorating activities *après-chasse*. That might explain the huge, over-stuffed couches, I thought, but what did the women do with themselves while the men were out hunting? (During a 1995 lawsuit in Paris, Italian fashion designer Francesco Smalto claimed he had secured a $600,000 per year tailoring concession with Gabon in exchange for providing a steady supply of Parisian prostitutes to the president. Smalto was being sued by one of the prostitutes because she was never paid, purportedly because she refused to have sex with a commonly uncondomed Bongo. Bongo, in turn, defended himself during the international scandal that ensued by declaring it was "public knowledge that many figures outside of Gabon could be involved in comparable para-commercial practices." How true.)

Lunch was soon brought in, along with beer to drink, and so we all sat down on the lion-paw couches with plates on our laps: four consultants and the pair who had come with us on the helicopter, the tough and the not-so-tough guy. The not-so-tough guy was an assistant to the tourism minister, a very pleasant-mannered older man—for some reason we began referring to him as "le conseilleur"—and the tough guy was the new director of Wonga-Wongué. He was young, and he had a simple and direct manner that made him seem trustworthy. I liked him. He was dressed in camouflage fatigues and black combat boots, and he had a wedge-shaped face, a heavy jaw, wide mouth, light skin, and straight hair cut in the military style.

He said (speaking always in French) that he had recently replaced the previous director, a Frenchman named Eric Pradel. The president, when he wanted something special—fresh meat for a special dinner—used to send some of his soldiers out to Wonga-Wongué in a helicopter. They would fly around and shoot whatever the president asked for. But then Pradel sent a message that it was better just to fax the order. He would take care of it. Less disruptive that way. So that was an improvement, but Pradel himself was a Rambo-type character, the new director went on, who liked to show off. Visited one day by some French soldiers he hoped to impress, Pradel chased an elephant with his car until the creature was near collapse. Then he boldly walked up and pulled the animal's tail. The elephant turned about and gored him in the heart. So that was the end of Pradel, who had lived in his own house elsewhere in the reserve, along with his wife and mother. After his death, the wife left, and the mother stayed. Perhaps we should go out and visit Madame Pradel, the new director added.

We talked a good deal more during that long and relaxed meal, and afterwards, as the conseilleur and the new director prepared to leave, the latter asked Karl, "What do you not want us to hunt?" I don't know what Karl said in response—but the question explained the two high-powered hunting rifles in the back of the helicopter, and later on, after the machine, carrying the pilot and copilot, the conseilleur and the director, had emphatically beaten its way out of there, it explained the dark puddle of blood in the bed of the truck. We noticed the blood later that afternoon, when we went down to borrow the truck.

※

We used the truck then and over the next few days to explore Wonga-Wongué with an eye to finding scenes and circumstances that would entertain tourists. Martha hoped to locate signs of gorillas and assess how easy it might be to make them habituated to gawking humans, so we spent some time driving from woods to woods, looking for signs of gorillas. John was there to find a good place to build a lodge and think about the logic and logistics of such a project, so we spent more time driving from savanna patch to savanna patch, looking for a good place to build a lodge. Karl was there to be himself, I think, so he took photographs and commented on what could go right and what could go wrong in the near or far future; and I was supposed to be taking notes, which was hard to do while sitting in the bloody bed of a bounding truck and watching the dust rise up and the world pass by.

For Martha's sake, we got up before dawn and crossed the savanna in the velvet darkness, while nightjars hunting for insects on the dirt track and terrorized suddenly by our head-lighted advance would turn bright white and leap up, scattering out into the black sea of air around us. We smelled the sweet wet grassy smells of the savanna and then the damp fecund smells of the forest. Daylight arrived in a pointillistic transition along with a cool breeze, a twittering and piping of birds, and the fragile rolling engine of crickets. No sign of the gorillas, though, although Martha was certain they were there, surely somewhere in the two-thousand-square-mile reserve, and could eventually be persuaded to show themselves.

For John's sake, we spent some time just touring the place, or a representative sample of it, and in that fashion, we finally found the ideal spot to build a lodge: a small lake, a patch of forest, a rolling sweep of savanna. The lake was as smooth as glass, which then started to be broken by the pebble toss of a light rain.

Another time, while driving out finally to visit with Madame Pradel, we found the logging camp—or one of them, at least. President Bongo took in around $30,000 a month from logging in the reserve, according to someone, and the main part of the camp, where the workers lived, consisted of a bleak series of rough-slab shanties with corrugated tin roofs, the slabs gray or black with creosote, the shanties lined up severely in rows on a flat, open acre of yellow sand.

Thirsty, we stopped at one of the shanties, which also served as the company store, for a Coke, thereby finding four young girls, teenagers or nearly so, their hair in snaky plaits, laughing and joking with three young boys at the store's open window. The girls stood in a circle, seemingly delighted with themselves or life, wearing clean clothes, one of them with a baseball cap on backwards. Also at the store were two small children, barefoot, wearing simple dresses and looking mildly forlorn.

Back on the track to Madame Pradel's house, we crossed a long stretch of rolling and flowing savanna, bare and with the occasional handful of fat and romping forest buffalo looking confused and surprised, running away and towards and in front of us in our rattling, rumbling, dust-tailed manifestation. We crossed the line of a big grass fire, and then we followed an edge of the savanna, where it collided with forest. After traversing more savanna, we stopped to consider a big splash of white laundry on the yellow grass and brown earth. Elephant bones, it turned out: white ribs and white vertebrae and white femurs and a white skull tipped ignominiously nose-down into the dirt like a tipped-over doghouse, with the tusks gone. These were giant bones, mainly, but there were also some miniature ones in the scatter, including the delicate V-shaped jawbone of a baby elephant—or, more likely, a fetus. Then, a couple of miles later, we come across another scattering of white laundry in the brown earth and the fire blackened grass. Another skull tipped over. The ivory of this one gone as well.

When we finally arrived at Madame Pradel's house (serenely perched beside a long oval lake), she told us over cups of coffee and tea that last Christmas five of the hippos in the lake beside her house had been shot, while six elephants in the area were also killed: the hippos for their meat, the elephants for their tusks. Ever since her son died, she said, things had gotten entirely out of control. Now, nobody confronts the poachers. According to her other son, who works in Nigeria, up there they shoot poachers, dig a hole and throw them in. Here if anyone shot a poacher, all hell would break loose. In most cases, there would be the guys behind him to think about. Take guns from a poacher, and you have taken guns that belong to the governor; and so it's the big guys who have a specific interest in poaching.

The sight of Madame Pradel sitting solemnly at her kitchen table and keeping up appearances bravely in her lonely house, and then the story of the hippo and elephant killings, all seemed bleak and depressing to me, but Karl was keeping a positive face on things. Maybe eco-tourism is the way to conservation, he was saying on our ride back to the lodge. And he was not convinced that poaching was totally out of control. "I'm sure that poaching has increased, but it could be still manageable, maybe even sustainable."

Wanga-Wongué is very remote. Madame Pradel claimed lately to have seen vehicles that did not belong to the loggers, which wasn't possible before. One route had recently opened up, making it possible to get in. But, Karl was saying, if you could cut off that route, the poachers—at least those without a presidential helicopter—would only have the river to travel on. Anyone poaching would still have to carry the ivory or meat on his back and walk forty to fifty kilometers to get out to the markets. At that point, poaching becomes sustainable because not enough people are willing to go through that. At the same time, of course, tourists coming into the country would also discourage poaching. And, as Karl intended to tell the minister, tourists would not put up with the sight of criminals hauling off ivory or cutting up animals for meat . . . or the sound of big timber trucks rumbling day and night up and down the roads.

※

Certainly, President Bongo didn't need the logging income. He had been president for the last thirty-some years (by the time of his death in 2009, it would be forty-two years) and had prospered magnificently via a special relationship with Gabon's former colonial master, France. He was first placed into office, originally as vice president, after a preliminary interview in Paris with Charles de Gaulle himself. He was rescued by French troops from an early coup attempt and kidnapping. He was maintained through the rest of his presidency with the strategic support of more French troops, permanently based in the country. In reciprocation, his vast wealth secretly helped to underwrite numerous French election campaigns—including the 1981 presidential campaign of Jacques Chirac, according to Chirac's distinguished rival, Valéry Giscard d'Estaing. Meanwhile, operating under the well-known French principle of *l'etat c'est moi*, President Bongo (or El Hadj Omar Bongo Ondimba, as he came to prefer) managed during his long political career simply to forget the irritating distinction between public and private property, and following that undoubtedly pleasant state of amnesia, to become among the richest of the rich.

During his tenure, President Bongo oversaw the exploitation of Gabon's vast petroleum reserves through an exclusive association with the French oil conglomerate, Elf Aquitaine, and the returns were significant: suitcases full of cash (according to a former Citibank official testifying before the US Senate), as well as transfers of about $65 million per year into personal Swiss bank accounts (according to an Elf Aquitaine official testifying in a French investigation). A US Senate report in 1997 suggested that his family was spending around $90 million per year; his Citibank accounts alone contained $130 million. His presidential palace and other properties in Gabon were worth the best part of a billion dollars; his immediate family's three dozen luxury properties in France included ten in Paris, such as the mansion worth $25 million on the Rue de la Baume, conveniently near the Élysée Palace. To get from one property to another, however, required a fleet of limousines and sports cars, Ferraris and Mercedes and the like. He liked to pay for things with cash, but at least some of those luxury vehicles were paid for with checks from the state treasury of Gabon.

Politics in Gabon were simple enough, especially following Bongo's early decision to establish a one-party system. Such an inspired arrangement undoubtedly contributed to his landslide election victory in 1973, in which he and all the other unopposed party candidates won by 99.56 percent of the vote. Was it possible to improve upon such decisive figures? Yes, indeed. Bongo again ran unopposed in 1979, winning the presidency this time with 99.96 percent of the vote. Some minor political opposition during the 1980s was handled with arrests and jail terms, and then, in the 1986 elections, Bongo was once more returned to the presidency, this time with 99.97 percent of the vote. That was a total choke, of course.

Eventually, an opposition to his tenure became substantial enough that—following a series of strikes, riots, and so on—the national party's central committee and the national assembly amended the constitution to allow multiparty elections. It must have seemed like an enormous victory for Bongo's opponents, although one of the most vocal of them, Joseph Rendjambe, was too dead to notice. Others were too rich to care, finding themselves, during the next few months and years, welcomed to the trough, with profitable jobs and significant positions in the government. The most significant positions of all, however, stayed in the family. The president's daughter Pascaline became director of the presidential secretariat. A son-in-law, Paul Tongire, became minister of foreign affairs. His son, Ali-Ben Bongo, became foreign minister, then defense minister, and finally—upon his dad's death in 2009—the next president.

So it goes.

٭

On our last day there, the helicopter—along with the conseilleur, the director, and someone else—came back to pick us up. This time we had a new pilot and copilot. The pilot was wearing the same one-piece suit with the big zipper that the last one did, but he had a small face, a bulbous nose, and an impatient manner. He was not happy. He was in a hurry. He had things to do, a life to lead, business to take care of. We took off.

Flying high above the savanna, we spied three gray elephants on the run. We circled over the logging camp, saw from above the creosoted shanties lined up in rows over the bleak flat acre of sand—and John commented sardonically: "Can't have a tree there. Might give the wrong impression to the workers."

Madame Pradel, meanwhile, had radioed in a request for a ride in the chopper—she needed to do some shopping in town—so that was where we were headed now: flying over some lovely rippled, waving, olive-green stretches of savanna followed by some long stretches of dark green forest, with the definition between savanna and forest almost perfect, very precise, and then there were smaller patches of forest looking like dark green fluffy buttons on a soft olive blanket. We found the long oval lake and, just beside it, the house and outbuildings of Madame Pradel, and we flew down low over the lake, circled noisily over her house and truck and outbuildings at the edge of the lake, and finally descended, exciting a frantic waver in the grass, on a hill above the house.

A grass fire was burning in a dark and smoky line between the house and our landing spot, moving slowly in our direction and in the process turning the soft, bluish-green grass into scratchy brown grass, but a winding track led from the house to the strip, and it looked open, snaking beyond and around the fire, so we all stayed inside the machine, rotors spinning, waiting for Madame Pradel to drive up the track and meet us.

She didn't, and the pilot was unhappy.

Finally the pilot shut down the engine, the rotors came to a stop, and we all hopped out. The grass fire was moving slowly, but the wind was rising, getting stronger, and the wall of smoke was being blown in our direction. Eventually, after several minutes of seeing no one, we started walking down the hill. It was farther than it had originally seemed. We walked for a quarter of a mile until we were far enough across the hilltop that we could easily see her house on the other side of a moving, billowing, smoking, crackling line of fire. No sign of her. "Something's not right," Karl said. We continued walking, leaping over the fire line now into a blackened blanket of charred grass, walking through sooty earth now, yet still high above the house and quite far away. The conseilleur called out: "Madame Pradel! Madame Pradel!"

No answer. Karl said, "This is not right. I'm afraid something is wrong here."

We kept walking until finally we saw someone leaving the house, going to the truck, getting in. She's there! We turned around, walked back up the hill, leaped across the fire again and eventually got back to the chopper. Soon Madame Pradel appeared, driving her truck. She with brown hair, big arms, and a big jaw and bony face with a mole right between the eyes. She leaned out and started talking. Long conversation. She was angry because she had thought we were going to land next to her house instead of up here. The pilot said, in French, absolutely not.

Ignoring him, she said she had to go back and get ready. She'd just driven up here to see what was going on, she said. And before anyone could argue any further, she drove away to get her things together.

We all had a long discussion with the conseilleur, who concluded, philosophically, "Out in the bush, things don't always happen as you wish." The pilot, meanwhile, was drumming impatiently, more and more vigorously, on the nose of the helicopter. First with the fingers of one hand. Then with the whole hand. Then with both hands.

Fifteen or twenty minutes later, Madame Pradel showed up again, dressed now in a blue skirt, colorful blouse, and blue jacket, ready for town and carrying a shopping bag. She climbed out of the truck. We climbed into the machine. She was the last—but suddenly she was refusing to get in. If she were to leave her truck up here, she said, it would burn. She demanded that the pilot fly down to the house and pick her up. Without waiting for an answer, she jumped away from the machine, ran and jumped back into the vehicle, and drove back down the hill. At last we went down too, riding in the chopper, raising with our rotor wash a high cloud of black dust over her house, setting down just long enough for her to clamber clumsily in.

3: THREE DAFT BLANCS

Back in Libreville, Karl and I one morning took a taxi out to the Lalala market. We instructed the driver: "*Le marché de Lalala, s'il vous plaît.*"

We arrived early and were met by the powerfully built market manager, a pleasant enough man who shook our hands. The Lalala was a small market located alongside a narrow estuary and lined with trash. Because we had arrived too early, its wooden tables were not yet loaded with wares except for, on the top of one, a single large piece of meat, which was just then being worked on. We tried to figure out what kind of meat it was. "Too big to be a monkey. Is that a tail?" Karl said.

We went out for tea and came back twenty minutes later. Now the market was active, but the manager explained, in French, that the women back there didn't want white people—*les blancs*—coming into the market. Women run these markets, so what they say generally goes. A police officer nearby joined in the discussion. The manager repeated his assertion: "The women don't want any whites down there." The officer nodded his head in agreement: It must be so.

Karl argued first with the manager, then with the policeman, and finally they both got tired of arguing with Karl and gave up. We walked through the Lalala quickly, noting the sliced and diced python, the duikers, bushpigs, monkeys, giant pangolins, as well as some beef, pork, and other domestic cuts. We priced the python and, for comparison, the beef. Python was more expensive. But when Karl tried to expand the discussion with a question about the wild animal meats, the beef butcher claimed ignorance. This was a cul-de-sac market, so you could feel trapped back there, and I was glad to finish the tour and get the hell out of there.

✤

My impression is that many black Africans consider most white people to be generally harmless and irrelevant if a bit daft. Daft: What kind of person would spread paste on herself before going into the sunshine? Who would spray evil compounds all over his arms and legs and hair and neck every time he goes somewhere, just in case a little insect should start to buzz about? Why do certain people stick perfume under their arms, and how do they still manage to smell like raw potatoes? Where does all that money come from? Why do they never really smile? They're scared of the sun, insects, sweat, even of just being relaxed and smiling: Why are they so scared? And how about those conservationists, the blancs who leave behind air-conditioned homes and three-car garages in order to get themselves dirty out in the bush. And for what? Supposedly to save animals. But why? Why do they waste so much money on animals when people, lots of people, could use some?

These are fair questions that suggest an ordinary level of daftness, but I suspect the daftest thing of all about les blancs—at least in the eyes of many Central and West Africans—is their attitude about meat. Les blancs like their meat disguised. They want it wrapped up in little packages and refrigerated so thoroughly that it looks and smells like soap. They would like to remain ignorant about where meat comes from, and they will spend their lives never thinking about the transition from well fed to good food. They're disgusted by the ordinary sight of a dead animal, and they turn up their noses at the prospect of good organ meat. They insist on taking their meat from a tiny spectrum of the most boring species—cows, domestic pigs, and the like—and they would never dream of experimenting with different cuts or new species.

It happens that the big city markets in Central and West Africa have plenty of the boring domestic meats available, if you happen to prefer that. But if you want meat that will remind you of your cultural heritage, meat that will recall a time when your family lived out in the village rather than in the big city, meat with real flavor that comes from an interesting wild animal of some kind, meat taken by skilled hunters from the forest or bush and maybe cured by a slow and flavorful process of smoking, meat with a real story behind it—*bushmeat*, in other words— you will have to pay a premium, as you would for any other luxury item.

※

Karl and I took a taxi one afternoon out to the Libreville suburbs and past a sign that said, Vétérinaires Sans Frontières, entering a large compound of boxes and pens and pavilions that confined several kinds of animals who were, I supposed, being quietly encouraged to have as much sex as possible. It was a breeding project run by the borderless veterinarians, and we met and talked to one of them, a Frenchman named David Edderai.

David reminded me of a well-bred antelope. He was lean and graceful, with green eyes and a lean face. He was sockless, wearing a white t-shirt and black pants, and although his English was distinctively imperfect, it was still a lot better than my French, so we spoke mostly in English. He said that there are fifteen major tribal groups in Gabon, and, within those, many smaller tribal identities. These groups and identities will include traditions about what is good to eat and what is not good to eat, what is taboo. But generally, David went on, the Gabonese don't eat dogs or cats. No frogs. No small lizards. No owls—because of various witchcraft beliefs. And no giant land snails. The Vétérinaires Sans Frontières, meanwhile, have been trying to established new domesticated species that might replace some of the old wild animals currently being hunted as bushmeat. The new, experimental domesticates included cane rats, giant rats, bushtailed porcupines, red river hogs, and antelopes such as sitatunga and duiker.

"Many people tell us," he said, "that 'It's beautiful what you are doing, but it's not exactly the same meat.' So we want them to see that there is no difference between the one we are breeding and the one they are finding in the bush." They were conducting taste tests.

They were also trying to teach people to grow their own; but, unfortunately, there is almost no tradition for animal husbandry, so the idea of raising livestock seems foreign to a lot of people. David gave an example. They had been teaching a few individuals to raise cane rats, whose meat is considered desirable. A young man graduated from the cane rat breeding course they had offered, and upon graduation he was given six rats to start his own breeding stock. Three months later he came back and asked for another six. David asked him what happened to the last lot. Oh, there was a funeral, and he had to go back to his home village for two weeks, leaving the rats at home without food. When he came back they were all dead.

Then there was the production problem. They wanted to find species that would be economically appropriate for breeding. The Gabonese actually prefer bushtailed porcupines. People like that meat. But bushtailed porcupines eat expensive tubers, such as manioc. Too costly. And they only have one baby per litter, plus the gestation period is more than three months. Too long. No good. "Right now, it's only on cane rats that we can do it," he said. Cane rats are promising. People like the taste. They're otherwise a nuisance. They eat grass, which is nearly free. And they are polygamous, so they breed quickly. The giant forest rats, by contrast, don't seem to breed at all in captivity.

Could this kind of project have a significant impact on the market? I wondered hopefully.

No, no, no, no, he said, unhopefully. It's not much. It's just one species. Just the cane rat. And only even fifty breeders working: no way to have an impact. Maybe breeding can have an impact, but in fifty years. They would have to have a big, big volume of domesticated bushmeat to be produced to have an impact. And there are many things more that have to come to help the bushmeat breeding become a substitute for the bushmeat that now relies almost exclusively on hunting wild animals as a source. You would need to have a real policy against poaching. You would need a policy on the prices on the bushmeat, in the market—taxes on the meats that have been hunted, so the one that has been bred can be cheaper. And a volume that is productive, of course. One thing is to make the price going up, he said. If the bushmeat is very expensive, much more expensive than the meat of other kinds, then they can try to make the market for the other kinds not going up.

Raising the price of bushmeat, in other words, would require other meats being available that people can buy at regular prices. The problem is that in the villages there is no other kind of meat. It's the only source of meat one can find. So maybe people should be thinking about this, trying to develop breeding of poultry, rabbits, and everything like this. To propose something different. Because people really like to eat bushmeat, but it's difficult to go into the forest every two or three days. And if sometimes they could go only once a week and have poultry around the house, they might prefer it—so that's one solution. The second problem is that Libreville is more than half the population of the country. People living here in the big city, their culture calls for bushmeat. So there is a big market here, even though it costs more, and for the people living in the villages, it's their main source of meat.

✳

I asked David some things about traditional cooking in Gabon, and he delivered a long explanation, which I will make very short here. The meat will be flavored with vegetables and sauces and boiled in a pot. It is never grilled. The vegetables may be limited to what you have in the garden, although you can often choose from a wide variety at the market. The starches are standard ones: manioc, plantain, rice.

The meat dishes come in three basic styles, based mainly on the flavoring or the sauce. To make a bouillon ragout, for example, you mix palm oil and water. You sprinkle in finely chopped vegetables—maybe onion, tomatoes, aubergines— and hot red and yellow peppers. The meat is prepared simply, and pretty much the entire piece goes into the pot. (Thus, for example, with porcupine, you'll see a little paw in your bowl. With chimpanzee, you might see a hand or two.) And finally you add the flavoring of a bouillon cube (manufactured by Maggi and coming in three flavors: chicken, shrimp, and onion-spices). Boil all this in the closed pot until the meat is thoroughly cooked.

Nyembwe is a sweet, thick sauce that will result in an entirely different style of meat dish; and in this case, the meat is often fish or chicken. The sauce is made from oil palm nuts. You take palm nuts and boil them, and then you pulverize them in hot water. You end up with the fiber of the nut and a lot of fat that makes oil. You then boil the sauce again and it becomes thicker during the cooking.

Finally, there's odika. This remarkably potent and sweet sauce is made from the ground-up seeds of the wild mango, and it comes in a small cake at the market. You can make it yourself, or you just buy the cake and then, when you're cooking, add in scrapings from the cake. This produces a very rich, earthy flavor—like peanuts, only richer. Maybe a little like chocolate, only more elemental. Actually, David said, it tastes like Africa—whatever that means!

✳

Since I wanted to find out what Africa tasted like, Karl and I went one evening to a restaurant called The Odika. Located in the city center just across the street, more or less, from the offices of an international conservation organization known as the World Wildlife Fund (WWF), The Odika was open to the cool night air and city traffic. Situated on a wooden platform surrounded on three sides by a short wall and wide railing topped with potted plants, the restaurant was protected from above by a roof and a ceiling with slowly spinning ceiling fans. There was a bar, faced with mahogany and rattan, and decorated in African themes with masks and other carvings of wood and soapstone; and it had room for about thirty people seated at half as many tables. The tablecloths were decorated with more African themes. A radio played African music, but quietly, as if in deference to the moderated sensibilities of the clientele—including one African woman with one white man, one French man, a family of ex-pats who were probably French, a middle-class African family, as well as Karl and me.

I studied the menu and found it was possible to order chicken, duck, and beef, along with seafood and several kinds of bushmeat (crocodile, porcupine, python, antelope, bushpig)—and all the prices were roughly in the same range. Beef was the most expensive of the domestic meats. Although slightly more expensive than antelope and bushmeat and porcupine, it was about the same price as crocodile, though distinctly less than python.

I ordered python, along with a Coke, and half an hour later found myself face to face with bundles of white meat curved around snake ribs, all of it bathed in odika sauce and surrounded by frites. The meat included a layer of fat and gristle. It was white, like chicken, but tougher—more like shark—with a gamey flavor that reminded me of the smell of urine but tempered with the odika sauce, which tasted like a sweet and tangy peanut-butter sauce with a hard-to-define earthiness. Like the taste of Africa, maybe. I don't remember what Karl ordered, because I was so distracted by my own meal and then by his insistence on taking photographs of me eating the python. But I've never appreciated french fries more in my life.

David Edderai had told us that The Odika restaurant was mainly for Europeans anyway, and if we really wanted to experience a bushmeat restaurant for Africans, we should go elsewhere. He told us about a place, drew us a rough map for getting there, and in the end decided to accompany us. Thus, on the day after I ate my odika-flavored python dinner, we rendezvoused for lunch with David in a less prosperous part of town. David was still green-eyed and lean-faced, still looking like a well-bred antelope and wearing the same white t-shirt, black pants, and sockless shoes he had worn before; and the three of us walked down a side street somewhere, through a region of rubble and dog feces until we came to a two-tiered open porch, a concrete floor, and a tin roof on wood posts that were painted green. The tables were simple and made of wood, the chairs of plastic, and at the stove, to one side, the pleasant woman running the place showed us six pots that contained the six items on the menu: blue duiker (small antelope), bushtailed porcupine, cane rat, monkey (of some sort), as well as manioc and ndolé (pulverized greens mixed with a sardine-like fish). We ordered beers—Régab—and contemplated the menu, which was written in French on a blackboard nailed above the six pots.

I ordered the duiker, manioc, and ndolé, altogether too much food, as I realized only after it was served. The blue duiker tasted a little like dry beef with a hint of beef liver, and it had been cooked in a light stew, a bouillon. The manioc was boiled and very bland, pressed into long baguettes—"batons," David called them—looking rather like white sausages and having a chewy, sausage-like texture. The ndolé was like creamed spinach with anchovies.

Karl had ordered porcupine stew, and, yes, I could see some little paws floating in the mix. I tried a taste—but we both let David finish off his cane rat all by himself.

Our conversation turned to bushmeat. "Do you see in the markets," Karl asked, "the protected species: gorillas and such?"

"Oh, yeah, yeah," David said. "All the time. You just have to go. You can see wild red river hog. Maybe chimpanzee or gorilla. Elephant."

"Why can't the Gabonese go and confiscate protected species on a daily basis?"

"Yeah, that's a good question. It's a question of political . . . because all the people that are the top of the poaching system are important people here in the country, so that they give guns for the poachers to use."

"Can we get law enforcement? I mean, Gabon has officially a six-month closed hunting season. Why can't they shut down the markets during that period?"

"It's cultural problem," David said.

"Laws are part of their culture too."

"Not those laws," David responded, spearing a piece of rat and chewing thoughtfully, then adding honorably, "It won't be by repression that we will change the way."

Karl: "But with repression you tell the people you have political will. I always say that you can't go and tell the hunter not to pull the trigger if the governor is eating gorilla meat. The governor gives the poacher the gun. And you go to the little guy and say, 'Don't shoot the gorilla.' He says, 'Go to the governor and tell him not to eat gorilla, and then I won't shoot any.' But none of us goes to the big guy and says, 'Hey, you have to change culturally.' We all have pilot projects working with the little guy, but the problem is—."

David: "Of course. But it is the same in many places in Africa, not only on bushmeat. Because people are not sensitized about the problem of conservation. They don't even imagine that maybe this kind of animal can disappear. It's something they never thought about. So in Central Africa, I think, it's new: talking about conservation, caring for wildlife. I mean with people in the country, and maybe in the young generations, we can see even in young generations, I mean in Libreville, not in the villages, the taste for bushmeat is not so important as it is for the elders."

Karl: "Has there ever been any law enforcement as far as putting a poacher in jail, in this country?

"No, never. I don't think so," David said, and he went on to tell us a story about riding the train from Franceville, in the interior, to Libreville at the coast. It happens that there are many wild mango trees at one part of the railroad line. Elephants eat them sometimes, and when the mangos are overripe, they have an alcohol content. The elephants get drunk and slow, so they walk along the tracks and are sometimes hit by the train. David said that while he was on the train, there was a lurch, a shock, and then the train stopped. He was sitting in First Class, and he watched through the window as the second and third class carriages emptied out, with people rushing forward wielding knives, machetes, baskets, bags. He wondered what was going on. *Is this a war?* he asked himself. So he stepped off the train, looked ahead, and saw that the train had hit and killed an elephant, and the people were all rushing out to get their free meat. He was very surprised by how quickly people were able to strip the carcass of all the meat. There were small fights over the trunk, which is a desirable piece. People prefer the trunk and tail. Some people like the ears, though they are mostly cartilage. The engineer got the ivory since, after all, he made the kill. It took less than an hour to strip the elephant to the bone, and, David thought, it's spectacular to see how quickly they can cut the carcass. So culture, yeah, bushmeat is part of the culture.

✳

After finishing our meal, we decided to take David's truck over to the Mont Bouet market. The Mont Bouet was big enough that I never did grasp how big it was. Maybe it covered a city block. Maybe two. Or three. Or four or five. Maybe it has only become larger and more imposing now, in my memory—but it was still plenty big enough in reality. We entered the market by wrestling our way through a tightly crowded street and then by inserting ourselves into a dark and complicated tunnel that turned into a giant, sprawling department store run by a few thousand independent merchants, women mostly, each with her own stall or table or spot and her own wares on display.

It was a warren of passageways and pockets, with immense crowds of buyers and sellers, gawkers and hawkers—who knew how many thousands or even tens of thousands of people, all of them, it seemed (except for the pale and awkward three of us) African and utterly comfortable in and familiar with this labyrinthine world. But we joined that slowly moving current of human flesh, passed through endless pockets of new smells and glanced at a long procession of spices, peppers, aubergines, tomatoes, onions. David pointed out the odika cakes, which I sniffed and considered. We stopped to look at the oil palm nuts, orange and the size and shape of garlic cloves, that after being tortured with a little pounding and boiling make up the ingredients of nyembwe. We moved past a hanging garden of garments, proceeded through a region of cloth in bolts of every color, then a region of shoes and eyeglasses, then a cornered tailor and his sewing machine, a dozen haberdasheries, an exotic netherworld of women's underwear, frilly and fruit-shaped, and a tedious overworld of men's. We turned a corner, passed a bent old woman trying to sell flip-flops, turned another corner, another, another, squeezed down an alleyway, slipped through a chute, were pressed by crowds along the wall of a vast fortress of stacked and bagged flour, were pushed around a corner until, suddenly, we popped out into a dark barn full of chickens in stacked cages, the concrete floor worn and dark and wet.

After more wandering, more corners and corridors, we arrived at an open room and a large butchery: domestic meat, most of it already chopped into bright red chunks and slabs. And after yet more disorienting twists and turns, corridors and alleyways, the crowds pressed us into the bushmeat section of the market, a large and steaming cave that presented itself first by the smell and flies and then by the sight of many hundreds, maybe thousands of dead animals presented on hundreds of gray and tippy wooden tables arranged end to end to form long corridors. Some of the meat was chopped and stacked and bloody: anonymous blocks of red and white, purple and gray. Much of it was not so anonymous.

I saw a python, chopped and bloody and presented as wheels of snake with the skin still intact. I walked past bushpig parts, dismembered duikers and bushtailed porcupines, whole cane rats and giant rats. There were unidentifiable haunches and torsos in various shades of red, purple, and gray. I noted half a large sitatunga (antelope) with the hair still on. I observed three baboons with the hair singed off, exposing a cream-colored skin. They were bloated and grotesquely puffy, like naked dogs with babies' heads, and the faces were locked into rigor-mortis rictus.

David spoke briefly to one woman, talking about prices and species as she chopped off the heads of duikers, hacking away with a cleaver. And in the area that displayed monkey heads, four young women, laughing and seemingly delighted at the comic spectacle offered by three daft blancs, thrust some monkey heads at our faces and cried out: "Eat this! It's good! It's good!" But the laughter was gentle teasing, so it seemed, and we all laughed back—or tried to.

We came upon some elephant trunk that had been sliced into wheels, rather like wheels of cheese only looking spongy inside, with a welling of blood. We were told the trunk wheels cost ten thousand Central African francs, or five thousand CFA per kilo (about ten dollars at the time), and after a good deal of disputatious negotiation, Karl brought the price down to three thousand CFA for one of the two-kilo wheels. It was a huge piece, about ten inches in diameter, with a fatty, gristly inner core surrounded by a radiating circle of red meat and then an outer rind, like watermelon rind, of thick skin. It was wrapped up in a sheet of newspaper and handed to Karl, who told me he intended to photograph it.

Meanwhile, he was quietly telling me to look at the leg farther down one aisle. It was a big hairy leg. Trying not to make a fuss about it, we both moved more closely to examine the piece more thoroughly. It was not any kind of antelope leg. Far too broad and muscular. Not a monkey or baboon leg. Too big. And the fingered foot at the end was a dead giveaway. It was an entire chimpanzee leg, of that I'm certain, severed at the hip, stretched out across the table, looking huge and hugely muscular, like a gorilla arm, and indeed the fingered foot was curled up into a half-relaxed fist.

But David, meanwhile, had become engaged in a spectacle elsewhere. The spectacle, as it turned out, was mostly him, as he squatted inside a wire-mesh pen where there was a still living male duiker, a rather big one about the size of a small deer or a medium dog, lying on his side, breathing fast and bound with some twine wrapped around his four legs. It was the best way to keep meat fresh: still alive. This was bay duiker, David said, and he needed male bay duikers for the breeding project, but he thought this poor creature was nearly dead.

He huddled over the animal, felt his legs, one by one. Slowly, he unwrapped the legs from the binding—the duiker quiet, looking up at him with large dark eyes. David ran his hands carefully over each leg in turn. "It's not good. This leg is cold," he said. I could see that the one leg seemed swollen and stiff. The duiker may have been bound for a couple of days, perhaps, David thought. Probably too long. But he massaged those legs slowly and gently until at last the creature emitted a long, rasping groan. Then another. Another. And another. David picked him up, carefully tucked his legs under, holding him upright, and I could see the duiker shifting his muscles and testing his weight, and soon he was hobbling and then, obviously fearful, had stumbled over to the wire mesh side of the pen where he began bashing his head against the wire mesh.

By now a couple dozen people were standing around, a small and excited crowd of onlookers. One man asked if we were going to kill the animal. Others suggested we should. Still, David negotiated with the owner and bought the duiker, and then, having gently wrapped him in the softest cloth available, he located a *carteur*—a free-lance wheelbarrow worker operating as porter for over-laden shoppers—and then gingerly placed the wrapped animal into the wheelbarrow. The three of us followed our carteur back out of the market, Karl carrying his newspaper-wrapped elephant trunk slice under one arm.

We look like fools, I thought. And as we followed our carteur up this corridor and down that alleyway, around one corner and through another passage, carefully and sometimes stumblingly negotiated and penetrated the streaming crowds of shoppers and sellers, once in a while I would hear the voice of someone trying out his or her high school English: "Hello! How are you? Where are you from? What are you doing?" There was commentary, gesturing, some laughter, much studied indifference, but little antagonism, I thought, mostly amusement, tolerance, and curiosity.

4: TRANSIT MOODS

On our way to the coast of Cameroon, Karl and I were dropped off by the airplane at and spent some time in the glass-enclosed international transit lounge of the airport at Yaoundé (Cameroon's capital and second largest city), stuck there—*in* Cameroon but not *of* Cameroon—as non-official nonentities suspended inside a rectangular fishbowl. As we waited for our flight out of Yaoundé and on to our final destination, the port city of Douala, therefore, we languidly lounged, listlessly lingered, drank coffee, ate peanuts, walked about, kept an eye on our luggage, walked about some more, and looked out the fishbowl windows onto a view of the lower level of the airport. The lower level was shadowy and, according to Karl, the site of a prostitution ring operating out of one of the restrooms.

He pointed this out to me as we both stood next to one of the huge rectangular columns that framed the windows overlooking the lower level—saying, quietly enough, "*Mmmm mymmy mmlllt.*" He was mumbling, I supposed, out of consideration for the other lingering loungers.

"What?" I responded.

"*Mmmmm mmy mmmy* there."

"I can't hear you."

"*Mmmm mmmm uh uh* there."

"What?"

"Prostitute. There. Watch."

I looked where he seemed to be looking—but he had a clear view of events that were simultaneously blocked from my own clear view by the rectangular concrete column. I realized that fact later. At that moment, though, I was just mystified. "Where? I don't see anything."

"Down there. Prostitute. Watch: She's taking customers into the ladies' toilet."

"I can't see."

"Just look. See that?"

"Sorry: I can't see anything. Where is she?"

Karl exploded with a roar: "**ARE YOU FREAKING DEAF AND BLIND???!!!!**"

※

My first impressions of Cameroon made it seem not, all things considered, a happy place. That's a short explanation for the unhappy moods we were both experiencing during our seemingly interminable wait in the airport transit lounge that day. A longer explanation takes us back to Karl's original involvement with this bushmeat business we were supposed to be investigating.

After receiving a regular education in Switzerland, he enrolled in the Cornell University School of Hotel Management in the United States, played on the soccer team there, took his degree, and then signed up for his first job at the InterContinental Hotels as operations analyst for their African division. He was sent to Kinshasa, Zaire, where he began analyzing operations and, in the meanwhile, tasted bushmeat in the hotel restaurant: an ordinary sampling of antelope, crocodile, and python, alongside the boring Western fare. No big deal.

The Kinshasa job was followed by hotel management positions elsewhere in Africa, including one in Egypt, another in Kenya—and then he quit hoteliering altogether, fell in love with a glamorous blonde from California named Kathy, and the two of them married and set up tent-keeping in Kenya's Masai Mara. At the time, the Mara was still relatively undeveloped, a big and sometimes convincing representation of East Africa wilderness, and the newlyweds worked out of their tent for two years as volunteer cheetah researchers, creeping steadily through the grass while watching cheetahs creep stealthily through the same grass, and trying to determine something or other about those lean and fast predators for the benefit of what would become the Kenya Wildlife Service. It was what Karl considers the ultimate experience, although paying for it required every cent of cash he had earned in the hotel business. Their social life in the Mara was limited to occasional meetings with pilots and guides and others of that ilk, and everyone they talked to or hung out with appeared to be preoccupied with cameras and photography. There was a lot of canny insider talk about f-stops, aperture settings, shutter speed, film speed, depth of field, field of vision, field of dreams. Karl bought a camera and started taking pictures.

Such was the start of his next career, which became more reasonable after he entered a business arrangement with some Masai friends and oversaw the creation of a luxury tented safari camp in the Mara, which was called the Intrepids Club. Since those days, the Intrepids has metastasized into a mass-tourism lodge, but back then it was just right, very beautiful, and also financially rewarding enough that he could afford to try photography more seriously.

He also became involved in a couple of other tourism projects. First was another Intrepids operation that would bring out well-heeled tourists from Nairobi by private plane to stay in a luxury lodge in eastern Zaire near the Virunga Volcanoes, where they would then be taken out in small groups to see the mountain gorillas. On paper, it was a nice idea. Karl put a lot of work and enthusiasm into it, but the wind slipped out of his sails on the day a Cessna 404, carrying a dozen tourists and their luggage (plus an extra pair of missionaries who had begged a ride) failed to gain altitude when gaining altitude was called for, and everyone on board was killed.

A partner in the gorilla viewing project had been the Zairean President Mobutu's son, and Karl's next project emerged from that fortuitous connection. The Democratic Republic of Congo (in those days, Zaire) is a possibly ungovernable country with a notoriously weak infrastructure and absurdly bad roads. The country's one functional transnational highway is the Congo River, which finds its headlands in the African east, snakes north and then east and then south for nearly three thousand miles before discharging 810,000 cubic feet of water per second off the West coast into the Atlantic. It's the deepest river in the world, the world's second in volume, Africa's second in length (behind the Nile), and it slides like a coiled and silvery snake through the second largest rain forest in the world. Little good can be said about the Democratic Republic of Congo's former colonial masters, the Belgians, but at least, upon bidding farewell in 1960 to the subjects they had robbed and the land they had stolen, the Belgians left fifteen riverboats capable of navigating the mighty river from Kisangani, the big city at the eastern end, to Kinshasa, the big city at the western end just above a set of impassable cataracts leading to the sea.

The fifteen riverboats were big tugboats, but anyone could expand their capacities greatly by lashing on a few double-decker barges. By the time Mobutu's son began thinking about them, there were only four tugboats—the other eleven having been cannibalized in order to keep their more fortunate siblings alive—but those four had been for some time offering one of the most underexploited adventures in Africa. A number of intrepid backpackers had already made this trip, over the years, but an unwashed young person going alone with only a few dollars and a grateful smile did not produce significant tourism income. What if someone turned the riverboat trip into a luxury excursion for tourists with money?

Karl's job was to answer that question, and in order to do so he was given an opportunity to ride on the riverboat, first class, for free. He brought along Kathy, and together they began their big adventure, starting at the quay in Kinshasa in the hot afternoon of February 16, 1989. They climbed a gangplank onto the *Col. Mudimbi* and were shown to their first-class cabin, which they scrubbed and sprayed until it seemed tolerable, and then they stood on deck and watched the world pass by.

By the time this boat had churned its way upriver and out of the shadows of Kinshasa, and the afternoon had cooled into evening, the *Col. Mudimbi* had been transformed into a giant shopping mall and party boat. The boat's generators spread power and light everywhere, and out on the lashed-on barges, merchants and shopkeepers set up their pharmacies and stalls and shops along with restaurants, bars, brothels, and three different discos with competing loudspeakers. At Kinshasa, around two thousand passengers had boarded the boat, but as they moved upriver, during the next several days, more and more passengers arrived—turning up alongside the *Col. Mudimbi* in boats and pirogues and climbing aboard. Shoppers and merchants also paddled up, buying from and selling to the merchants and shoppers already aboard; and fishermen and hunters appeared as well, tethering their fragile vessels alongside the floating city and offering their wares for a good price, then relaxing for a couple of beers at the bar before climbing back into their fragile vessels and casting off again.

The fishermen tossed up catfish, eels, tiger fish, and so on. The hunters hauled aboard bags and bundles and backpacks full of fresh and smoked meat: bats, birds, crocodiles, duikers, grubs, lizards, monkeys of several species, snakes, snails, and swamp-dwelling antelopes. The monkeys were sometimes smoked, their brains and eyes removed; the fresh ones were presented with their tails wrapped around their necks as a convenient handle. The crocodiles were enormous, the bigger ones twelve to fifteen feet long, and often they were still alive, a rope wrapped around the mouth for safety's sake. Karl had seen bushmeat before, and had even tried some at the coffee shop in the Kinshasa Intercontinental. But now he was amazed not only by the variety but by the sheer quantity of it. There were thousands of primate carcasses on that boat, some of them smoked but a lot of them fresh. Every meat trader on board had his own enormous freezer, and the fresh ones were all tagged with the owner's name and dumped into an even bigger freezer room in the main tugboat. It was a huge commerce, which until that trip Karl had not been aware of.

After about a week of travel, Karl and Kathy watched a hunter paddle through the swirling brown water in his small pirogue, lash up to the sides of the floating market, and toss aboard some wrapped meat. Chimpanzee meat. The hunter also brought on board a cheap plastic travel bag that, unzipped, revealed inside a sweet infant—the baby chimp he had just orphaned—that he offered for sale along with the meat. The infant chimp was too small to be worth much as meat, but in Kisangani he might be stuffed into a birdcage and sold as a pet for as much as fifty dollars, or its equivalent in Zairean currency. A day later, another hunter appeared with another chimp orphan, this one a male with a strangely wrinkled face. A couple of days later, after one of the twin propellers fell off the *Col. Mudimbi* and a replacement was brought down from Kisangani in another boat, a hunter on the rescue boat brought aboard a third chimp infant.

Two of those orphans were soon bought by traders who intended to resell them once the boat reached Kisangani, and the third—the wrinkle-faced male— Karl and Kathy bought for five dollars. Chimpanzees most fully resemble people in their infancy, and this one seemed a lot like a desperately needy little child. He leaped into Kathy's arms and climbed right up to her face, latching himself on with spindly arms wrapped around her neck, holding onto this new mother as if his tiny life depended on her, which it did.

They had bought the baby chimp as a spontaneous act of compassion, but now what were they going to do with him? First they tried to find a suitable place for him in Zaire, and when that didn't work out, Karl acquired the necessary permits and brought him out to Kenya, carried by Kathy for the cost of a baby on a regular commercial flight. Back in Kenya, they began caring for the little ape in their own home.

Little apes usually grow into big apes, and even medium-sized ones are dangerous. Still, Karl and Kathy built an enclosure outside their house and allowed Mzee to come inside during the afternoons. Soon he had learned to use the toilet and brush his teeth, and he had begun sleeping in bed between his two adopted human parents, holding hands with each as he drifted sweetly off to sleep. What else could they do?

※

As Karl began to understand, hunters were creating large numbers of ape orphans across Africa, and a small number of orphanages had already been established by well-meaning people to care for some minor fraction of them. He set out to learn about the orphanages, see if he could find one that would take Mzee. In the company of a German friend named Helmut, Karl traveled out to West Africa to visit a couple of orphanages, in The Gambia and Sierra Leone, then it was on to Central Africa, where he and Helmut traveled in Gabon.

From Libreville, they took the train west to Franceville, Gabon, where they were shown inside a large, French-financed biomedical laboratory that had been doing various kinds of research with about seventy-five chimps and gorillas. Most, possibly all of them had been acquired as bushmeat orphans: sold after their mothers were shot as meat. The director of the lab told Karl that people continued to bring ape orphans to the laboratory, but by then they didn't need any more, so the donated babies were put down. Karl watched as a worker in the lab shot at the chimps with an air gun. It was a management technique for persuading them to move from one part of their prison to another.

While riding in a bush taxi out of Gabon on their way to Congo, they stopped in a small town to stretch. Soon they were surrounded by a crowd of curious onlookers with nothing better to do, and so Karl asked if anyone had seen any chimpanzees or gorillas lately. Oh, yes, someone said, there was a gorilla baby in that hut just across the road.

The gorilla baby may have been a year old, and she lay still, lethargic and curled up into a hairy ball on the dirt outside the hut. The gorilla's owner showed up and told Karl that he had killed the mother three weeks back and gave the baby as a toy to his children. They had first kept the gorilla tied up to a post with some string, and the string had eaten through the baby's skin, creating an open sore that became infected. The children, meanwhile, had grown bored with their toy, and so now the hunter was left with a useless and dying baby gorilla, and what could he do? Karl said he could take the baby to an orphanage in Congo and see that she received medical treatment for that infection. The concept of medical treatment for an animal was completely alien to this poor hunter, of course, nor was he interested in giving the creature away for free. Why should he? At last they negotiated a price, the equivalent of around eight dollars, which, the hunter declared, fairly represented the cost of bananas he had already fed the gorilla.

So Karl left Gabon in a taxi with a baby gorilla in the backseat. As they passed into Congo-Brazzaville, they were stopped at the border by a guard who, obviously bored, spent two hours questioning Karl and Helmut and searching them and the taxi and their luggage. He was curious about their cameras, radios, and just about everything else they carried—but not about the dying baby gorilla in the backseat.

At last they arrived in the small town of Mbinda, where they found rooms at a local mission, then located a veterinarian who treated the gorilla with antibiotics. Karl also acquired some baby food, which he began spoon-feeding to the baby. But the baby was dying . . . and then she wasn't. She perked up. She seemed better. She climbed onto a table to get some slices of apple, and suddenly this little gorilla was lively and energetic. Karl named her Mbinda, in honor of the small town where she had recovered.

At the time, two ape orphanages had already opened in the nation of Congo-Brazzaville, with a third one in the planning stages. Karl and Helmut headed for an expanding chimpanzee orphanage—dozens of baby chimps—that had been created and was managed by a tough and passionate Frenchwoman, Aliette Jamart, in the coastal city of Pointe-Noire. Chimps and gorillas don't usually mix very well, and Madame Jamart advised Karl to take his gorilla to the capital city of Brazzaville, where, she said, there was already a well-run gorilla orphanage, financed by a rich and eccentric Englishman named John Aspinall.

Helmut had gone back to Germany by then, so Karl bought a ticket for himself for the two-hour flight from Pointe-Noire to Brazzaville, and he kept Mbinda inside his zipped up jacket. That worked for a while, although he attracted a lot of curious stares from people who must have wondered why he wore a jacket when it was so hot. He was sweating profusely, and when he finally boarded the plane, he unzipped the top of his jacket, giving both him and the baby gorilla some fresh air. Unfortunately, a stewardess then saw the gorilla, and she began to fuss, saying, "You have a monkey." This was the start of a long and vigorous debate between Karl, the stewardess, and then an airline official, which was finally resolved when Karl bought a child's ticket for the gorilla. He then buckled little Mbinda into her seat next to him, and the plane rolled down the runway and lifted into the air.

Finally, then, the tiny gorilla was taken to the John Aspinall orphanage in Brazzaville, where she was cleaned, coddled, and cared for—but died anyway. And Karl, meanwhile, returned home to Kenya and that rapidly growing young chimp of his. For a while, he became involved in the establishment of yet another ape orphanage, a place called Sweetwaters in Kenya, and he placed Mzee there with several other chimp orphans. But after one of the Sweetwaters chimps—Charlie, an older male—died from shigella, which Karl believed could have been prevented with better hygiene, he and Kathy decided they would not expose Mzee to the same risk. They removed the chimp from Sweetwaters and brought him back to their home. It soon was his home, too, and they were both as attached to him as regular human parents are to their own human children. . . .

Mzee had his own pet dog, for daytime play and companionship, and when he came into the house in the late afternoon, he would take a bath, get a drink from the refrigerator, sit in a chair and leaf through magazines, turn on the telly, and so on. "The relationship has evolved," Karl once told me, "and we are family now, just like any other family. We seem to have a retarded child, but so do other families."

※

That relationship could be one piece of the puzzle having to do with Karl's mood that afternoon in the Yaoundé transit lounge. We had moved into the heart of bushmeat country: a wide-open, Wild West sort of place where you can still find chopped-up chimp meat for sale in the public market.

Another piece comes into focus once we consider Karl's more recent career as a photographer. After that trip on the *Col. Mudimbi*, he had a compelling enough sequence of photos to accompany an article about the Congo River and the wildlife trade he had witnessed. Pretty soon a second article, based on his trip to visit the ape orphanages, was being readied for publication by *BBC Wildlife* magazine in England. As a result of those two articles, some people in London associated with an animal protection group contacted Karl and asked him if he would be willing to investigate the Central African bushmeat trade more deeply and take more photographs. He said he would do that.

By the summer of 1994, then, Karl was back in Kinshasa, traveling with a guy from the animal protection society named Gary Richardson. The two of them found a restaurant that illustrated its menu with pictures of the species being served, which included chimps and gorillas as well as elephants. Karl took pictures. While snapping more photos of some big, bloody packages of bushmeat arriving at a local Kinshasa airport, though, they were arrested by a couple of soldiers. After some arguments, struggles, a near car crash, leveled guns, a gathering crowd, and the payment of a couple of significant fines, they crossed the river north into the city of Brazzaville (in Congo-Brazzaville), where Karl photographed gorilla parts for sale in one of the markets. From Brazzaville, they flew north by commercial jet to the small town of Ouésso, population eleven thousand, which was a major center for meat draining out of the northern forests, much of it routinely moving south to Brazzaville on the same commercial jet they had just taken. The meat was sitting there in big blood-soaked sacks as they walked down the steps from the plane.

The local meat truck would arrive in Ouésso twice weekly, routinely offloading carcasses of dozens of different species; and on the day Karl and Gary were watching, the load included an entire silverback gorilla, already cut into pieces. They filmed one of the giant ape's giant hands.

It was standard operating procedure in this part of Congo-Brazzaville for any obvious new arrivals, especially daft blancs, to have their passports confiscated upon arrival at the airstrip. The only way to get them back was go to the local police department for an extended session of grilling and bribe-paying. Thus, after Karl and Gary finished filming the gorilla hand taken off the truck, they went to the police station to retrieve their passports. The police chief had already gone home for the weekend, however, so Karl and Gary went to see him at his home. There they explained to the chief that they were intending to continue north by pirogue on the Sangha River in order to visit Congo-Brazzaville's famous new national park (Nouabalé-Ndoki) as well as a very large German-run logging operation in the same area—but the chief explained that such would not be allowed. Instead, he said, they would take a pirogue west on the Ngoko River until they had been deported from his country and dropped into the adjacent country of Cameroon. To make sure this happened as he intended, the chief continued, he was providing them with the pirogue and an escort (which, of course, they were required to pay for).

Karl and Gary were taken down to the river in the company of a gunman dressed in a tracksuit. The pirogue was a large log that had been hollowed out and given a square stern, where a single outboard motor was screwed on. They stepped into the log, along with the gunman and a boatman. The motor sputtered, smoked, and came alive, and then they began moving up the Ngoko. Soon after they had left the outskirts of Ouésso, however, they tied up at a small riverside settlement and on-loaded a large bag containing something that clinked. The clinking was of a distinctive timbre: raw ivory, Karl understood, realizing soon after that the police chief's gunman was there to escort the ivory, not him and Gary. Eventually, Karl was able to look inside the bag and count around twenty small elephant tusks.

The police chief's ivory was dropped off two to three hours later, still on the Congo-Brazzaville side of the Ngoko, and soon after that, Karl and Gary were deposited on the other side, in Cameroon. Before them was a logging camp called Kika and a dirt road next to it, and eventually on the road along came a bush taxi. The driver took them down the road into a heavy rainstorm and, after slipping off the road and being stranded in the middle of nowhere for a few hours, they finally made it into the town of Mouloundou, where they stayed overnight in a mission. Next day, they took another bush taxi north but were stopped at a place called Mambálélé Junction by the police, who pulled them out of the taxi, searched them, and required them both to fill out some papers. The taxi, meanwhile, pulled away, so they were stranded for the rest of the day in Mambálélé Junction: one or two shipping containers and a few shanties built of rough wooden slats that housed the police station, a small restaurant, and a few roadside shops. The dirt road there served as a conduit for trucks carrying logs, and in fact one such truck had broken down right at the junction, so at least Karl and Gary had someone to talk to: the trucker. The trucker was hauling timber on contract for a northern Congo-Brazzaville company called CIB (Congolaise Industrielle du Bois)—the very German-owned operation whose concession Karl and Gary had intended to visit when they were in Ouésso, only had been forbidden to do so by the police chief. And, they asked, had the driver ever seen chimpanzees or gorillas during his trip from the CIB concession in Congo-Brazzaville?

Well, yes, he had. In fact, the driver went on, he had just bought some chimpanzee from a hunter, which he stored in the engine compartment of the truck. He flipped open the great hood of the brick-red vehicle and pulled out some arms and legs. Karl took pictures.

That same afternoon, someone mentioned that a hunter at Lepondji, a small village just down the road, had recently killed a gorilla, so Karl and Gary walked to Lepondji and talked to the hunter. The hunter was too poor to own a gun himself, he said, but the police chief in Mouloundou had sent him one along with his order for gorilla meat. After he found and killed the ape, the hunter sent the gun and most of the meat back to the police chief, and kept for himself the head and one arm, both of which he was about to cook. In the hunter's rough kitchen, Karl and Gary found the head resting in a shallow bowl with a basket on top to keep the flies away. Karl removed the basket and took pictures.

The police at Mambálélé Junction pulled Gary in for some additional interrogation on the next day, which meant that the pair missed that day's bush taxi—and in the afternoon, they heard that someone had a gorilla baby in a logging camp a few kilometers down the road. They rented a couple of motorbikes, biked out to the camp, and found a man who claimed to be the owner of the gorilla baby. He kept the baby inside a suitcase during the night, the man said, and during the day let him out but tied to a string. Unfortunately, the baby died that morning, and so his owner had just thrown him into the bushes. Karl and Gary found the body, put it into the open suitcase, and Karl took pictures.

✳

Karl's early travels into West and Central Africa—first to look at the orphanages, then to look at bushmeat and take pictures—can be considered a bit of random sampling done in ape territory, where everywhere he went, or so it seemed, he was soon stumbling upon ape body parts and dead or orphaned babies. Karl's random sampling seemed to suggest that hunters were killing large numbers of apes, and thus, the question became: Was this a serious problem?

The answer would depend in large part on the numbers of living African apes and their ability to endure, through the surplus of normal reproduction, some degree of loss from hunting. The numbers of living apes, however, are not great. Maybe 5,000 to 50,000 bonobos left in the universe. Probably fewer than 115,000 gorillas of all types. Twice that figure for chimps, more or less. Those are small numbers, especially when compared to the 6 billion-plus population of their human cousins, who are adding to that figure by around 80 million each year. It also happens that the African great apes reproduce very slowly, and thus a reasonable person might be concerned that the bushmeat trade was out of control, that all three apes could be sliding on the slippery slope to extinction.

Karl's "random sample," as I call it, was not a scientific study, and where were the scientists during this time? In fact, Karl and Gary came across a biologist when they were in Ouésso and filming the meat truck as it unloaded various pieces of meat including that butchered gorilla. An American researcher was standing there, writing down the species in his notebook and estimating amounts by weight. Some of that gorilla, including the hands, ended up in a nearby restaurant, and so did Karl, Gary, and the American. They had a few beers and talked a little about what they were doing, and then the discussion moved on to the matter of apes and orphans.

The American's research documented that the people in the town of Ouésso were taking in an average of 5,700 kilograms of bushmeat per week, which averaged out to around a half kilo per person. The meat was taken from thirty-nine species: bats to bushpigs to eagles to elephants, along with seven kinds of monkeys and two of apes—chimps and gorillas. During the eleven-week period in which the

American conducted his survey, three chimp carcasses had arrived while gorilla carcasses were appearing at the rate of 1.6 per week. That's a lot of dead apes, and the methodically collected data the American provided and eventually published in a scientific journal was useful in considering the impact. His study, along with a couple of others, confirmed what Karl already strongly believed: that the traditional consumption of wild animals in Central Africa had recently turned commercial in a major way, and it had now become the biggest conservation issue in Africa.

Conservationists should have been talking about it, publicly. They should have been spreading the word openly. But they weren't. Why? What was the nature of this resistance or denial?

Karl began to get some sense of the matter as he tried to find someone in the United States willing to publish his photographs accompanied by a written text. Everyone turned him down. The *National Geographic* wasn't interested. The editor of a monthly glossy called *International Wildlife* explained to Karl that his pictures were "simply too disturbing for our audience." *Wildlife Conservation* magazine rejected it, with an editor commenting that Karl's pictures were "gory" and lacking in "cultural sensitivity."

Karl had uncovered what was probably the most significant conservation story of the decade, and yet those conservation publications, and the organizations behind them, were unwilling to acknowledge it. Nevertheless, his story slowly broke through—first in England with publications by *BBC Wildlife* magazine. And finally in the United States, in the 1996 issue of a photography magazine and a 1997 issue of *Natural History* magazine.

After Karl and an American journalist witnessed the aftermath of a gorilla slaughter—an entire family killed for meat in the forests of Cameroon—his photos of the event appeared in a May 1999 issue of the *New York Times Magazine*. Steve Gartlan, a former director of World Wildlife Fund in Cameroon, wrote to the paper, insisting that the article was based on "flimsy, insubstantial and mainly anecdotal" research. In a subsequent letter, Gartlan complained that Karl was suffering from "Western values," chided him for keeping a chimp in his "mansion," and declared that he was "exploiting" the dead apes he photographed, since "the market for emotionally charged photographs and films is so large and so lucrative." Indeed, Gartlan suggested discreetly ("it has been alleged"), Karl may have even paid hunters to kill those gorillas.

That was uncalled for, but I'm running out of paper, so let's just return to the transit lounge in the Yaoundé airport and the subject of people's bad moods. This must have been Karl's sixth or seventh or tenth trip to Cameroon, back once more to look at the same old story. He had been privately threatened, publicly insulted, openly ridiculed, called a racist, been roasted on the Internet, and so on.

In some ways, it might be said that he had by then begun breaking through a wall of denial, first in Europe and then in the United States. At least his photographs had begun winning prizes. He was starting to be recognized in a positive light. That was progress. Maybe. And maybe I represented some of that progress, since I was coming on this trip to illustrate his photographs with a text that would become the first accessible book on the subject. But Cameroon, at least my early impressions of it as gathered from inside the transit lounge, seemed pretty bleak.

And so there you have it: the two of us sitting in Yaoundé transit, both sunk in the funk of a very bad mood.

5: TO THE BOONIES AND BACK

After finally transiting out of Yaoundé and on to the port city of Douala, we tripped up some stairs, joined a line, and finally, after the usual gymnastics, officially entered Cameroon. Moving from the comparatively rich country of Gabon to its more-than-ten-times-poorer next-door neighbor, produced an almost palpable shift in ambient wealth, like a sudden change in barometric pressure. Our wallets barely fit in our pockets.

While eating our dinner that evening at a sidewalk restaurant in the center of town, we began looking for a moneychanger among the street's seething crowds of passers-by and hangers-out. We found one, along with a small posse of his buddies, and after dinner they led us through a door and into a dark, dead-ended hallway of some spooky building where, in my brilliant assessment, we were suddenly too vulnerable. The government-backed exchange rate was official robbery, and had we settled for unofficial? The moneychanger and his posse engaged in a flurry of conspiratorial whispering. Karl and I responded with our own conspiratorial whispering. Then, as casually as we could, he and I each pulled out a few hundred American dollars, spread and counted them, whereupon the dealer sent someone away and someone else returned with the promised wad of francs, and so the furtive exchange was made. It was like a drug deal.

The next day, after renting a Toyota Land Cruiser complete with its own driver, a quiet and earnest middle-aged man named Pierre Effa, we left Douala and turned east towards Yaoundé. It was the rainy season in Cameroon, and the sky was filled with gray and the road with logging trucks looming out of the gray, headed in our direction and looking monstrous. We were going full blast down the road in the rain, cataracts on the windshield, a heavy fog closing in behind us—and, seeping in through a cracked-open window, the sweet smell of rain-soaked earth and vegetation.

The sun: a white wafer behind swirling clouds.

The trucks: huge yellow behemoths with logs the size of oil barrels welded end to end.

We passed a wrecked truck in the bushes and the burned-out skeleton of an old car, and we drove for a long time through a crumbly carpet of farm bush: rough secondary growth marking the pathetic echo of a forest that recently was.

Karl, meanwhile, was telling me about a zoo in Yaoundé, underwritten by the Bristol Zoo in England, where the English donors had been told they're educating the people of Cameroon about the importance of not eating apes. The zoo has a bushmeat education project, and a sanctuary for orphaned apes. "There are illegally held chimps within fifty meters of the zoo," Karl said. "That's a total choke! How can you pretend to be active on the bushmeat front, on the basis of education? I think very little is being achieved." He continued: "All these sanctuaries are screaming 'education, education, education.' But the impact is minimal and too long term. The education component is one or two generations away. All these are false hopes, these pilot projects. . . . Nobody faces the harsh reality that none of these projects has the answer. It's only for the donor ready to pull out his checkbook and write his fifty-dollar check. He will feel better handing over that check and then getting a good night's sleep. Sure, sanctuaries might play a role in terms of animal welfare, but in terms of conservation their impact is minimal. It's a choke!"

We fell into a mutual silence—me quietly trying to scribble, unsteady pencil on bouncing notebook, the details of his rant—and then he started up again. "The 'real conservationists' attack these ventures as wasting money which could be going to save apes in the wild, while the sanctuaries are satisfying the bunny huggers: raising apes which would live fifty years but are already 'genetically dead' in terms of the wild species. What these conservationists ignore is why, with all their money, they are not getting on top of the bushmeat crisis and the production of more and more ape orphans. Why should the public spend more money on them, if they clearly do not have the answer? Conservationists have to admit they have failed, and that we might not have the answer. The answer is beyond the traditional conservation approach!"

At last we arrived in Yaoundé, capital of Cameroon, with crowds of people lounging around and looking sullen. No one laughing, no one smiling. The streets filled with deep potholes and open sewage gutters, and all around us heaps of garbage and litter. We drove past an enormous building under construction, or at least half-built and surrounded by construction barricades. According to Karl, it had been overrun by squatters who set up their own government inside, a very unpleasant one. People called it the "building of the dead." A woman was held hostage in there for weeks, raped repeatedly, and the police were afraid to enter. She gave an interview on the radio.

Karl: "People have no respect for anything because the big guys at the top are the biggest thieves, crooks and liars, the biggest everything, so the attitude filters down." The local director of an NGO in Yaoundé told Karl he finally got a second phone. It cost 100,000 francs, but the real problem is paying the bill. You have to hire somebody to go out and pay the bill, and it takes about three days.

✳

We stayed at a big hotel in town and, over the next two or three days, met a number of people, including a former gorilla-hunter named Joseph Melloh. Joseph came to our hotel and chatted with Karl a while, saying things in an accent I couldn't crack and in currents I couldn't follow, though I got the general drift. My first impressions of Joseph: small, quick, birdlike, with a gentle manner. He had a lean, triangular face, a finely trimmed mustache, and a quick and musical way of talking in a Cameroonian English that was sometimes hard to understand.

He said: "Nothing has changed."

And: "The so-called military man has just sent some people in the forest these days, which has brought some ivory."

We planned to rendezvous again with Joseph once we got into the boonies farther east, and I hoped that the second time around some of his thoughts and information would be decrypted.

✳

We left Yaoundé at last, driving east and dropping, soon, from tarmac onto a red clay road that became increasingly unreliable and inclined to gaps and gashes, ruts and holes. Past car and truck skeletons littering the roadside. Past small villages made of stick-and-mud houses, with open fires for cooking, a few wandering goats for being cooked, a few people sitting in small groups along with, occasionally, peanuts spread out in a circle on the ground to dry in the sun.

We arrived at a place where the forest had been ripped open into a shattered maze of rust-red dirt roads, with trees being trucked out of the maze. We passed dueling white butterflies, a sign forbidding bushmeat—*Bracconage Interdit*—and entered a logging camp owned by a French company called Pallisco. There was a radio playing, a baby sitting on a tree stump, and two workers' villages: a bare clay clearing and a few regimented rows of shanties made of rough-sawn planks with galvanized tin thrown on top. Pallisco had two or three hundred employees who, of course, had brought out their families, so around a thousand people lived in those two villages.

Karl had once embarrassed Pallisco with a film, shown on French television, about their operation. The film dramatized what can happen when a thousand non-forest people suddenly show up in the forest and the company provides no meat. The company gave guns and ammo to hunters, who killed any animals they could find. It was supposedly free meat from the forest. This free meat included, as Karl's film documented, some adult chimps who were cut up and stuffed into baskets. Along with the dead chimps there was a baby, too small to be worth very much as meat and therefore still alive, waiting to be transported back to the base in a truck driven by one of Pallisco's French managers. Karl took some footage of Joseph Melloh sitting alongside the chopped-up adults and gently cradling the dazed baby in his arms. As a result of Karl's film, Pallisco had put up road barriers and signs and also plastered signs on their trucks that said *Transport de Gibiers & Passagers Interdit*. And they started a chicken farm. We were shown the chicken farm. We were told that the plan was to have two thousand chickens for starters, but at the moment the farm consisted of a couple of screened beehives filled with a few hundred chirping yellow balls of chirping feathers.

In the meantime, the car had started chirping, and so after looking at the chicks we drove over to the Pallisco garage and machine shop (wooden-framed tin-roofed garage, blue and white ELF oil barrels, a giant pincers on wheels powered by a rumbling orange thorax spewing black puffs of smoke) where a burly Frenchman with suspenders and a flattened nose replaced our fuel filter.

After leaving the Pallisco concession, we eventually arrived at a rough settlement called Lomié. Telephone service had not yet arrived in Lomié, nor had any other kind of service, but the place was distinguished by being close to the Dja Faunal Reserve, Cameroon's only UNESCO World Heritage Site, and it was and is within striking distance of a few urban centers to the east. You can go north to Abong-Mbang. You can go south to Ngoyla. You can go farther east to Yokadouma.

We stayed in a no-star hotel: the Hotel Rafia, which was a long stucco shed with about ten wooden doors, each providing a room protected overhead with a tin roof and underfoot with a tile floor. Giant cockroaches scuttled across the tile. The place had seatless, flushless toilets; and, in a courtyard of baked red clay stood an exhausted palm tree and a mango tree filled with an eager choir of weaverbirds.

In the morning, I was awakened by roosters and a suffusing morning light, and after a quick breakfast I went out to see Mark Van Der Wal, a Dutch foreign aid worker involved in conservation, who lived in a small house in town with some nice Pygmy crossbows on the walls and was responsible for, among other things, Project Joseph.

Project Joseph had been designed a couple of years earlier, and the basic concept was to keep Joseph Melloh the gorilla-hunter out of trouble.

Instead of killing gorillas, as he had formerly done, Joseph would, one hoped with an equal efficiency, run his own gorilla conservation operation, underwritten by the International Fund for Animal Welfare. Working with the people from two villages right next to the great Dja Faunal Reserve, Joseph would locate family groups of living gorillas and, over time, make them used to being watched by people. Those people would eventually be tourists with a good deal of money, so a new economic potential would be introduced into the area, solving human and conservation problems simultaneously. Great idea. Mark was soon telling me some of its less promising aspects.

To begin with, the Dja Faunal Reserve, this remarkable UNESCO World

Heritage Site nearby, was a "black hole." Completely overrun by hunters. In theory, there should have been a buffer zone extending thirty kilometers away from the actual reserve. In truth, the reserve was surrounded on all sides by villages, and on most sides by roads. Inside the reserve, you could find snare lines, spent cartridges, evidence of elephant and other big game hunting. People hunt elephants using ordinary shotguns with a bamboo spear jammed into the barrel. The trigger is pulled. The cartridge explodes. The bamboo spear penetrates the elephant's hide and splinters into a thousand sharp pieces, leaving a very big hole. In the northern parts of the reserve, Mark said, you can sometimes find the remains of those bamboo spears. There had been an American research site that covered an area approximately five-by-five kilometers, run by Tom Smith from San Francisco State University, and the presence of those American scientists seemed to protect that particular area for the seven years or so they were there. But recently they had pulled out.

Mark told me about one village he has become familiar with, Dgabosten, which specializes in the bushmeat trade. Dgabosten has about 600 to 700 villagers, including women and children, and around sixty are professional hunters who send out tons of bushmeat a month. The village is "not an exception," Mark added. "It's just a case that we know it well." About seventy-five percent of their kill is caught with snares, the rest by shotgun. "So if something moves they shoot. Gorilla, chimp, it doesn't matter. The bigger, the better." Still, the bulk of their meat always comes from small animals. Small forest antelopes, and so on.

"Wherever you travel," Mark went on, "it's the same story. Wherever there are forests, the story is the same. Bushmeat is easy meat, low investment. The guns are often locally made. The snares are very cheap."

⁕

Joseph showed up at the Rafia wearing a blue-and-black striped nylon soccer shirt, and soon the three of us—Karl, Joseph, and I—had climbed into the car and, with Pierre at the wheel, set off to find Joseph's old hunting camp. Franceville, he called it.

We followed a road that gradually disintegrated until it became a violent red furrow blasted through the forest. After a while we stopped, and Pierre tucked the car into a discreet little spot just off the road and then prepared for a snooze. Karl, Joseph, and I walked for an hour or two along an old track that had grown fallow. It was brushed over now with vines and bushes and a few trees chest and head high, and on either side was the broken forest, recently logged and open to the sky with a heavy sea of secondary undergrowth. We heard a perpetual rattle of insects in the bushes, the chirping of a few birds in the trees, and, on occasion, the ratcheting of a hornbill.

We finally reached Franceville, which was just about nothing, nearly gone, completely disintegrated. A few hundred feet farther down the track, however, we found a fresh new hunting village: a few huts, two of them mud-and-stick, the others of palm frond and bark over poles. A few chickens wandered around, pecking in the dirt, and one shabby dog was lazing around, nose resting flat in the dirt.

The new hunting camp was called Djodibe and the dog named Plaisir—so we were told by Mbongo George, one of the three hunters who had built and now occupied the place. The others were Mbongo's brother Desire and a colleague named Dieudonne, who were both elsewhere at the moment. There were also some wives and children living in Djodibe, who all concentrated on keeping themselves hidden, while fleetingly shooting out curious gazes now and then from inside one or another of the shadowy huts.

Mbongo George was a young man—in his thirties—wearing shorts, flip-flops, and a red sport shirt. He had a broad and handsome face, a calm smile and steady gaze, and a very pleasant manner that I found relaxing. He also had the disconcerting fidget of wavering his legs open and shut as he talked. He spoke of gorilla hunting and gorilla eating freely, in a casual, matter-of-fact way, and our conversation involved a lot of questioning and answering that would be translated from Africanized French to English and Americanized French and back again in reverse.

Mbongo told us that bushmeat traders are now supposed to have licenses, which allow them to trade in A and B species, with apes and elephants and the like illegal. Between country and town are road barriers supposedly manned by Eaux et Forêts officers. The licensing system identifies the quantity and species a trader can buy—not above sixty pieces of meat per week. If you have more, they will confiscate. The traders used to pay bribes, but now it's more complicated. If you don't have a license, they just take all your meat. If you have one and show it to one of the Eaux et Forêts officers, he says, "I can't eat your license," which is a circuitous way of saying, "Give me a cut of your meat."

Gorillas are fragile, compared to chimps, Mbongo said. If you shoot a gorilla out of the tree, he will fall down heavily. The fall kills him. If you shoot a chimp out of a tree, he still manages to run off. And if a young gorilla happens to get his or her hand caught in a snare, which can happen, the gorilla family will hang around for a day, and then they'll leave, and you can kill the gorilla with a spear. Gorilla meat is special, he went on. "It's a good meat to eat, but the women don't eat it." Why not? The women eschew gorilla or chimp meat because they think those animals are too close to human. At the same time, the men like it because it gives them strength and power.

Mbongo is a member of the Zime tribe, from the bigger group of Kozime, and he went on tell us some of the beliefs and customs his people maintain regarding the mystical power of gorillas. Sometimes they will take the bone of a gorilla and tie it to a newborn baby. It's a way of making sure the baby will grow up strong. To cure a backache, you burn the bones of a chimp and pulverize the burned results— then add oil, make a paste, and rub the paste into someone's back. If a young girl gets pregnant, you tie a chimpanzee's pelvic bone to her hips, and she will have no problem with labor, even if she's very small. If it's dry season and you want rain, you can walk around with a chimpanzee skull, and it will rain.

Does chimpanzee or gorilla meat taste better than, say, duiker (forest antelope)? I wondered. Mbongo's answer turned economic: If you kill a gorilla, the director of the local secondary school will pay 35,000 francs for the meat.

Best part to eat? The hands and feet. True for both gorillas and chimps.

A part they don't eat? They leave a male's testicles.

Cooking a gorilla? To cook a gorilla, you first butcher it into pieces, singe off the hair. Put the meat into a pot of boiling water and oil, and cook for two hours. Add salt and spices. That's the muscle flesh. As for the head, you can put the whole thing, including brain and eyes, in its own pot of boiling water and oil, and the flesh falls off and becomes part of the stew. The skull you might save and later use for fetish (symbolic medicine and magic) purposes.

The spices? Wild spices include wild pepper. They also sometimes put vegetables in the stew: bitter herbs, cassava leaves, cocoyam leaves, and masepoh (rather like basil or sage, sweet and pungent), and anchea (local vegetable about the size and shape of a tomato, but orangish or purplish in color).

❋

We left Djodibe and began the long walk back to the car, but before we had gotten very far, we met Marcial, an old friend of Joseph's. Marcial was carrying a full pack—a wicker backpack—of meat just taken from his snare line. He maintained about one hundred snares, he said, and his pack was bulging with carcasses, which he pulled out to show us: three porcupines, one red duiker, one blue duiker, two mole rats. Marcial told us that his camp was called Karefou, quite a few kilometers away. Karl asked him why he had gone such a long way, and he said there was not much wildlife to kill in between. Now he had to go very far.

We gave him a ride in the car to his rendezvous with some market traders, and during the ride, he told us that before he used to go out on the logging trucks to where he emptied his snares, and then he came back on the logging trucks, but now he has to walk because SEBEC, the company that operated in the area, had closed down. He confirmed that hunting was no longer very profitable, very hard work. In the old days, it was much easier. He also said that recently some officers from Eaux et Forêts confiscated his meat and told him to stop hunting, and he asked them, "What else can I do?" They said, "Go to town and find a job." Marcial went on to say that gorillas and chimps get caught from time to time in the snares, but only the young ones. The older ones tear themselves out of the snares—but these are cable snares, and often the cable becomes tightly wrapped around fingers or a wrist, and so the fingers or hand become infected, rot, and then drop off.

Continuing our bouncing ride down the red road through the forest, we passed an old man wearing bib overalls and struggling with a large wicker backpack that had a set of duiker legs sticking out the bottom. We stopped and talked to him, and in the process noted the signs of something still alive and struggling near the top of his pack. The old man said he had a live pangolin, and Karl and I talked briefly, in English, about buying the animal and setting him free. But then the old man opened the pack to reveal two pangolins, both badly injured and in death spasms. Beneath the pangolins were a couple of large duikers on top of each other. The bottom duiker had her throat slit, tongue hanging out. The old man's name was Fabrice.

We gave him a ride, and pretty soon picked up another hunter carrying another wicker backpack of meat. His name was Mboum Joseph. He said he used to be a mechanic at the logging company known as SEBEC, but then they stopped logging. Only their sawmill was working now, because they had no concession to cut wood. Mboum said he had a gun but no cartridges, and at the moment, he was just hunting with snares to maintain his family. He had gone today to empty his snares, but he didn't get much. In the old days, he used to get much more.

We discovered, next to the road, a small hunting camp with the hunter gone, his two sons playing games on top of a pile of logs across the road from the camp. The boys, Romeo and Judas Nkankan, posed for photos on top of the logs, which were giant—at least four feet in diameter—and told us their father was out harvesting meat from his snares. They were sweet kids, I thought, and Judas was the younger one, maybe five years old; Romeo may have been three or four years older. They wore T-shirts, shorts, flip-flops, and Judas kept a small slingshot tied on a string around his neck. The boys showed us inside their meat-smoking house, which was made of palm fronds and sticks, and filled with smoke and bees. A few porcupines and half a dozen duikers—"bitches," as the boys called them—were being smoked on a wooden rack with a smoldering fire beneath. The duikers were split wide open at the chest, the heads also split in half, and the divided carcasses were spread open into a dark and lumpy pancake. A cross of bamboo kept each of these carcasses flattened open, while swarms of maggots on the meat were wriggling and waving in distress. . . .

A while later, we came to a small village—a Ba'Aka Pygmy village—consisting of beehive-shaped huts made of sticks and leaves, with about a dozen adult inhabitants, men and women, plus a few children, everyone very unhealthy looking. Several of the men's teeth had been fashionably filed into pointed triangles, like shark's teeth, and two of them had scrubby beards. They were dressed in tattered rags, barefoot, seemed lethargic, and the children were large bellied. "These are the most marginalized people in Africa," Karl commented quietly.

They said they didn't own a gun, so they were only hunting with snares. One of the men had a deep infected cut on his forehead, and he showed me a thick lump on his inner thigh. He asked for soap. I seriously regretted having none. One of the women let me look into her cooking pot, which was on a fire and boiling.

Just then a giant Mercedes Benz truck with some giant logs chained to its carriage rumbled by while raising an unpleasant cloud of red dust, and Karl said: "They watch millions of dollars worth of trees go by, out of their forest, and they don't get a cent."

In the pot I saw cassava and yams, some kind of yellow vegetable ("garden eggs," according to Joseph) wrapped in a leaf, and some pieces of duiker meat....

※

After moving on to a place called Bertoua and checking into the only hotel in town, the Mansa, then checking out the meat markets there and in Abong-Mbang—altogether a couple more days of this and that—we headed back to Yaoundé, where we would stay for the night before heading on, next day, to Douala and our flight out. Joseph stayed back in Lomié, needed as he was for Project Joseph, so it was just Karl and I and our driver, Pierre Effa, making the return trip.

Pierre had buggy eyes and arched eyebrows, and there was a vaguely troubled sense about him. He seemed beaten down, a little depressed perhaps, and he had been very reserved and quiet this entire trip. But slowly, I thought, he was getting more comfortable with us, and after helping us locate elephant meat in the Abong-Mbang market, he seemed interested in talking about bushmeat customs.

Speaking in French, Pierre told us that his tribe was Ewondo, and he declared that for him and his family bushmeat was a treat, although for ordinary, day-to-day consumption they ate domestic meat. He said his father had been a civil servant, and so he could afford to hire someone to hunt for him. This man would deliver meat—sometimes every week, sometimes every two weeks—but the gun belonged to his father and the cartridges were given by his father to this hunter. He wasn't as well off as his father, Pierre went on, so they ate bushmeat only once or twice a month, because it was a lot more expensive than beef or pork in Yaoundé.

I asked him what kinds of species his family ate now, and he declared that his wife would buy a porcupine or cane rat normally. Gorilla would be very exceptional, because it's too expensive. As for elephant, she might only buy a small piece, because elephant meat soaks up water and gets much bigger when you put it in the cooking pot.

Karl asked about taste: *"Quel est le viande que vouz préférez? C'est différent, le goût?"* Pierre said he preferred the taste of chimp meat. It's better, and he thought that maybe that better taste would explain why chimp was a good deal more expensive than gorilla in Yaoundé.

Among Pierre's people, the Ewondo, he said, gorillas and chimps are treated the same. Women will not eat the meat from either one when they're pregnant. If they do, it will affect their baby. They will, however, eat ape meat when they're not pregnant. "It's a custom. Don't know why. It's the tradition." He said that ape flesh is good for you, and if you cook the bones and pulverize them, you can use the results to produce strength in children. He started this with his first girl. You might put the powder of bones into a bath, or you can cut the skin and press the powder directly into the blood. His first girl was bathed regularly for her first two or three years with the powdered bone of chimp. . . .

Meanwhile, as Pierre continued to talk in a desultory sort of way, the road became muddy and more muddy, then it got muddier, and we came to a long, long downhill stretch that was crowded with trucks and buses pulled up alongside. "What is everyone waiting for?" we might have asked ourselves, but we didn't. Instead, we continued driving down that muddy road, thinking perhaps about time and distance, schedules and flights out of Douala, until the traffic jam became thicker and harder to negotiate. The land was very wavy there, meaning that the muddy road snaked up and down in waves, but still we moved farther into this land of sticky congestion until we came to the ultimate source of it: a massive petrol tanker on its side, jackknifed, and blocking the road. We had descended into a long valley while passing that long line of stopped trucks and buses and the occasional auto, and suddenly we could see, along the road moving uphill on the other side of the long valley, another long line of trucks and buses and the occasional auto: all stopped and pointed in our direction.

Karl said to Pierre, "Keep going."

We maneuvered closer to the wrecked petrol truck and then made a reckless break for it. Pierre threw the car into four-wheel drive, and, after a disconcerting bit of gear-grinding, the wheels churned into the mud and spun us up and up to the higher edge of the road, which was just a rutted muddy mess. Pierre was gunning the engine, and our wheels were spinning in the slop, our car sliding, slipping, sliding, slipping, sliding, slipping, and finally sliding down and landing with a crunch right onto the cab of the jackknifed petrol truck.

We got out.

The Land Cruiser was damaged—fender crushed—and stuck, wedged by the twin forces of gravity and mud against the tanker. Pierre got back in, raced the engine, spun the wheels, and the car rose up, levitating uphill while raising a spinning cloud of mud, and then slowly it slid back down, churning its own deeper rut as it spun and slipped and nestled back into place next to the overturned truck.

By now we had become a minor spectacle for bored crowds with nothing better to do than watch and chatter in a frenchified schadenfreude. Pierre again raced the engine, spun the wheels, and the car seemed to levitate once more, then, once again, it faltered and slipped back down, having dug an even deeper pocket into mud. Karl, now, began soliciting help from the bored crowd, and so pretty soon more than a dozen young men—Karl and I temporarily included in that category—were hugging the car on the outside, letting our feet and ankles and calves sink deeply into the mud before, in unison, heaving and ho-ing while Pierre raced the engine and spun the wheels. It took several more tries, but eventually the vehicle rose up, quivering, shivering, and then it spun out of the giant rut and away from the overturned petrol truck . . . only to be confronted by another overturned truck and—worse!—the sight of major traffic ahead of us that was slowly pressing and coagulating from jam to jelly.

It was now or never, and we chose now. Karl began freshly urging our young helpers on, and, in spite of the increasing number of muttered comments in French about crazy, craziness, impossibility, and folly, we managed to skittle, scuttle, and scurry with sufficient suction and traction that we passed the second downed truck and at last gained purchase on a stretch of less sloppy road. All this while, however, the traffic ahead of us and facing our way continued to inch forward, gradually forming its own brand of vehicular constipation, and so it seemed important to continue. Karl and I pulled out our wallets and began placing some extra change into the hands of those who had helped us, but the second our money appeared, a much larger crowd of people also appeared and soon were clamoring for their unearned share. Hastily, we climbed back in the car, tossed a wad of small bills out the window—and watched everyone dive for the scattering cloud of paper as Pierre gunned the engine.

We drove away, with Karl commenting sardonically: "Total choke: Everyone was prepared to wait there for the two or three days it takes to get the petrol lorry moved."

We drove on, quietly now, very little talk, just the view out the window: roadside villages consisting of clusters of mud-and-stick houses with thatched and tin roofs, a smoky fire, a few chickens scouring and chirping, a small herd of goats, perhaps, and occasionally a few pigs and bouncing piglets. The scenery looked bleak, and the overcast sky and the thought of our damaged car made it seem bleaker. About the only one who said anything, on that final stretch back to Yaoundé, was Pierre, who out of nowhere produced the following non sequitur: "I can find chimpanzee meat."

Pierre was very familiar with the Yaoundé meat markets, and his comment led us to hire him to carry out an experiment once we got back to our hotel in the big city. This is an experiment that I regret, one about which I have a sense of bad karma. At any rate, in the interests of illustrating vividly the important point that bushmeat is an urban luxury, Karl and I gave Pierre some money and told him to use his normal negotiating skills to buy various cuts of meat, domestic and wild, including chimpanzee. As a result, a few hours later there was a knock on Karl's door—I was sitting in his room, talking about something or other—and the door was opened to reveal Pierre, standing out in the hall with something bloody wrapped in newspaper.

He came in and told us the prices he had paid. I arranged the meat on a table—big piece of boneless beef here, big piece of pigs' head pork near it, smoked chimpanzee arm there, smoked chimpanzee hand next to it, unsmoked hand over there. Karl photographed the meat alongside labels with the prices written on them as a graphic illustration of the pricing issue, and here is what the prices were:

> Chimp hand (less than 1 kilo): 2,500 francs
> Smoked chimp arm: 2,500 francs
> Smoked chimp hand: 2,500 francs
> Big piece (at least 1 kilo) of boneless beef: 1,500 francs
> Big piece of pig's head (about 1 kilo) pork: 1,300 francs

Pierre said there was also a chimpanzee head in the market, which he didn't buy. It would have gone for around 12,000 francs. He also didn't buy a big piece of beef with bone, which would have cost around 1,300 francs. Normally beef is cheaper than pork, he said, but they hadn't gotten any beef in lately because of train problems. . . . But I don't remember any more of what went on. I mainly remember handling the limp, chilly, disembodied hand of the chimp. It was like a Halloween nightmare: standing in an open grave and holding a small person's severed hand.

✳ PART II

6: SPECIAL REGION 4

Two days after touching down in Bangkok, I flew north to Chiang Rai, where I met Karl at a hotel called the Dusit Island Resort. Karl! We shook hands and smiled. I was glad to see him.

We were headed to Burma (or, as the generals prefer, Myanmar) to observe timber elephants at work—as the start of our next book on the vanishing elephants of this world—but a couple of months previously, Karl had introduced a knot, the extended complexities of which I was now beginning to unravel. He wanted first to take a quick look at an odd bit of the country in the northeast and touching the Chinese border, a place called Special Region 4; and so, following an exhausting series of assessments and debates across the ether, I agreed to preface our journey to the timber elephants with a minor detour into Special Region 4, whatever that was.

We left Dusit Island next morning in a VW bus under the pale coin of a full moon, moving through the smell of wood smoke, passing palm trees and banana trees and strolling monks in saffron robes, proceeding into the hills and then an increasing concentration of morning traffic—including three schoolgirls on a motorbike, the middle girl steering, the girl in front leaning over the front and combing her hair, all three with satchels on their backs—beneath mountains looming, rough and toothy, out of the haze. "The first time I came here fifteen years ago," Karl said, "I went with two Americans who were drug control experts, who came here telling everybody they were interested in Buddhism"—adding, after a pause, "It's getting worse and worse, and they don't tell you that."

We came to a sign that said, KEEP AWAY FROM NARCOTICS AND PSYCHOTROPIC SUBSTANCES, and the traffic slowed and then coagulated at the border.

My visa application was based on an entry into Burma via commercial flight from Bangkok to Rangon, where I would be officially embraced by an official tourist agency, but Karl thought our alternative, unofficial route would work just as well: "I've done this four times before. I'm pretty confident that it will be OK."

It looked to be a long wait, but at the entry gate we were directed to the head of the line, where our passports were immediately stamped and handed back: the efficiency a consequence, I later realized, of money having passed from one unknown person to another. Yes, we had help from invisible handlers, and I will describe the visible ones now. First was the silent adolescent driver of the VW bus, who never said his name. Second was our voluble and more mature guide, translator, and general fixer, whose name was Lose: a small, slight man with a pleasant manner, semicircular eyebrows, an orange-brown tint to his skin, and high cheekbones that combined with thin cheeks to give him a concave face. He wore black Levi's, the cuffs rolled halfway up to his knees, and a red-and-black jacket with, on the back, an embroidered cowboy and, on the front, the embroidered word Marlboro. He was a dedicated smoker who said he spoke a dozen languages, was thirty-six years old, and happily married with two children. Maybe he would have no more, he added, possibly because, as he several days later revealed, he grew up with seventeen siblings.

Karl and I also had taken along a traveling partner: a young Swiss national who had rendezvoused with us back in Chiang Rai, and who was now, inside the bouncing VW bus, videotaping everything. His name was Andreas Gehriger. "Call me Reas," he said. He was a freelance video journalist working with Karl on a project for Swiss television, an undercover exposé of nefarious criminals and illegal trafficking in endangered animals and their parts from Burma into China, which explained why we were headed to Special Region 4 instead of the timber elephants.

Reas had a clean-shaven face that, in a beginners' drawing book, would be blocked out as an inverted triangle, with one straight line across for the eyebrows, another straight line for the mouth. In profile, another triangle would define the Roman nose. He was dark-eyed and had thick, dark, close-cropped hair, wavy and distributed like a cap. He liked to have his smokes, I soon discovered, and he also liked to talk. He and Karl seemed to have a lot to talk about, starting with their plans for the Swiss television film.

They would videotape in the markets, Karl said, where a lady will try to sell you tiger penises. Once you pull out a camera, people can get really upset. "But that's good. The hand in the camera"—Karl gestured a hand grabbing at a camera—"can be a good shot." But it's not only tiger penises for sale, it's everything—everything!—and Chinese resource extraction doesn't stop with wildlife. "Anything which has any value: manganese, coal, timber." Meanwhile, so Karl and Reas agreed, they would avoid the BBC when it came time to sell the English-language version of their film, since the BBC had stopped doing serious investigative journalism as a result of their lawyers. Last time Karl sold a film to the BBC on the bushmeat trade, it went through seventeen edits, and the lawyers wouldn't let him name the logging companies or even identify which country they were from. "The lawyers say that the best story is the one you don't get sued for. The full result is wishy-washy."

Chattering thus, we passed through a scrubby landscape, mud-covered, with slow-moving water buffalo wandering through the mud—and then we followed a rocky, olive-brown river, as our little bus methodically chugged uphill and again uphill while negotiating a cliffside highway half washed out in several places, moving higher into the hills and then mountains, past houses on stilts with thatched roofs and woven bamboo walls, past pigs along the road, and then past whole valleys arranged into a jigsaw of rice paddies and terraces and more water buffalo.

Here and there were a number of settlements and road blocks, too, the obvious purpose of which was to raise money—the police and army version of sidewalk lemonade stands and PTA bake sales—which Lose was good at dealing with.

Karl: "What are we doing here?"

Lose: "To pay the some special army."

Another stop, and Lose said: "A bill."

"What for?"

"Car washing. He sees that this is a foreign car."

"Is he army? Police? Immigration?"

"Nothing."

We paid a lot of taxes and bribes that day, and as our reward, late in the day, we arrived at a very beautiful place: a great, broad plain of green and brown rice paddies and grazing buffalo, where conical-hatted famers bent at the waists in the slanting lemon sun, pulling up clumps and bundles of green rice and slapping them into the brown water. Surrounding this great plain, at some distance, was a wall of rugged mountains shaped like ripped pieces of paper, first gray-green, then gray, then whitish-gray fading into a far distant haze.

We also saw, in that same magical lemony light, a farmer dancing out in his field with a pair of giant ping-pong paddles. We stopped the car to watch this spectacle more thoroughly. The paddles had wooden or bamboo handles, with circular pieces of cardboard cut from a Sanyo television carton and fastened to the handles with a loop of bamboo. The farmer stood barefoot in the middle of a pile of rice on a large bamboo woven mat, using his feet to kick up a cloud of dusty rice, then swooping gracefully down with the paddles, and thus winnowing the dirt and husks from his crop of rice.

❋

At last, we pulled into a town called Kyainge Tong and checked into a hotel, also called Kyainge Tong. This was the middle of January, I should add, but a big plastic Christmas tree stood in the hotel lobby, decorated with strings of flashing lights and a red and gold tasseled tinsel banner that said, MERRY CHRISTMAS HAPPY NEW YEAR. Another sign gave notice: PLEASE DON'T MAKE PLAYING-CARDS & OTHER GAMBLINGS IN THIS HOTEL. THESE GAMES ARE PROHIBITED BY LAW. THANK YOU.

I slept very badly that night, and we took off right after breakfast, stopping briefly at a government office to get the special visa for Special Region 4, then snaking our way out of town, with Lose taking on the role of tour guide: "So on the right side is the city hall. It is a big beauty." We passed a school: "In the raining time all the water is going into the school because they don't fix the water."

And after a long drive north into the mountains we arrived at a road block and guard post where, after the usual passport and visa examinations, a steel pipe was lifted and we entered Special Region 4, which at first looked like the unspecial place we had just come from: the same road twisting through the same mountains of swaying forest and swirling bamboo followed by the same sudden dropping away of vegetation to reveal the same vistas, then the same road again turning past the same Buddhist shrines, temples, and monasteries. We stopped at a small village in the mountains called Wan Ha Tapond, the villagers members of the Loi tribe: an old man smoking opium in a bong, several women wearing silver-bauble-and-coin helmets. And we stopped at a monastery and had a conversation with a pipe-smoking monk.

Karl to Lose, who was doing the translation: "Ask him if he minds having all the trees cut down."

Lose: "He don't understand."

But from my limited perspective, the setting was serenely pastoral, and since we were traveling during the dry season, the predominant color was brown, while the main smells and tastes were subtly associated with dust . . . until, suddenly, from out of the dry land and the brown-watered valleys emerged a flood of lush green grass neatly cropped and surrounded by bright green shrubbery and trees. It was a golf course, immediately followed by an imposing fence and gate, a pair of nasty-looking armed guards in military fatigues, and then, beyond the fence and gate, the unfolding vision of a great green lawn and a big white McPalace: a Greek-revival heap of stocky rectangles and white stucco.

Karl: "A lot of New York City junkies paid for this."

Here is what, after a few keystrokes, anyone can learn about Special Region 4 and its relationship with the New York City junkies. The place was created in April 1989 as a semi-autonomous piece of mountainous northeastern Burma after a ceasefire between the Burmese national army and the Marxist guerrillas led by certain drug-dealing criminals. Special Region 4 now has its own visa requirements, its own civil service and army, its own SR4 license plates. Because it shares a border with China, Special Region 4 has also taken on a distinctly Chinese flavor. The telephone signals pass through Chinese networks. The currency is the Chinese yuan. Most ordinary conversations take place in Chinese, and in fact, most ordinary residents having those ordinary conversations are Chinese. The guy in charge (and the owner of the McPalace we just passed), General Sai Leun, was, while a young man (then named Lin Mingxian), a Red Guard actively fomenting chaos on behalf of Mao's Cultural Revolution. From those youthful origins in China, Sai Leun matured into a serious contender in Burma: a rising star with enough "starisma" to warrant his own mug shot on the official United States' wanted list of international thugs, murderers, and drug dealers. . . .

※

Green reverted to brown, and the road rambled and wavered until we had reached the town of Mong La, which is the jewel in the crown of Special Region 4. We stopped for lunch at a Chinese restaurant, open to the street, and while savoring green tea after fried vegetarian rice, we relaxed and watched traffic on the street, which included a large number of bicycles and motorbikes (old farmer riding past, conical straw hat hung onto his back by a chinstrap, ancient iron-headed hoe slung over one shoulder) and several Toyota Corollas interspersed with the occasional Chinese truck run by a single-cylinder, front-mounted engine that (no hood, no fender, a huge flywheel) made noise and spewed fumes. And then along came a brand new blue-and-white garbage truck, a modern one with fancy hydraulics, backing up to some bags of garbage outside the restaurant and warning us with an electronic chime sounding like an ice-cream truck but playing the happy tune of "Santa Claus is Coming to Town."

Christmas was starting to seem like a theme in this part of the world, but Mong La is at heart a Buddhist town in a Buddhist country, and after lunch and then a check-in at our hotel, we drove to the top of a hill at the center of things and climbed to the top of a great golden temple and pagoda.

Mong La was surrounded by high hills, but the upside-down ice cream cone of the golden pagoda reached high enough to rival those hills, and in the late afternoon, we stood up there and looked over the town, while the sounds of puttering motorbikes and chugging Chinese tractors, of children's high-pitched voices and laughter and a cacophony of cocks competitively crowing—those sounds rose and turned insubstantial, and a mild breeze attenuated the heat of the day. Lose, standing next to me, pointed to a green and watery area at the edge of the river flowing through town, and said, "All those rice fields used to be poppy fields."

After seeing about all we could see from the top of the great golden pagoda, we climbed back down, got in the car, and drove over to the pink and spiky drug museum.

The drug museum included dramatic photographs of dead addicts and live interdiction personnel, and, beneath cracked and taped-over glass, we could observe small samples of dried poppies and the narcotics manufactured from them. An extensive diorama illustrated, with the help of dressed-up manikins, the degrading effects of drugs on addicts and the curative effects of intelligent medical treatment and law enforcement. The drug museum's historical section, meanwhile, described the arrival of opium poppies on ships run by Arabic and Portuguese traders during the fifteenth and sixteenth centuries, and it explained that nineteenth-century British colonists finally shipped in the addiction, which was part of their overall plan to enslave the populace. At last, though, all was well: "The state has raised the momentum of efforts in all sectors for prevention of the scourge of narcotic drugs, the enemy of all mankind."

Special Region 4 used to produce nearly nine thousand kilos of raw opium annually. The opium was refined into morphine and heroin, smuggled through the mountains and across the border into northern Thailand, transported south to the hub of Bangkok, and then passed into the jet stream by Chinese criminals. On April 22, 1997, however, Special Region 4 was officially declared a drug-free zone—after a combined agreement between the Burmese generals and General Sai Leun—and to celebrate that auspicious moment the narcotics museum was opened, whereupon the momentum of efforts in all sectors for prevention of the scourge of narcotic drugs began.

First was the police work, which consisted of decapitating plants, burning fields, apprehending criminals, and smashing refineries. Second was the economic work. Opium was a major cash crop in this part of the world. The opium poppies, *Papaver somniferum*, grow easily and well in these mountains, and a tribal farmer could make as much as $250 per year farming them, a sum that is at once pitifully small and significantly better than any income he could hope to earn from any other crop. Still, the government introduced alternative cash crops for the small-plot farmers and provided, in the language of one government report, "income generating enterprises" and "other suitable business enterprises."

✳

Income generation? Suitable business enterprises? The Las Vegas-ization of Mong La happened quickly, and it began with a paving of the streets, followed by wiring for electricity to power the flashing lights that flashed happy thoughts in Chinese and English, such as, "Oh! That's wonderful!"

Dozens of enormous casinos, discos, and hotels were built. A non-stop pornography channel was cabled into the hotels. Prostitutes from Thailand and eastern Europe were shipped in, their phone numbers displayed prominently in each hotel room. Most famously, a glamorous Thai transvestite revue, commonly known as The Ladyboy Show, was organized. ("After the shows," Karl recalls, "the transvestites would take these Chinese guys into the toilet and ask five dollars to show them their equipment. A lot of the Chinese guys couldn't believe they weren't women.") For family-oriented entertainment, meanwhile, Mong La offered an amusement park, the Mong La National Paradise, complete with Ferris wheel, a herd of polo-playing elephants, broad lawns and a large pond with plastic paddle boats for rent, and even a great barn containing a bear farm.

So the new Mong La, though built with money from opium and heroin, was by the start of the new millennium making money through gambling and sex (with a bit of amphetamine thrown in for good measure, this new drug being produced in hidden labs to the east)—and the Chinese living staid lives on the other side of the border began to buy. Suddenly there was, according to a reporter from Toronto's *Globe and Mail*, "a new economy of casinos, karaoke bars, golf courses, brothels, hotels, bowling alleys and tourist gimmicks such as the elephant polo." Outside of town, dozens of luxury condos were under construction, while (according to the same Canadian reporter) "the night sky of Mong La is brightly lit by the neon lights of the gaudy casinos and posh hotels." As many as 600,000 Chinese tourists with several million dollars worth of yuan in their pockets were annually arriving on day-trip buses, eager to sample Mong La's exotic wares.

Then one day the beloved daughter of a well-placed Chinese official returned home from Special Region 4 humiliated and poorer by the equivalent of $100,000, so the Chinese army was called out. Troops marched to the border, and, for those day-trippers without any sober or boring need to enter, the border was closed.

Mong La's booming economy instantly went bust, and now, as our little group of ostensible sightseers and industrious videotapers visited the place, it was still busted. The one luxury hotel still operating—where we stayed—stank and was badly run by a skeleton staff. The Ladyboy Show was gone, the transvestites sent back to Thailand. The eastern European prostitutes were no longer in evidence, except for a single tawdry dance show just down the street from our hotel. The flashing lights no longer flashed, and the palatial casinos and discos were looking worn and weather-stained, with only their noble profiles yet reflecting architectural ambition and a few big signs still recalling delusions of grandeur—for example, the Myanmar Royal Leisure Company. Even the amusement park, Mong La National Paradise, had fallen on hard times, with the polo-playing elephant herd reduced to a single, sad elephant and the plastic paddleboats beached and bleached and cracking in the sun, while, as we would eventually take note, a dead cat floated in the pond's green scum.

According to Lose, Special Region 4 included about eighty-five thousand residents, so even as the decaying casinos littered the center of Mong La, it was still operating as a real place with people to feed and business to transact. Actually, the Thai sex workers still gathered dutifully in the red light district next to the central market, and one evening we spent a half hour walking past the extended row of sex boutiques, saying hello to some of the more friendly prostitutes and trying to estimate their numbers: a few to several dozen slender young women inside the boutique stalls watching TV, talking to each other, looking bored, a few of them playing net-less badminton in the dark street outside the stalls. But where were the customers?

Although all the high-stakes casinos were closed down, the night brought out a smaller-scale, more amateurish sort of gambling with, inside one rough shed I entered, thick crowds of cigarette-smoking men, a few women, all of them sweaty and wild-eyed as they gathered around eight homemade tables marked with crudely hand-numbered squares. You placed your money on a numbered square and set your hopeful gaze upon three giant wooden dice temporarily restrained by a rope at the top of a washboard-style slide. The giant dice were released one at a time, whereupon they rolled down in a wooden racket and came to rest on the numbered squares, instantly generating a human racket of raging shouts, cries, and screams. That seemed to be the big excitement in Mong La.

After dinner that night—more fried vegetarian rice—I called it a day. My room was 221, and so I walked past the doors numbered 207, 209, 211, 268, 215, 217 . . . until I finally found my own foul-smelling cubicle, unpleasantly hot with a window opened onto a potentially less hot alleyway and the penetrating sounds of a party, mainly bass and drums, stealing into my room and then my head until around two o'clock in the morning. I couldn't sleep. What to do? What else but look at the porno on television.

I saw fish-white, sunken-chested, pot-bellied men with small—tiny!—penises, who looked like the illegitimate offspring of gangsters and nerds pulled out of a T.B. sanatorium. The women were frail and utterly failing in their sad attempts at faking passion, pleasure, or even focus. *Is it over yet?* their dazed eyes kept asking. On the positive side, however, I was permanently cured of any interest in sex, more or less.

✳

One day we ran into a couple of Australian tourists, two beer-drinking guys with bug-eyed sunglasses lashed on with color-coded cords, bored and eager to leave, but aside from them, I never saw any obvious tourists, other than ourselves, for the entire time we were there. Meanwhile, we were required to declare ourselves actual tourists, rather than, for example, actual spies or journalists, so we showed up at the Department of Tourism and had a long chat about tourism with the director. He introduced us to the woman who would be our official guide and translator, a pleasant and attractive youngish woman, as I remember.

I don't remember much, probably because she didn't actually spend much time being our guide and translator. That was fine with me, since I was by then growing paranoid and thinking she might be working for the secret police, whose presence I occasionally imagined. (Yes, you: man in the white poplin jacket, taller and better dressed than anyone else in the market, drifting about in the style of an absent-minded shopper while single-mindedly appearing ahead of us, behind us, ahead of us, behind us, and occasionally drawing in close enough to listen, in a overly friendly way, to our casual conversations with merchants.)

Possibly the most touristic thing we did was visit the official border crossing into China. The Chinese customs and immigration building was emphatically modern looking—glass-and-steel sort of thing—while the Burmese building made a much quainter impression. Not counting, that is, the still-standing ancient border gate, which was flanked by life-sized elephant and castle statues and decorated with a couple of upward-looking dreamy angels and a seven-tiered flaming flowing roof with a tower on top.

Altogether, it seemed like a sleepy border crossing operating alongside a slow-moving, silvery river . . . across which we could observe a rambling chain-link border fence and some bears. The bears were on the Mong La side of the border, so we drove across the river and down a windy dirt road until we came right up to seven big-nosed and long-tongued Asiatic black bears in seven tiny cages, plus a house, and a man and his wife who lived in the house and also owned the bears. We had come at feeding time, it happened, and as the man brought out buckets of sloppy gruel to his animals, they grunted and groaned and whimpered and spun around in wild excitement. The cages were so small, the bears had just barely enough room to spin, all except for one slightly more fortunate fellow with a slightly larger cage, who hopped around and around at the edges of his quarters, as if he couldn't stand all that room. The bears slobbered and gobbled up their gruel, and afterwards, as the man sprayed them and their cages with water from a garden hose, they madly kissed and bit the water. They seemed to love the spraying of water into their mouths and their cages, and while they were thus momentarily distracted, some wandering chickens gathered together enough foolhardiness to peck inside the cages, pilfering some final scraps of the bear food.

The bear man said his name was Lao Chang Yangjo and explained that in the old days, when the Chinese gamblers were coming into town in big numbers, he was selling many bears for much money. It was easier to get bears then. The hunters would bring in babies. Now the bears had pretty much disappeared, having been nearly hunted out. Yes, they were much harder to get—but they had also gotten harder to sell, so that kind of balanced out. Since the Chinese started turning away gamblers at the border gate, business had gotten a lot slower, but he would continue feeding the seven big animals he had because sooner or later some rich customer from China would have a wedding and want to show off by roasting a bear. At that point, he would kill one, butcher the carcass, and send the pieces across the border.

With Lose as translator, I asked the wife how they killed the bears when they were sold as banquet meat. She raised an arm and mimed firing a rifle into the cage. (Karl later told me they slaughtered their bears by electrocuting them.)

Karl asked how they were able to get the meat across the border, since it was illegal to send parts of an endangered species across an international border. The answer: Sure, the Chinese still kept the border closed to gamblers, but nobody cared about stupid animals. Anyhow, his house and the seven bears, though located across the river from the official gate, were still right next to the chain-link border fence and in fact about twenty feet away from that big hole in the fence. China was just on the other side, and as we could see, people passed back and forth through that hole all the time.

It was true. As we watched the bears and talked with Lao and his wife, we were able to look over to the dirt road leading to his house, and the dirt path that the road became, and watch people coming and going along the road and path, and passing through the hole in the fence separating China from Burma's Special Region 4. Reas and I even tried this little trick ourselves, and so I made my first tentative entry into China.

⚹

During the next few days, we found as many as a hundred live bears in Mong La, most of them kept in cages so small they could barely turn around. You could walk down a street in certain parts of town, peer into a courtyard or an alleyway, and find the mute brutes tucked away like rotten gym clothes tossed into an old gym locker. But about half of those hundred bears were prisoners in a single ghoulish operation very optimistically called the Bear Farm, which was open to the public and located within the grounds of the town's amusement park, Mong La National Paradise.

The Bear Farm consisted of a very large, cinderblock-walled, corrugated-iron-roofed barn, with a nice reception lobby at the front to receive any visitors and customers. We parked out front and walked through a glass door into the lobby: three gawky Euro-American types carrying a camera, a video camera, and a notebook. The lobby was exposed to the outside by a glass wall. Wooden furniture had been arranged on a red tile floor, and the business side of the lobby—containing one antique cash register and one subdued cashier—was separated from the customer side by a long row of glass cases displaying the farm's one important product: bile taken from the bears' gall bladders, which was used to con sick people into spending money. There were cans with pills, red and gold boxes containing powders, and fancy maple-syrup-style bottles containing a pale yellow liquid.

I started examining labels and soon found some translated into an English that explained why anyone would spend his or her last yuan on this kind of egregious scam. The literature cheerfully declared that bear gall-bladder bile would treat almost anything. It would "protect the liver and brighten the eye, clear up and remove evil heat, diminish inflammation and relieve pain, benefit the gall and remove stone," as well as cure "various acute and chronic hepatitides, icterus, hepatomegaly, cirrhosis, cholecystopathy and biliary tract, aphta, glossitis, gastritis, bronchitis, stagnated fire, mania and spasm in children"—and so on. *Stagnated fire!* I liked that one.

Karl and Reas had passed through a door in the lobby and down a few steps into the barn proper, where the bears were. I followed them into the shadowy interior of the place, which was filled with the stench of too many animals crammed into too-small cages. I counted around fifty bears, almost all of them in solitary cages looking like a combination shopping cart and bird cage and lined up in four parallel rows, with a fifth and perpendicular row at the far end of the barn. These were cages of steel, with barred walls, barred ceilings, barred floors—each less than five feet to the side, I estimated—raised off the floor by three- to four-foot legs with wheels on the bottoms and, at one end, narrowed into a bottleneck or squeeze. The Bear Farm was not so much a farm as a factory, with bears being the primary moving parts.

As if to mock the animals, or perhaps to insult the intelligence of any normal human entering the interior of this factory, the far cinderblock wall was painted over with a giant, happy-thought mural showing wild bears playing gaily in a forest, which was the exact opposite of what was really going on. What was really going on: imprisoned bears, raging and pathetic, rubbing their faces raw by swaying helplessly back and forth, back and forth, back and forth, back and forth, back and forth. All these bears had catheters surgically embedded into their gall bladders, and now, as we three watched—and photographed, videotaped, and took notes—a white-covered senior Bear Farm technician, his mouth and nose lurking behind a white mask, entered carrying in one hand a large canister and in the other a giant syringe. Accompanied by a young female assistant, he began walking from cage to cage, bear to bear, and gradually if industriously retrieving the factory's daily production of bile.

The bears would be suckered by food into the bottleneck end of their cages, where access to food was traded for upper body mobility. They jammed themselves in there, in the process exposing their bellies and the catheters embedded therein to the reach of the technician, now squatting beneath the cage, and his syringe. The bear ate. The technician drew away a syringe full of bile, squirted the contents into his container, and then—as the assistant moved ahead to feed and immobilize the next bear in line—he followed, proceeding to squat beneath the next cage for the next hypodermic milking.

It was disturbing to watch, but soon enough the technician, working away on the factory floor, cage to cage, bear to bear, began to seem disturbed that he was being watched—and photographed, videotaped, written about in a notebook. He stopped, giving us significantly unhappy looks. We ignored him, and soon the assistant was detailed to come over and ask us, in her high school English, to leave. Karl replied: "No problem here. We're just interested in what's going on. What do you have to hide?" And he continued taking pictures, while Reas continued videotaping. The assistant silently returned to assisting the technician.

After milking the bile out of two more bears, the technician looked up again to see us still there. He shook his head, then handed the syringe and canister to his assistant, and waved both hands and arms in a gesture that was clear enough: *Go away! Get out of here! No pictures!*

We didn't respond.

The technician returned to his work, but after milking three more bears, he stopped again and turned to see that we were still there and still being a terrible disturbance, and now he began waving his arms vigorously and shouting vociferously at us in Chinese, saying things that may have translated as: *Get the hell out of here, running-dog shitheads and unspeakably filthy pigs, before I fucking call the fucking police!*

Karl just shouted back: "What's the problem? What are you worried about? We're tourists! We're tourists taking pictures, and when we're done we'll leave." Reas's style was different. He was a master of the sheepish smile, the gentle and wordless apology of the face, the sweet curl of the lips projecting an agreeable fool's unquenchable ignorance, as if to say: *Oh, sorry! Was that me? Did I do that?*

※

In the mornings, we would go down to the big market in the city center: a large rectangle made of a series of corrugated tin roofs raised on steel posts and enclosing a car park in the middle. Here, amid a chaos of smoky, open-air restaurants, we all five (including Lose and our silent adolescent driver) paused to eat a hot breakfast and drink sweetened Nescafés.

Then (as our driver excused himself to wait by the VW bus, leaning and twisting up close to the left side mirror in order to tweeze away all the irritating new hairs that had begun sprouting out of his face since yesterday) we four toured the markets, examining the vegetable produce and the meat and the animals about to become meat—fish, chickens, snakes, a large python, turtles, trembling pangolins, birds of all sorts, a small leopard-looking cat, civet cats—as well as the various animal parts, such as skins and claws and paws and bladders and penises, a dog's head, and all kinds of dried snakes and bird parts meant to solve this or that medical problem. Live puppies were also for sale, as were live birds: the former for food, the latter for fortune. Good-luck birds.

When I saw a large, dark-feathered bird in the market one morning, still alive and tethered with a string passed through the nostril hole of his beak, I paused—distressed at the mindless cruelty on display—and the woman who owned the bird smiled and made a flapping motion with her hands, meaning: Free him and get good luck in return. We negotiated the price down to twenty yuan, and then, taking the bird out of the market and out of town, we stopped the car on a country road, got out. I untied and drew away the string that had been passed through the nostril hole and released the bird at the edge of the road. After a brief hesitation, he flapped his wings and flew weakly across a ditch, then dove into a thicket. I hoped he would survive.

As we drove away, I asked Lose what kind of bird we had just freed.

Lose: "They like to live on the bag of the barflow."

"Bag of the barflow?"

"Bar floor."

"Bag of the bar floor?"

"Yes, they live on the bag of the bar floor."

"Back of the buffalo? You mean cattle egret?"

Meanwhile, though, Karl and Reas had been trying to track down the big traders. By the time they made a connection, I was beginning to feel sick to my stomach, and so I slept late and missed the visit to a dealer who had a new leopard skin and four bear paws for sale (two thousand yuan each for the paws), and who said he had just sold a nice and very rare tiger skin for fifty thousand yuan and a crate of tiger bones for eighty thousand yuan—skin and bones altogether, Karl estimated, around fifteen thousand dollars.

But the three of us jointly spent a lot of time looking at penises. Penises were very big in Mong La, and they were used for . . . what? "For the man energy," explained the nicely dressed, poised, and attractive young woman behind one pharmacy counter.

Tiger penises were worth many yuan as traditional Chinese medicine, she added, very excellent for putting the purr and growl back into a man's sex life, but since, alas, the tigers had already just about been wiped out, their penises were now only rarely showing up. Instead, we would have to settle for other sorts of penises, such as—for example—some lovely but efficacious deer penises, which were displayed before us under glass within elaborate red-and-gold gift boxes. She could sell us deer penises, if that was what we desired. We priced them, and thus discovered that older was better than younger. One more than ten years old was selling for the yuan equivalent of about ninety dollars, while a much younger penis would fetch little more than half that figure. What a happy thought.

As we pressed her, the woman repeated: No tiger penises. But they did, she assured us enthusiastically, brew and sell tiger wine. As a matter of fact, we could see the brewing process right back there in the next room: those twenty-gallon fish tanks filled with whitish ginger roots and a few curved bones within a brown-tea colored brew. The bones, she told us, were guaranteed to be from a tiger, and they would lend a tiger's powerful chi to the final concoction, which was bottled in those fancy decanters so neatly arranged on the shelves right before us.

※

The animal extraction business in Mong La worked like a giant vacuum cleaner hoovering through the forests of Special Region 4 and the rest of northeastern Burma, sucking out, mainly for Chinese middle-class consumers, animals common and rare, endangered and not endangered, live and dead, whole and disassembled. This was Economics 101, that page in the textbook where the downward curve of disappearing supply is mortally stabbed by the upward spike of mindless greed.

Both China and Burma have signed the international treaty known as the Convention on International Trade in Endangered Species (CITES), which is meant to protect species threatened with extinction, such as tigers and Asiatic black bears, from a trade across international borders. It would seem that much or most of the wild animal business in Special Region 4, as it serves Chinese business and markets, is illegal and ought to be stopped by the governments of China and Burma. But aside from the legal aspects of a business that continues to violate CITES restrictions, there is a very worrisome public health aspect. A visit to the town food markets one morning turned up, as I mentioned earlier, a couple of dead civet cats. Civet cats are actually unrelated to cats, and they look more like big weasels or raccoons. They are also the direct source of the Severe Acute Respiratory Syndrome (SARS) virus that appeared and began spreading among humans in southern China during 2002. By 2003, the SARS virus had spread globally and killed some eight hundred people before a radical series of quarantines and an official Chinese prohibition on "the slaughter, cooking and selling of wild animals like the civet cat" succeeded in curtailing, at least temporarily, the developing pandemic.

The public health issue may be the most obvious cause for alarm in considering the wild-animal capitalism of Special Region 4, but what upset me most immediately about this whole business was something at once harder to describe and to justify: my own personal sense of the simple, stupid cruelty involved. Greed and lawlessness are common enough, but here, in this little corner of the world, I saw a cold callousness: a strangely hard attitude I observed among those happy-faced purveyors of tiger skins and bear bladders and deer penises, of live snakes and birds and monkeys and dogs, of reptiles and amphibians . . . a smiling callousness that just sneaked up and surprised me. I had come to a place where many things human and all things non-human were for sale, live or dead, whole or dismembered. A place where the stimulation and feeding of human appetite was the reigning force, the sole significant value and motivation. A place where the party goes on, where the happy-thought sign in flashing lights always says, "Oh! That's wonderful." Yes, I was feeling a serious cultural disconnect. Surely, I thought to myself, I am moving among a strange and frightening people who have no sympathetic feeling for animals, not any kind of sympathy for any kind of animal whatsoever.

On the final evening of our stay in Special Region 4, that disquieting feeling came into its sharpest focus. This time we visited a street Lose told me was called Live Animal Restaurants Street, and we slowly strolled past the restaurants there. They were sidewalk restaurants, with the tables and chairs spilling out in the open from under a roof, with the concrete floors drifting out as well until they become sidewalks terminating at the curb.

At curb's edge the menus were all on animated display.

Proceeding from restaurant to restaurant, we examined the menus, which included but were not limited to: a pair of fluffy brown-and-white slow lorises (small primates), two or three dozen cobras rearing and weaving inside mesh-topped baskets, some fat owls blinking serenely inside owl-sized cages, a pair of diamond-scaled pangolins curled into self-protective balls, a trembling baby raccoon-like creature, numerous large toads in plastic bags, turtles, a writhing monitor lizard, one tiny baby rhesus monkey on a chain, several fat little white dogs, a large caged eagle. . . .

The third restaurant along led in the competition for customers, with a lively boisterous crowd spread inside and on the sidewalk, everyone dressed to kill in dark suits and bright puffy dresses. It was a wedding party, and the bride and groom, sleek and shiny and full of real promise, were the center of attention, while the honeymoon car (cream-colored luxury sedan with roses taped in long aerodynamic rows along the sides and a large bouquet of red and yellow roses packed into the shape of a valentine heart taped onto the vehicle's hood) waited at the curb. Members of the wedding party, meanwhile, were slowly settling into their seats and tables for the grand dinner to come, and in the process shifting through a series of social tableaux: kisses, hugs, wrapped arms and bright smiles lit by flashing cameras.

The night was early, so perhaps appetites and business would pick up soon enough. Still, as we moved up the street, looking at the live menus and trying to identify species, we reached the last restaurant, where, away from the noisy comings and goings of the wedding party, things were much more sedate. At this final restaurant only four or five customers were seated, while the woman who appeared to be both cashier and waitress occupied herself by sweeping down the restaurant floor and sidewalk. She ignored us, as we paused to examine the menu at curbside, including four cute little white puppies, but when we bent down to look at a pangolin inside a cage, pathetically trembling and hugging a turtle in the same cage, the woman furiously stepped over and began jabbing with the end of her broom handle at the pangolin, trying I suppose to wake him up for our benefit. But it seemed just cruel. "Stop. Stop it. Stop! Stop!" I said, then shouted, but she obviously didn't understand English and in any event didn't care. She did at last stop after I grabbed the broom and risked a tussle and a scene.

✸

After another of my fried vegetarian rice dinners that night, we all turned in. Karl and I both happened to have rooms located in the same general part of the same corridor of the hotel, and as we both passed in the direction of our doors, we suddenly noticed two solemn-faced, furtive, and surprisingly tough-looking men quickly pass us from the opposite direction. "They just came out of my room!" Karl said—and he thought they were secret police. It was a very worrisome idea, actually, partly because Karl earlier, in Thailand, had been in touch with some dissident leaders who gave him information and maps showing where the Special Region 4 amphetamine labs were hidden, which for some reason he had been carrying around with him all this time.

As we drove south through the mountains on the next day, at last passing out of Special Region 4, sighing that interior sigh of relief that comes with the rearview sighting of a quietly descending border pipe, and with the rising sense of a decisive passage from horrific police state to merely horrible police state, Karl commented philosophically: "This country induces introspection. It's all pretty slow. It's a good thing sometimes to get away from the rush of the world. . . . But I mean if they had found that file, all those documents by these dissidents, showing where the opium fields still are, showing where the amphetamine labs still are, it would have been a different story."

7: THE BURMESE TIMBER ELEPHANTS

Burma was building a brand new international airport in Yangon that would, I was sure, some day be fine, but the airport we waded through now was a Dickensian edifice built for the purpose of abusing orphans. *Please, sir? May I be excused from all this?* you wanted to ask. We slowly passed through another immigration—my sixth or tenth since arriving in the country—and then waited in a smoke-filled non-smoking lobby for the bus to take us onto the tarmac. Jet engines screamed outside, and every once in a while a man came in waving a stick with a sign on the end that said things like, AIR MANDALAY 501.

At last our own flight number was waved on the stick, and we pushed our way out to the buses and then clambered onto the plane. We flew at first over rice paddies and an ornately serpentine silver river, followed by more rice paddies and a long expanse of farm plots and more rice paddies, pulling above the clouds now and proceeding to a place where the clouds dissipated and the land rose and wrinkled and turned green with a stubble of trees. According to Karl, we were now passing over tiger country, only the tigers had already been wiped out. Finally, we sailed out over a blue, blue sea and began turning, following the coastline, looking at an edge of land silhouetted with palm trees, then turning again and nosing down onto a sandy runway, pulling up finally before an airport the size of someone's beachside bungalow. THANDWE AIRPORT, the sign said, and we crawled off the plane into hot air and terra softa-sanda. We went through immigration once more before at last finding our baggage.

Bags in hand, Karl and I discovered our escort and driver. The escort was a broad-faced, cleanly dressed man who greeted us in English; the driver was a small and oily haired, sunglasses kind of guy who never said much. He drove a small Toyota Corolla that seemed instantly overloaded with our bags and the four of us, as we bounced along the sandy, rutty road away from the airport.

Our guide turned around to talk from the front seat, said he was taking us to a good beach hotel where we could, as he phrased it, "have relax," and then he passed out his business card, which said *Moe Sinn Mung (Dr.).* "You can call me Moe," he said.

"What kind of doctor are you?"

"Doctor of Veterinary Science."

✳

It was still dark when, next morning, we piled into the little car and drove away. But the air was pleasant and cool, and as the darkness peeled away, a yellow sun angled its light into the misty fields on either side of the road. Farmers in conical straw hats were walking along the road, while other people pedaled ancient bicycles or drove even more ancient Chinese trucks and motorized carts, or urged motion into arthritic beasts drawing wooden-wheeled carts. A woman balanced a basket of bright yellow flowers on her head.

Our driver pressed a tape into the car's tape player, and soon some sincere syrup was being poured onto a cheap pancake: "You have no right to ask me how I feel," the singer moaned, "you have no right." But we were headed into town now, a place called Oat Shit Pin, and the road became increasingly populated. Women, girls, and sometimes boys walked past with yellow paste dabbed into triangles, circles, and swirls on their cheeks. Dogs, chickens, goats, and sometimes pigs rose up to join the people walking—or, if not walking, then balancing themselves on antique bicycles and also, now, riding in motorcycles attached to tinny old sidecars containing extra passengers. Our driver honked, people moved, and the traffic became thicker and more stubborn. A rough box pulled by a single-cylinder engine chugged along beside us. A giant steel bus with human flesh popping out of glassless windows came into view.

After breakfast and tea in an Oat Shit Pin cafe, we returned to the car. The driver slipped in another moaning tape: "One more time, one more time, one more time." And we drove away and soon made it to the far side of town, where we were stopped for our second or third official checkpoint of the day—a few small buildings, a scattering of trees, a barrier across the road, a ragged gaggle of languid men with guns and mustaches. Our guide, Moe, got out, papers in hand, and conferred with the official apparently in charge. (We were moving into an area officially closed to foreigners, I should mention, but Karl had been there twice before and was able to get our permits based on various friends and high-level connections; he was planning to produce a story and documentary film on the Burmese timber elephants.)

The tape player started up again—"Can this be love?"—and we left town and dropped into a different century, a quieter one with few engines and no electricity, where people lived simple lives harrowed and refined by hard work. This was a peasant society, where farmers in dried-out rice paddies pulverized muddy clods with the help of yoked and humped white bullocks dragging old wooden sledges. Where the road, built by British colonialists more than a century ago, still needed work. The car would periodically fall into one of the many potholes with a heavy bang of metal on metal, but the road was gradually being repaired— or so I concluded from the regular heaps of rough gravel deposited along the way. Soon I saw that the gravel itself was being repaired. We came across a heap of larger rocks with a man in rags knocking at them with a sledge and making them smaller.

We drove past rice paddies guarded by bamboo houses on stilts, and then the road began ascending. The driver downshifted, and the car began grinding into hills that were green with trees and yellow-brown from bamboo. The road became steeper, and the traffic, always light, nearly disappeared, save for an old banged-out bus or the occasional rickety logging truck transporting great boles of timber. We kept grinding up and up and up, higher into the mountains and sometimes onto the unfolding of a great view with a frightening drop-off at the edge of the road and an expanse of green far off at the horizon. The road curved and rose. It ran out of tarmac and turned into a long lingering trail of dirt and stone, and then our driver stopped the car and popped open the hood and, after an appropriate waiting period, poured in what I had thought was our drinking water.

We made a second stop for cooling the overheated engine, a third, a fourth, and, then, at some point in the early afternoon, our laboring car made a final turn up the disintegrating mountain road, and someone said, "The elephants!"

✳

The car pulled over at the roadside hamlet of Nyaung Chay Htauk—shade trees, a few bamboo sheds and shelters, some snacks and soft drinks for sale—where a minor cluster of bystanders and onlookers turned to paint us politely with a collective, curious gaze, and where, as I saw now, a small forest of gray-skinned flesh was quietly swaying. We climbed out, stretched, and ambled towards the elephants.

But Karl and I were just then stopped by Moe and introduced to the elephant doctor, a lean and bespectacled young man named Dr. Min Bang Ow. We turned again to look at the elephants: a big gray puddle that included, I could see now, two babies, maybe one or two years old, who were about the size and shape of Volkswagen Beetles and as cute as anything. Standing between us and the elephants was a small, tough-looking man, who grimly held out an iron-tipped spear—ready, it seemed, to poke out the eye of any person or elephant who should get out of line.

I tried to count the elephants, and you'd think such big creatures would be easy to count. But there were people in front of me, elephants in front of other elephants, and at the same time I was watching the man with the spear and the babies and the onlookers and bystanders. The adult elephants came complete with men sitting on top: mahouts—or *oozies*, as the Burmese call them.

I counted three adult elephants and the two Volkswagen babies.

The oozies were lean, jockey-sized men wearing simple cotton shirts and dark longyis, and they sat on top of the three adult elephants, their legs wrapped around the elephants' necks, their bare feet half-hidden behind the elephants' slowly waving cabbage-leaf ears. And then, after one of the oozies bawled out a few incomprehensible syllables and poked his bare feet emphatically into the inside folds of a pair of gray ears, the eyes between those ears momentarily pulled into focus. A head raised, and then, step by step, an elephant painstakingly shifted the beams and boulders of her body in a manner that moved her forward until she had reached the edge of the road. She stopped, stood there quietly, as if she had fallen back asleep, with only her trunk still awake and animated, fidgeting restlessly.

Karl, now walking towards the giant creature, drew a bright fruit—a tangerine, I think—out of his pack. He pressed it forward in a gesture of presentation. "A gift," he said to the elephant. He held the fruit up close to the creature's vacant eye, then brought it right up to the tip of her trunk.

The elephant seemed oblivious, utterly uninterested.

Karl paused before tossing the fruit onto the pavement in front of her, right beneath the working end of her trunk, whereupon that great flexible column of muscle and gristle curled, arched, and uncurled. It lowered the sniffer end until it was directly above the fruit. With a slow *whuff*, then, the elephant pulled up a column of air and olfactory molecules, then paused, as if in thought, before slowly raising her trunk, slowly shifting her weight, slowly elevating her right foot, and slowly lowering the same foot until it had reached the fruit and pressed down to pop it open, splattering a crown of juice onto the pavement. The elephant paused to *whuff* the splattered juice, then showed absolutely no further interest.

Now the oozie on top began shouting some serious commands—"*Hmet! Hmet! Hmet! Hmet! Hmet!*"—and, in response, the great beast began to lower herself. First, she folded her rear legs, which were hinged at the knees just like a person's legs, so that she was kneeling, her back sloped down, just as a person might kneel. After more commands, she began to kneel with her front legs, which were also hinged at the knees like a person's legs, only a person facing in the opposite direction from the first person.

A wooden rack the size of a small bathtub was resting on her back, insulated from her skin with a dark red and woolly protective padding (pounded Napé bark) and fixed in place with a couple of ropes that wrapped around her neck, another rope around her chest just behind the front legs, and a final rope that looped (with the help of a charming little carved piece of wood apparently meant to reduce the friction in that sensitive area right above the anus) beneath her tail.

Several pieces of luggage and Karl's photographic supplies were soon being tossed into the wooden rack with the high assistance of the oozie, who stood barefoot on the elephant's shoulders and was judiciously arranging and balancing things. And then Karl climbed up. I watched him place one foot on top of the elephant's kneeling and horizontal front leg, then, hoisted part way up by Dr. Ow from below and the barefoot oozie from above, he put another foot on the elephant's neck and climbed into the rack, turning around and sitting down in the center, knees up and facing forward. The oozie then settled back down onto the elephant's neck, shouted several emphatic commands, and the beast rose once more. More commands from the oozie, and the elephant—by then joined by a Volkswagen baby—moved away. They were soon replaced at the same spot by a second mother elephant accompanied by a second baby.

The oozie sitting on this creature's head shouted, and she too lowered herself on folding legs. Luggage was passed up and arranged, and now it was my turn. I stepped onto the top of the elephant's horizontal front leg, hoping the soles of my shoes were not too rough, and—pulled by the hands of the oozie, pushed by the hands of Dr. Ow—rose to place a knee onto the back of the elephant's neck and finally, from there, stumbled up and into the wooden rack. Then I turned around and clumsily sat down, knees up, jammed between all the luggage bundled on either side. The oozie looked back, gestured for me to hang on, and I, slow thinker that I am, got the idea just as the whole front of this astounding creature began rising suddenly and sharply. I nearly fell out of the rack. Then the back rose up, and soon the fully standing beast began to sway and lumber and then to locomote monstrously, in the style of a portable earthquake.

A third elephant, this one without calf, moved into place. More luggage was piled on top, and Moe took his position in the rack.

So, all loaded up now, and having said good-bye to our driver, we set off, with Dr. Ow, the elephant doctor, cheerfully following on foot. It was very exciting to ride an elephant, and my elephant, her baby following alongside, walked with a steady, shifting weight. I was swinging hugely from side to side, front to back—feeling as if I had become stuck inside a giant washing machine—as she proceeded at her steady, steady pace: one leg column replaced by the next leg column, one foot barrel followed by the next foot barrel, shifting and settling that great tanker of a torso with each step, massively swinging an enormous weight.

The oozie, a boy of maybe fifteen or sixteen and small for his age, kept looking back to smile reassuringly and make sure I hadn't yet fallen off. We started to descend, and he gestured that I should reach back and brace myself by grasping the back of the rack. Then we started to ascend, and he gestured for me to hold onto the front. It was indeed a precarious business, but of course I had the front and back of the rack to hang on to. The oozie just sat there balanced right behind a bony, boulder-sized head, a leg behind each ear—or sometimes shifting his position to sidesaddle, with one leg dangling behind the ear and the other leg casually folded across the top of the head.

Sidesaddle like that, the oozie easily turned to look back at me, smiling exuberantly now, as if he completely shared my own delight. And what an astonishing experience it was indeed, to ride an earthquake-maker like this, one who walked so quietly, foot after foot after foot, quietly stepping on those flat and padded foot bottoms. The oozie urged me to hang on again, and soon we were climbing again, step after step up a steep and very narrow trail. Now the oozie turned and urged me to hang on at the back, and this rocking, enormous creature began descending.

The oozie held in his left hand an iron hook attached to a wooden handle, the full implement about the size of a carpenter's hammer, and every once in a while he kicked the elephant behind the ears with his bare feet, shouted some emphatic words, and then clobbered her on the head with the broadside of his hook—bonk!—a wooden sound. And yet she seemed not to respond to the pain or indignity of it but, rather, just stolidly to continue in her plodding ways.

The elephants took us along a narrow ledge, almost too narrow for a person even, but they walked evenly, shifting their weight methodically onto each foot in turn.

But suddenly we stopped, all five elephants and all four people stopped there on the precariously narrow trail. Why? I looked down to discover a gray Volkswagen nudged and parked beneath my elephant. The baby wanted to nurse. After about ten minutes of quietly urgent activity below, we continued—with the trail now turning steeply down a mountainside in switchbacks, each hairpin turn navigated carefully by each beast: stepping down, placing her weight, turning her whole body then to face the new direction. So down we went, turning at last into a ravine and then into a narrow rocky canyon with some deep steps up and down and over boulders. Then we turned up again, climbing heavily up another steep hill, across another ledge and ridge, and now down an astonishingly steep trail with, once again, precipitous switchbacks, as well as deep elephant stairs made by dinner plate feet. I shouted out to Karl, who was still on the elephant just ahead: "Now I know how Hannibal crossed the Alps!"

Karl shouted back: "And they do it when it's pissing down rain. You couldn't walk down these hills without falling on your ass three or four times!"

The steep descent gradually turned less steep until, finally, the hairpins straightened out, and we came into an open valley, then approached a few bamboo houses on wooden stilts, followed by some cows and chickens, then people—and shouts and greetings—and then our elephants lumbered up to a house built on a hillside steep enough that its front porch, elevated on stilts with a bamboo railing, was almost exactly one elephant high. The elephants pulled up to the porch, one at a time, and from each elephant baggage was tossed off and onto the porch. We, then, very sore-bottomed and knotty-backed, awkwardly climbed off and tossed ourselves over the bamboo railing and onto the porch.

✲

This was the base camp, Lay Te Camp, an oozie village and supply depot, and here was our house, a guest house: with rough slab floors, split bamboo walls and bamboo roof, and divided into four sleeping cubicles, each with a pair of rough slab beds. We chose our rooms and beds and dumped our packs. The latrine was located just a few steps away, inside a simple bamboo hut with a rectangle of woven bamboo for a door.

Downhill from the porch, a tea-green river slowed and widened into a pool, and soon, as the late-afternoon light turned thin, the oozies had un-racked their elephants and led them down to the pool for a bath. An elephant walked into the water, the oozie walking alongside, then the elephant lowered into the water, soon kneeling and listing sideways a bit, three quarters submerged. The oozie began splashing water all over the animal, splashing and scrubbing with his hands onto the still dry areas of skin—getting the top of the head, top of the back, the ears, and even (like a good mother would) carefully scrubbing behind and inside the ears.

Karl and I took some time to bathe ourselves at the river, and finally, as the light began its pointillistic dance with the dark, the elephants were fitted up with their night chains and bells and led down the trail to their night release and retreat in the forest. Here they would find their own food and wander at their own pace, free— for the night—though dragging their chains with them. Their bells were carved out of wood, hollowed, and fitted with wood clappers, so the distant clanking of the chains alternated with the *clonging*, single-note xylophone sounds of the bells. They seemed like a line of children, all washed and ready for bed . . . or maybe a line of prisoners, all fettered and heading for the cells. Soon the elephants had turned a corner into the trees and were now far enough away that the sounds faded and then disappeared.

We had our dinner—rice, veggies, some canned fish—by candlelight. After dinner, Karl showed off his new mosquito-net tent. This piece of high-tech magic he bought at a fancy camping store in Bangkok, and it came conveniently packaged in a small, flat, circular case the size of a large pizza. Karl unzipped the circular case, pulled out the circular object inside, flicked his wrist, and—presto!—the thing exploded into a fully formed half-cylinder, a cocoon of mosquito netting given shape by a series of flexible plastic ribs. I was amused and impressed. The rest of us, meanwhile, were stuck with the old-fashioned dishrag sort of mosquito nets you tie up high and tuck in low; and now, by flashlight, we retired to our respective cubicles to curse the mosquito nets, inflate the air mattresses, and roll out the pads and bags and blankets.

Back on the porch, evening cups of tea in hand, we settled back into an environment of stars, crickets, and candles while Moe talked about elephants. There were two thousand wild elephants still left in Myanmar, he said, and about five thousand in captivity, mainly employed by the logging industry. There were three reasons to keep catching wild elephants, he went on, pausing graciously for a moment while I pulled out my pencil and notebook to write it all down. The first was to reduce the number of wild elephants. Two months ago, wild elephants killed two people and destroyed six villages. The second reason was to feed the elephants, for their own survival. The third was to protect people from the dangers of wild elephants. People were moving deeper and deeper into the forests, and so you captured the elephants to protect the people.

Those were the three reasons, and although I dutifully wrote them down, they still seemed to me more like one reason repeated three times, but before I had a chance to think on the matter further, Karl asked Moe whether the timber company would capture and train any more elephants during the year.

In the coming summer they were going to train three elephants, he said. They catch the wild elephants when they're young, from ages four or five until about the age of twelve. Otherwise they're too old to train.

Now, upon my urging, Moe described the training process, which goes something like the following. After a capture in the forest, and with the assistance of a mature tame elephant, a young wild elephant will be roped, dragged, and then immobilized with ropes inside a crush or cradle, which is a giant tripod made of poles and at least one standing tree. The training commences with the goal first of exhausting the animal and breaking down her resistance, accomplished by withholding food and water for two or three days. Then a pair of trainers working in shifts begins feeding and watering her, sparingly at first, while chanting lovingly in a special language—the Khamti language, Moe said— from five in the morning to eleven at night. The trainers will keep the elephant awake, and they'll touch her all over her body, even, while hanging from a beam at the top of the cradle, standing briefly on her back. They also use food as reward and punishment, first testing the foods to see what the elephant really likes, and feeding her accordingly. "If she's angry," Moe added, "they cut the feeding, make her depressed."

After ten days to three weeks of such treatment, the young elephant will be subdued and ready for a more particular training. Released from the cradle, hobbled at the forelegs with a length of cane, he or she will, over the next three months, be taught some of the simpler commands and responses required of a working elephant: *hmet* (lie down), *how* (be careful), *myauk* (lift), *pway* (carry), and *ya* (be quiet). . . .

✹

We started the next day with a simple breakfast, which was dinner warmed over, and listened to the morning sounds: running water from the river below, yelping dogs, and a far off burst of elephant trumpeting. Meanwhile, Karl was still packing—or trying to. The problem was the high-tech mosquito-net tent he had so proudly exploded open for us last night. It had begun life as a coiled, circular object fitting into a carrying case the size of a large pizza. It had been transformed, in a burst of kinetic energy, into a cylindrical pup tent. But how to turn that big cylinder back into the smaller circle? The carrying case had a set of instructions on the side, drawn in the universal language of cylinders, circles, floating hands, and pointing arrows. Staring at the instructions, Karl attacked, dropping to his knees and wrestling with the thing, pushing, twisting, falling on top of it. He tried again, once more dropping, wrestling, pushing, twisting, falling on top, this time managing to get the tent flattened into a circle, but too big a circle to fit into the pizza case. He tried again.

"Here, let me have a try." I looked at the directions, looked at the tent, looked at the case. The trick, obviously, was to torque those flexible plastic ribs into an extra twist or two, transforming their big circles into smaller circles; and so, considering the directions once more, I grabbed the ends, then twisted, dropped, squeezed. After a couple of tries, I succeeded, and we inserted the folded tent into its pizza carrying case and zipped it shut.

"How'd you do that?"

"I don't know."

✹

Lay Te Camp, the base camp, served a number of satellite camps where the real work takes place, and we planned to go visit one. Now we were entirely packed, our bags distributed on the porch. Soon we heard clanking chains and clonging bells, and we watched in the predawn haze as three elephants walked single-file along a trail and splashed into the pool for their morning bath. Then, as the first ribbons of sunlight dropped across the railing and planks of the porch, three male elephants— minus their chains now—quietly pulled up. They were gray the color of river rocks, a dull gray with a rippling of wrinkles: loose skin cast over a moving machinery of enormous bones and muscles. Their expressionless faces gave the impression they were living in another world and entirely removed from our flimsy needs and flimflam plans. They looked like somber intelligence housed in rock, and all the people around them—the oozies sitting on their necks, a handful of busy people on the porch—all of us seemed by comparison nervous and jerky, like unbalanced birds. The elephants barely looked at us, merely curled and flipped the ends off their trunks, sniffing discreetly in our direction and quietly stealing all our secrets.

The one first in line appeared simply enormous, a hulking presence with sixteen-inch-long tusks, who happened to be—according to Dr. Ow—an eighteen-year-old male named San Sein Aye. His oozie was a young man named Aung Htay Win. Bags were handed over the bamboo railing and placed onto the back of San, and pretty soon Karl had climbed on as well, and so Aung kicked his feet and San moved away.

Next up, an amber-eyed sixteen-year-old male named Shu Khin Kyaing, who was nicely tusked as well. The oozie riding Shu was a boy with fuzz on his upper lip and a shy smile—thirteen years old at most—named San Lwin. But he seemed perfectly at home behind an elephant's head. More luggage was loaded onto Shu, followed by me. The oozie, San Lwin, shouted a few words, kicked his feet, and, like a ship casting off from a wharf, we slid away from the side of the porch and turned to follow the wake of Karl and his elephant.

Finally, the third elephant was loaded up—entirely with bags and supplies, since both Moe and Dr. Ow insisted they would walk—and the caravan began its slow and loping trek. This was a fifteen-mile, five-hour excursion through steep, dusty, dry-season hills. The terrain seemed a lot like yesterday's, with steep hills and precariously narrow trails, along with some tight switchbacks and deep ravines, and then we navigated an obscure maze of dry river beds. As we walked uphill, my elephant used his trunk to test the ground in front of him, first sniffing with his nostrils, then turning the trunk and probing the soil, as if testing its firmness. And when the trail became really steep, he seemed to lean the thicker part of his trunk against the rising earth before him, as if using that remarkable organ as a temporary prop for his mammoth skull, as a steadying fifth leg. The elephants stepped heavily over fallen trees, climbed up and down huge boulders, but as we proceeded through one series of impossibly steep switchbacks, I began thinking, *If this guy falls, I'm done for. There's no way I can jump off at the right time. I'll be crushed to death by six tons of flesh and bone.* A few seconds after that, my elephant slipped, stumbled, and dropped to his knee—but, as I soon realized, it was only one knee out of four, only one leg out of four, and he recovered and kept right on lumbering.

My oozie that day, San Lwin, kept (in a woven bamboo sheath tied to the rack) a short, dull-edged machete, which he routinely pulled out to whack the elephant on the head. He yelled some mysterious command—"*Ma wickie widdle waho wao!*"—then *clonk* went the machete.

Sometimes, when we came into an open spot in a dry riverbed, the oozies and their elephants converged in a brief tight conference, where cheroots were lit, puffed, and passed around. And sometimes San would stop Shu, signal the oozie behind us to hold up his elephant, and then very, very quietly reaching back into a little cloth ditty bag he kept tied to the rack, he would pull out his sling shot and fire a small stone that splashed into a leafy thicket—and a bird would fly out.

Moe and Dr. Ow went to the same veterinary school, and although Moe had given up animals in favor of tourists, they still had a lot of gossiping and catching up to do. So they were walking behind us and happily caught in a deep and extended conversation. Meanwhile, I was beginning to understand why they preferred to walk. I was cramped and trapped inside that wildly oscillating rack. When the beast started to climb, I would lean forward and hang on for dear life at the front. When the beast started to descend, climbing down with enormous steps that periodically drew his back alarmingly close to the vertical, I would hang on for dear life at the rear. The muscles in my back were soon rebelling fiercely, knotted up and painful, and after a couple of hours, both Karl and I tried walking as our trail followed a winding dry riverbed. But for the final hour we were back on the elephants, passing through a wide canyon with high walls on either side and moving beside an actual river with olive-green water made transparent by the sun, and we crossed and recrossed that river several times.

By mid-afternoon, we had arrived at the satellite camp: a few bamboo houses gathered at the edge of the slow-flowing river and surrounded by high hills. The trees had lost most of their leaves, and the sun was lighting the tops of the hills and casting yellow spots onto the greens and browns of the forest. Pop music emerged from a battery-powered radio somewhere, while the moving river produced a more steady and melodic sound. The air carried the smell of wood smoke; and down by the river's edge, five children—two little girls, three slightly bigger boys—were racing wildly about, playing ecstatic tag and who knows what else.

Meanwhile, the elephants were unloaded, their racks and woolly bark saddles taken off and left on a few old logs stuck in the mud by the river, where four skinny brown dogs lurked and sniffed.

We tossed our things into our bamboo guest hut and washed ourselves at the river. Then Dr. Ow put on a clean white shirt and did the rounds, visiting the oozies and their families and checking on the elephants—and he invited me along. There were six working elephants in camp, Dr. Ow told me as we walked between the houses, and eleven men to work them, including oozies and assistants. Also, there were wives. An oozie can only have one wife. He's not allowed to have the usual "small wife" because tradition says it's dangerous. Of the eleven men working this camp, eight had wives, and at the moment, six families were in residence. Being an oozie is a family business. The job is learned early and passed from father to son. And this village—eight houses, plus a large common house, and the small guest hut—was built last summer. The elephants were kept here. There was a high rack for loading elephants, a place for pounding the Napé bark that makes elephant blankets. And at a slight rise above the rest of the village, there was a shrine to the *nats*, or spirits, especially the nat named U-Dae, who overlooks the fate of both elephants and oozies.

The shrine looked like a small bamboo birdcage surrounded by a small wooden fence.

This satellite camp, located at Plot 44 of Pataung Township along the Buyoe River, was temporary. The men started this village, at this spot, in July. Just the men came at first, and it was very rainy, but when it became drier they built the bamboo houses—all bamboo, including the structural posts and the roofs—for their wives and families, who came later. They located and marked their work site in June, built the camp in July, marked and cut all the trees from July to December. From January to March is extraction time, when they drag out all the timber—with a production goal of eighty to one hundred metric tons of timber, mostly teak, per elephant per year. One metric ton equals about fifty cubic feet. And from March to May is the hot season, when logging stops and the elephants have their vacation, time off to rest, eat, and do whatever else it is that elephants like to do.

The wood smoke in the air, I could see now, was partly a result of cooking fires burning inside holes in the ground in front of some of the houses, but mainly the consequence of a fire that had been slowly blackening the top of one of the hills—a fire set by some of the people in the village, who hoped to expose the hideouts of monitor lizards in order to dig them up for food. A cool breeze started in the late afternoon, raising the flames and smoke on the burning hill, and causing the leaves to waver in the sunlight on the other hills; but after dark the fire seemed to burn itself down, while the breeze turned into a chilly and then a cold wind. It seemed even colder than the previous night, and I was awake most of the night, shivering and curled up like an anxious monitor lizard inside my too-thin sleeping bag.

✳

We were up again before dawn, and, as a faint dusting of light developed, we watched the oozies prepare the elephants for work. These were four simply enormous pachyderms, including a couple of males with tusks three or four feet long and thick as a man's arm, yellowish white with darker cracks. The oozies greased up the elephants where the harnesses rub, added the woven-rope harnesses and the chains that attached to them, and tossed on the bark padding and small saddles. Yes, these were the working elephants, big and strong, and even the oozies now seemed, if not bigger, then at least older and more serious than the ones from yesterday.

A yellow Komatsu bulldozer with a rusty steel blade in front had clanked and rumbled past the camp yesterday, following the river out and plowing through the shallow parts as it went, having already plowed through the dry parts of a feeder tributary—thus putting in a temporary road for the logging lorries to rattle through. And now we and the elephants followed that temporary road out of the village and up the dry tributary.

After half an hour or so, the elephants and their oozies turned off, finally, to climb a steep trail, with the rest of us following. We climbed halfway up a hill before stopping at a spot where some workers were waiting and where a few massive trees had some time ago been felled and sectioned into enormous twenty- or twenty-five-foot-long logs, each with a hole the size of a fist punched into one end. And now the first elephant in line was moved into place. His harness chains were drawn by one of the assistants through the log holes and wrapped into knots, and on the command of the oozie, that first elephant started to pull. It was a steep and narrow ridge there, and the elephant soon was dragging the big log downhill. The earth rumbled from the great weight of this huge shaft of timber dragging over it. But as the dragging continued downhill, the sound shifted, subtly at first. The dragging sound changed to a sliding one . . . and the log was moving, now, faster than the elephant in front of it, faster and suddenly about to crash massively into one of the elephant's rear feet. But the oozie shouted a command, the elephant deftly sidestepped, the log slipped past, and then, as the slack chain went taut again, the log was drawn off course to collide with and wedge itself against a standing tree.

The oozie shouted more commands. The elephant turned and pressed the bulky upper part of his trunk against the wedged log. He pushed once, twice, thrice. Then he moved back to the front of the log and resumed the dragging, and so the log was pulled free and continued down the narrow ridge of this steep hill. At last the elephant and the log behind him arrived at a saddle connecting this slope with another. It was a narrow saddle, with a steep drop-off on one side and a steeper one—a forty-foot cliff, actually—on the other. A worker now unchained the elephant from the log, and the great animal turned and, using his tusks, lifted and then pushed the enormous log off the edge of the cliff. It slipped, accelerated, tumbled, and then crashed massively down onto the dry riverbed forty feet below.

Meanwhile, the other elephants were chained up and drawing more logs down the same steep trail. And as some of the elephants dragged logs down, others were climbing back up the hill to fetch more logs—while I did my best to stand out of the way, listening to the shouts of the oozies and the deep rumbling in the earth as logs were pulled, the clanking of chains, the clonging of wooden elephant bells, the crackling of small trees being swept out of the way, and now the sound of an oozie singing softly to himself.

This was patently very dangerous work. A single miscalculation, a tiny slip, a sliding log, an unanticipated softness in the earth followed by an unexpected collapse. . . . It was easy to imagine the catastrophic accidents that could—must—sometimes happen in such precarious circumstances with such massive weights involved.

After a time, Karl and I descended to the dry riverbed, where a giant yellow forklift was spewing black hydrocarbon clouds and playing pickup sticks with great boles of timber, loading those sticks with a *thunk* and shiver into the bed of an ancient beat-up truck. The yellow forklift was a Furukawa FL230-II marked, on its side, with the silhouette of an elephant lifting a log and the letters MTE, the logo for Myanmar Timber Enterprises. Finally, when the truck had been entirely loaded, several people—including some logging workers, as well as Moe, Dr. Ow, Karl, and me—climbed up, positioned themselves carefully on and between and in front of the timber, and rode back to camp. The elephants finished work around noon, and thus as we were packing up for our return trip, they came back to camp as well, were bathed in the river, and then treated with tamarind-and-salt balls.

Our return to the Lay Te Camp that afternoon was like our trip the day before, only in reverse. But there was a lovely moment, while we were still following the wide wet river through its high canyon, when one of the oozies pulled up his elephant's bell and disengaged the clapper, so that the elephant suddenly fell silent. Soon the other two oozies had disengaged their elephant bell clappers, so that now all three elephants had gone silent. They stepped quietly, no sounds of crunching, no one-note-xylophone concerts, just the soft great round padded feet settling down and spreading out on the dirt and stone along the edge of the flowing river, so quietly. Then, with the sun overhead and in the bright glare and sharp shadows of the canyon, an oozie started singing—un-self-consciously, just singing for the pleasure of it, a mysterious tune with liquid words, until we came to cross the river once again, and the elephants splashed across noisily and then emerged on the other side quietly on a surface of stones.

Later on, we passed through a dry river bed that was strewn with a carpet of orange flower blossoms cast off from overhanging trees, a sweet-smelling, shadowy, dream-like tunnel that we moved through wordlessly.

Back at Lay Te that evening, we visited with the oldest oozie of the village, a fifty-five-year-old man named U Tun Nyan, who said he had worked for Myanmar Timber for thirty-seven years, having started when he was eighteen. Elephants are trained from the ages of five to nine, he told us, and then they work in transportation from nine to eighteen. From there, they become timber haulers and workers, remaining in that role except when, for the females, pregnant or nursing. Retirement comes around the ages of fifty to fifty-five. The oldest company elephant in this area, he added, was seventy-three years old: just about old enough to die. They bury their elephants after they die, having removed the ivory and stored it in a safe place maintained by Myanmar Timber.

One big change from the old days, U Tun went on to say, was that the forest used to be dark because it was so thick, but now there was light everywhere. The trees had all been thinned out. Another big change was the means of transport. Before they used the river to transport all the logs out, but in 1985 they realized they were losing lots of teak that way, so now the elephants transported timber to the collection point, where it went out by truck for some distance before being woven into rafts and floated down the big river. The last tiger he saw was in 1975 or 1976. Now there were too many people in the forest, people harvesting bamboo and even farming vegetables in plains near the river, so the tigers were gone.

✳

After an early breakfast on our last day at Lay Te, we were standing on the porch, nearly packed and expecting the elephants soon. "Dale, are you walking or take the elephant?" Moe asked me. Moe was sportily dressed this morning, wearing blue nylon pants, a cream-colored nylon jacket, a brown stocking cap, a white scarf, and white sport shoes marked with *www.wbute.com*.

"I'm not sure. Yeah, I'll take the elephant."

Meanwhile, I was listening to a stereophonic cock-a-doodle symphony—an a-root-a-toot-a-tooting from near and far, here and there—and hearing the distant trumpeting of an elephant. The sun was rising, and the trees in the hills around us were being pulled out of the darkness and in the process becoming scattered scratches in colored chalk.

Last night, Karl had asked for the elephants to be ready by six-thirty, and now it was almost seven. Again this morning Karl had been wrestling on the porch with his high-tech-mosquito-net-cocoon-tent, and again he was completely baffled by it. He studied the directions, wrestled, studied some more, wrestled. I tried, but this time I was lost, too. I'd completely forgotten how I collapsed the cocoon into the appropriately sized circle to fit in the carrying case, and after I made a few serious attempts and failures, Moe tried as well. Finally we all gave up, having managed to press the springy cocoon down into an approximately flat bundle of larger circles that wouldn't fit the case but at least could be bundled and tied up crudely with twine.

Now it was seven-thirty, but the elephants still hadn't arrived. Karl was getting anxious, then irritated. "Where are the elephants?" he said, and then, a few minutes later, "I wonder where the elephants are." And then, "The elephants are late." Then, "Should we ask where the elephants are?" And, hopefully, "I hear an elephant bell, far away."

At eight-thirty, Karl said, "I'm getting worried now. It's a time when, you know, we're going to have to rush, so there is no need to rush later in the afternoon. If there is any problem with the car, we've had it." Karl had been planning to catch a plane out of Yangon in the late afternoon.

When a single elephant arrived at a quarter to nine, Karl and most of his luggage and camera equipment were placed aboard, nearly everything except for the mosquito-net tent, which he gave to Moe as a gift. Still, Karl would have to wait for us at the road, and we had to wait on the porch for the other elephants. It was like waiting for a late bus, as we paced and chattered with each other desultorily, combining resignation and patience with indignation and impatience. The elder oozie we talked to last night, U Tun Nyan, was sitting on the porch this morning, sharing our tea and conversation, but even he had no idea where the elephants were—or if he did, I missed it, since he only spoke in his own local language and Burmese, and no one was willing to translate.

At around half past nine, we gave up on the elephants, oh, such unreliable beasts, and set off on foot—Moe, Dr. Ow, and I—all three of us carrying our various bags and supplies and assisted by a couple of tough young men from the village who were hired to carry the extras, including Karl's crudely tied-up, high-tech mosquito-netting tent. The two porters were walking fast, and they soon disappeared into the woodsy, bushy trail ahead of us, which seemed much steeper and harder and more intricate this time than it was when I rode it the other day on top of an elephant. Still, we kept up an elephant's steady pace, and at some point in the middle of a difficult uphill climb, we actually caught up with the two young porters, who were sitting on the ground, smoking cheroots and looking chagrined and dejected—having been stymied by Karl's tent, which, when they least expected it, spontaneously broke free of the twine and burst open into a big cylinder.

We laughed, wrestled with the thing, and finally subdued it sufficiently to clap on the restraints once more.

Back at the road at last, we found Karl and the driver and car patiently waiting—and the driver helped load our things into the trunk, and then, as we climbed in, he pulled down his sunglasses, chewed a stimulating chew, slipped a tape into the tape deck, and then drove like a complete maniac, bounding through the wrecked and wretched mountain roads, pulling onto a long, flat, and rice-paddied plain, and running down that road while honking at bicyclists, motor bicyclists, slow-walking peasants, hitting holes in the road with a bang and shudder, and in that manner racing all the way cross-country for five or six hours until we reached the airport in Yangon, where Karl was dropped off, and then the Summit Parkview Hotel, where I was.

8: GOOD-LUCK BIRD

Having an extra day in Yangon, I decided to sleep late, eat well, and, even if neither of those worked out, at least do one important tourist act, which would be to visit the famous Shwedagon Pagoda. At 321 feet high, the Shwedagon dominates the skyline of Yangon. Hard to miss. It's big and tall, as well as bright and shiny, being gold-plated and, near the top, encrusted with 5,448 diamonds and 2,317 rubies, then tipped at the very top with a seventy-six-carat diamond. More to the point, it houses, among three other critically important Buddhist relics (staff, robe, water filter), eight hairs plucked from the head of Gautama Buddha himself.

Traditionalists say that around 2,500 years ago (logically, at some time before or soon after Buddha's death in 486 BC), the eight hairs came into the four hands of two brothers, who, recognizing the enormous value of what they had just acquired, put them inside one golden pot with a golden lid on top. After much consideration, the brothers at last decided to enshrine the sacred hairs in the great pagoda. When it came time to remove the lid in order transfer them from the pot to the shrine, however, enormous quantities of light burst forth and reached up to the sky and down to the center of the earth. That was followed by lightning, thunder, earthquakes, a severe hailstorm of precious gems, and another storm of special miracles whereupon the blind could see, the deaf hear, and the dumb speak intelligently. The brothers finally managed to get all eight hairs out of the pot and into the shrine, and to put the lid back on the pot, so that was the end of that.

Archaeologists say the golden pagoda is younger than the traditionalists say, having originally been built sometime between 700 to 1100 AD. At first, it was only about twenty-seven feet high. Successive kings and queens piously rebuilt it, making it higher, and in the fifteenth century, Queen Shin donated her own weight in gold to begin the tradition of bolting gold sheets onto the brick underlay. So, by the time I walked out from the Summit Parkview Hotel and along some busy streets and through some big gardens to the great pagoda, there must have been an awful lot of gold up there, and the early morning sun, now shining directly onto a significant part of it, lit the whole thing up brilliantly and in that manner contributed to the aura of something very wonderful and grand.

I approached the entrance (one of four, as I later discovered), which was guarded by a couple of flame-edged lions each forty feet high, plus a few dragons and some blissful flying and praying maidens. After taking off my shoes and carrying them in my hand (as I saw other people doing), I walked inside, down a long, long hallway of high ceilings and giant gold and red columns, on for a football field or two until I came to some stairs, which I climbed.

I reached another walkway, this one lined with flower sellers and trinket sellers. "Flowers? You buy flowers?" "Thanks. No." And someone said, "Your shoes. Put them there." I saw a high wooden desk, the back of a shoe rack, and a man behind the desk and in front of the rack who pointed to a small box. "Donation," he said. I put in 1,000 byat, seeing a note of that same denomination already in the box. "Socks also," he said. I took off my socks, and he put them into the shoes. He had little pink plastic bags to put shoes in, but mine were so big they wouldn't fit.

Barefoot now, I continued walking, soon arriving at more stairs, a long flight of them—and with an alternative twin flight on the other side of a middle set of non-moving up and down escalators. It was still early. They hadn't yet turned on the escalators. I finally reached daylight again, and emerged into what looked like an amazing city of temples: a thousand golden exhibits and mini-pagodas and shrines and other religious exhibits and dioramas, each with a donation box in front, each with some kind of Buddha statue or a dozen Buddha statues or various alternative objects of devotional shock and awe—lions, dragons, elephants, clowns, and who knows what else?—each with people bowing down, making fervent gestures of pathos and submission, eyes tightly closed, hands pressed in prayer, doing repetitive calisthenics, fervent obeisances, and in general trying to make themselves humble indeed. I immediately understood I could get lost in the crowds and all this religious imagery and devotion, and so I tried to note what might be distinctive about my surroundings, in order, eventually, to find the exit and my shoes again.

I began irrationally to worry about the shoes. I asked myself: *What if I can't get back to them?* I had the tag, number 40, in my hand. I put that in my back pocket, and thought, *Well if I can't find my shoes again I can always walk barefoot back to the hotel. Maybe I can buy shoes there.*

Meanwhile, I was still trying to orient myself. The Buddhas in front of me: nice, but I could already see lots of Buddhas around. And now there were increasingly dense crowds of bare-footed people moving around as well. To my left now, I discovered a pair of distinctive statues: a pair of Vaudeville-style song-and-dance men wearing clowns' checkered shorts and looking vacuously cheerful, striking a pose of smiling extroversion. *I'll remember them,* I told myself, *and they'll mark the entrance and my shoes.*

I began walking: past the giant reclining Buddha on my left, and then the fat Buddha, and then the dozen Buddha clones. There was, in one exhibit, a gigantic bronze bell, tattered at the edges, obviously very ancient, suspended by a mirrored dragon, with an exotic cuneiform chiseled all around the sides of the bell. And just beyond that, inside yet another devotional pavilion, a whole crowd of worshippers bowed and prayed to a Buddha with flashing neon lights: red, blue, green, and white colors flashing and sweeping in exotic light waves ordinarily used to advertise beer or dancers. People were earnestly prostrating themselves before this neon Buddha. I moved along, walking down a long passageway that, I now discovered, ended at an elevator. I turned around, walked out again, and was pulled aside by a young woman. "Excuse me, sir, you have not paid admission."

"No."

"It is necessary to pay admission—and donation. Come."

And she drew me over to a cashier's booth, told me the cost would be six American dollars, which was both admission and a donation to the temple. I gave the cashier a ten, and she returned the change: two ones and a two-dollar bill. It was the first two-dollar bill I'd seen in about forty years.

I kept on walking, an admissions tag now on my chest, and as I walked, the place began to seem more and more like Disneyland, a religious theme park for Buddhists, replete with all kinds of odd Buddhist iconography, the gaudier the better. I saw, for instance, a golden flaming cable car, a toy, sliding creakily down a small cable and landing inside some pavilion—with a message? A coffee cup? Who knew? And then the golden pagoda itself came into view, and from this angle it captured the morning sun's blast, blinding me temporarily, and I felt dizzied and shaken. I put my hand before my eyes, walking away from the blazing light into a shadow where out of the bright yellow light appeared an old man, toothless and grinning fatuously, who said, "Hello."

"Hello," I responded, continuing to walk, knowing already that he was trying to latch on.

"How are you?"

"Fine."

"Are you American?"

"Yep."

"Where are you from? Minnesota?"

"Nope. Boston."

I kept on walking, kept on looking at the squatting monks, the bowing devotees, the gaudy statues, the gratuitous gold.

"This is for Tuesday. This is celebration," he said, vaguely nodding to some commotion to the right. "Do you know what day you were born on?" he asked, smiling.

"No," I said, and he responded with a bigger smile, as if to say: *Of course you don't, fool!*

"Aha! What year were you born?"

"1944."

He pulled out a little black book and, leafing through it, quickly found a calendar for 1944.

"What month?

"November."

"What day?"

I didn't like this. I was walking faster now, he walking faster to keep up. "What day?" he repeated. "Twenty," I spit out at last, begrudgingly.

"Aha! You were born on a Monday!" He smiled in triumph, then closed and pocketed the book—and continued. I knew what this was really about: money. My money. And so I walked even faster. He kept up. "And what is your planet? Mercury?"

"I don't know. I have no idea," I said, knowing how much of a mistake it was even to be answering his questions, then adding, "I'm a Scorpio."

"Yes, Scorpio! And your stone is coral. And your color is pink!" he declared, excitedly.

"Oh."

I was by now walking as fast as I could, intending to outwalk this toothless parasite, but he managed to keep up. "You have babies?"

"Yes."

"This is for babies," he said, pointing out some obscure sort of shrine, adding: "Stone. Sixteenth century."

I kept walking, trying to ignore him. "And this is elephant," he said, pointing to an elephant. I kept walking. "And this is reclining Buddha," he said, while pointing at a giant reclining Buddha . . . but hadn't I seen that already? Wasn't that one of the first things I saw, just after the Vaudeville song-and-dance team? And when we came to the giant bell, which I certainly had already seen, I knew we had somehow gone right past my exit—and my shoes. "This is a very big bell," my guide said. "Stolen by the British!" And I stepped into the pavilion to look at the bell in part because I wanted to confirm exactly where I was. I turned, knowing that if this was the same bell (which it surely was) as before, I could turn my head to the right and see the Buddha with the neon lights. I looked directly to the right and saw, yes, a big crowd bowing with awe and reverence before the flashing red blue green white neon lights behind a Buddha statue, and so I stepped out of the bell pavilion and started walking back to where I knew the entrance and exit and my shoes must have been.

"Where are you going?"

"I'm leaving," I said. "I came in back there."

"Oh, you are mistaken," he said, looking at the sticker on my chest. "You are the north entrance. Over there is the west entrance."

"No, you are mistaken. I came in over there."

"Oh, you lie!" he said.

I looked at him directly for the first time. "No, you lie!"

"Oh, you are very, very wrong. You will see."

"No, I'm not wrong. You will see."

And I walked past the reclining Buddha, past the song-and-dance vaudeville team with the checkered shorts, and past the Buddha clone cluster, and past. . . . But where was the entrance? Meanwhile, the toothless demon was still tagging along, still trying to insert himself more thoroughly, and profitably, into my life. "How long have you been here? Where are you going next? Have you been to Mandalay? When are you leaving?" I kept walking, saw another Buddha with neon lights, more worshippers—now I was lost! Or was I? And I kept walking until I did finally, finally find the exit.

I stopped there, pulled out my wallet, drew out a dollar, and handed it to the man, who accepted the money and soon had dissolved back into the circulating crowds.

And I walked down the stairs. But wait a second! Were these really the same stairs I came up? Had I seen those giant crocodiles before? Surely I would have remembered. And all those trinket vendors? Had there been so many before? And—this was the clincher—where were the escalators at the center of the long, long stairs I walked up? I descended a little farther, just enough to look down into a dark wide stairwell and confirm: no escalators in the middle. And I realized I'd gone down the wrong stairs, exited the wrong exit, and so I turned back and emerged into the sunlight and back into the circulating crowds—and I proceeded back in the rotating world of shoeless life and karma as far as the vaudeville clowns, the reclining Buddha, the giant bell, and turned back once more.

This time, at last, I found the right exit, which was confirmed by the escalators, now working, and I descended and soon found the place where my shoes were. The guy who originally took them was no longer there, however, having been replaced by an overweight and sullen-faced teenager, who looked at my ticket and said, "Donation." She pointed her chin at the box.

"I already paid my donation when I brought my shoes in," I said.

Her face remained inert. "Donation," she repeated.

"I already made a donation!"

"Donation," she said, steady and sullen as ever.

All right! I paid some byat. She handed over the shoes, making a histrionic grimace at their heft, as if to say, *You call these boats "shoes"?* And I took the shoes, socks wadded inside, walked with them in hand down the stairs and the long corridor to the final be-lioned entrance and the outdoor light when I heard a shout behind me.

"Hallo!"

I ignored it.

"Hallo!" And then I heard running footsteps. "Hallo, sir!" Two women were running down the corridor, one carrying a round basket about the size of a small cake tin, with, I could see now, a couple dozen tiny, seething birds inside. "You want sparrow? Sparrow fry? You make fry. Free sparrow, one dolla," one of the women said, and she sculpted her face into an eager smile and flapped her hands. She had me there. "OK. I'll free a sparrow." And I began pulling out my wallet while she upped the ante: "Two dolla, two sparrow."

I thought fast, recalling that I had gotten four dollars in change—the two-dollar note and two singles—but then I gave one of the singles to the toothless demon. I still had the two-dollar note, though, which I had been planning to keep as a souvenir . . . or something, but. . . . "OK. Two sparrows."

One of the women opened the top of the basket and put her hand through the opening, carefully drawing out two trembling little brown and white birds, holding them, so fragile, in her hand.

I pulled the two-dollar bill out of my wallet, handed it to the other woman, the basket holder. Her partner now held out the hand that clutched the two little sparrows, as if I should take them. I didn't want to. "You take?" She wanted to hand them to me so I could have the thrill of—or the good luck imparted by—freeing them by my own actions. I said, "No. You let them go."

So she opened her hand, and the sparrows, surprised or shocked perhaps at this new turn of events, froze, trembling. They hesitated, and then, boisterously batting the air with feathers, they burst away and out an open window at the end of the hallway, out into the rapture of light and freedom. The woman smiled into, or at, my face. It was a fake smile, a merchant's ersatz expression, as if to say, *How cool is that? How fun! How lucky!* It was a hokey smile, a hoax, the professional summation of an act of blackmail, and I imagined her saying the more complicated truth, which was this: *See. I've done a mean and stupid thing by capturing these two birds, and for only two dollars you were able to undo that mean and stupid thing. How lucky we both are—but excuse me now: I have to go out and capture more birds.*

I wanted to swat her.

9: SHIELDED BY A PRAYER

Head down, eyes closed: "Our Dear Lord, thank you for another beautiful day. Thank you for keeping us safe. We ask for your protection during the long flight ahead of us, and for your blessings as we head across the forests of Congo and into Central Africa, on to our mission at Zemio. We also beseech your tolerance for our frailties, and we look forward to your blessings over our lives. In Jesus's name, amen."

Head raised, eyes scanning the airfield ahead and, then, the prop below: "Clear!"

The prop turned with a *puck* and a *pook*. The engine coughed, woke up, and then roared. Prop spinning mightily. Plane shaking. We began to roll, shake, roll, bounce, roll, shake.

Our pilot, a missionary named Ron, wore white Levi's and a khaki shirt with epaulettes. He had a sun-reddened, longish face, a beaky nose, pale blue eyes, and sandy hair turning to gray. He looked serious, stern, preoccupied. Maybe, I thought, he was upset that Karl, Reas, and I had arrived in Entebbe (Uganda) late and was therefore worried about making it to Zemio (Central African Republic) before dark.

Let's be honest here: I retain, like a small but permanent toothache, an abject fear of flying. *Please, God, I don't want to die!* I cry out, or might as well, every time the plane jiggles a little—but my previous experience with missionary pilots has convinced me that their wistful flight-time prayers will be counterbalanced by the wakeful logic of steadfast sobriety and professional focus. All things considered, I'll take the missionaries.

Bedeviled by buffeting spurts and invisible spirits, our wings creaked and flopped and flexed and stretched, and then we lifted and mounted, turned and trod the air with a lighter and lighter tread, wheeling over tin-roofed and rust-stained houses ringed with banana trees and soaring above roads of shiny-wet red clay. We rose above Entebbe—green and edging onto the gray waters of Lake Victoria—and then Ron (his pale blue eyes suddenly illuminated by a shaft of sunlight) handed me (sitting in the copilot's seat) a plastic box of peanut-butter cookies recently baked by his wife. I passed the cookies into the back, where sat Karl and Reas, and then, upon their return, helped myself and placed the box beneath my seat. That cookie was just right, and I mentally recounted the remainders. Four!

Soon we had passed above a sea of white clouds with ahead of us a green sea of trees, and we flew over the northern edge of Lake Albert, with a sandy margin at lake's edge. But now came massive, towering, billowing white and gray clouds, dangerous ones, I thought, filled with weather, and Ron bravely piloted our little buzzing shell through a maze of corridors and passageways and tunnels past and around and through the white and gray obstacles. Below: an interminable, scrubby desert.

We landed at Arua, in northern Uganda, then took off once more and slipped into Congolese airspace. At one point, Karl poked me in the back and yelled above the engine noise and into my ear: "We're going to fly over an area for an hour without seeing people. Only a few places left in Africa where you can do that."

And soon, yes, we had left behind all marks of civilization. No roads, no houses, just a flat green surface of grass and stubble and a maze of riverine forests, and through it all, a deeper swath of riverine forest following a long meandering river. There was a long stretch of this dark green maze growing in lower wet areas, old riverbeds, like mold growing in cracks. Once in a while, though, I'd see a puff of smoke in the distance, or a brown spot, like a rotten spot in a green apple, where the trees had been cleared around a small cluster of huts: round and small with thatched roofs, looking like mushrooms. But mostly it was just green and green, light yellow-green of savanna patches and the dark malachite green of forest galleries.

It was all very beautiful, if also very noisy, with the wind whipping our frail windscreen, the engine wildly chewing away at its endless meal of air, and, inside the plane, Karl and Reas debating interminably in the back seats about elephants, meat, and ivory. At least that was what they had been debating about when I could hear what they were saying.

The last time we saw Reas was as we were coming out of Special Region 4, after which he returned to Switzerland and, with impressive efficiency, produced his Swiss television exposé on the illegal trade, from northern Burma into southern China, in live and dead animals. Having done that, Reas had been persuaded now, a few months later, to accompany Karl and me on our little African expedition. We wanted to see forest elephants appearing in a small opening in the forest at a particular spot in the southwestern tip of the Central African Republic, but Reas was also coming along in order to film another exposé for Swiss television on the illegal trade in elephant meat and ivory moving across the border from Congo into the Central African Republic. This bit of video journalism would, so Karl was convinced, demonstrate that elephants in central Africa were vanishing even faster than most of the experts thought, and that they were going down so fast because the average elephant brought the hunter more profit in meat than ivory. The difference was one of consumer responsibility: the middle-class Chinese citizen wanting to buy a trinket for his girlfriend or the middle-class Central African wanting a treat at the dinner table. My opinion was that meat and ivory were apples and oranges, both important but with very different pricing and marketing trajectories. Karl understood that, I'm sure, but he was impatient with the nuance.

I had listened to his perspective before, and so now was imagining a conversation I couldn't hear: *All these conservationists are blinded by their obsession with the ivory trade. No, it's not just ivory! It's not just ivory! If we stopped all the trade in ivory, would elephant poaching stop there? No. They're being poached for their meat, with in many cases the ivory becoming a by-product.*

Me: I was happy to have their talk take place in the back of the plane, while in the front I just looked out the windscreen and listened to the whistling of air and the rumbling of volatile hydrocarbons oxidizing intensively inside a hot block of steel, while occasionally Ron the pilot would point out something I seldom could see and shout something I usually couldn't understand. But he was interested in elephants, too, and so he would swoop lower down and wheel around to investigate. We saw nothing, however, and, after a few hours, we came to a town and screwed ourselves down to land on a bare strip of red earth covered with rotten mangoes and overrun with ecstatic children.

✳

That was Zemio, and since it was our first landing in the Central African Republic, we had to stop at the government offices—a one-story mud-brick building constructed in the shape of a small train, painted cream and open on one side with four doors, each with blue trim and billowing blue curtains—and say hello to the commandant and get our visas stamped. I knew he was the commandant because LE COMMANDANT had been stenciled in black letters onto the dirty orange stucco wall behind his head. His name was Jean-Claude Gbomango, so I concluded from the little wooden sign perched on his desk.

Commandant Gbomango seemed to know Karl and be an old pal of Ron's. The latter had brought in some kind of welcome package from the outside world, and so our friendly chatter, in French, was conducted quickly and happily until the rubber stamp was pressed, lifted, and dropped three times, after which we climbed back into the plane and flew for about ten minutes more before landing on an airstrip on a hill where there were more waving and yelling children and many more rotten mangoes from a thousand mango trees.

That was the Zemio mission, and it took me a few days to appreciate its size. It was big: over seven acres where rows and rows of trees, palm and mango, had been planted and were competing with the less organized planting of about a hundred buildings, many of them small, built from soil-colored bricks sitting on top of brick-colored soil and topped with corrugated tin. Ron said that the trees used to be filled with enormous fruit bats with six-foot wingspans in the old days.

After rolling the plane into the hangar, politely greeting a half dozen workers and hangers-around, and walking past a building from which emitted the sounds of a trumpet practicing the scales and then laboring over "Rock of Ages," we reached the guest house. A palm tree filled with weaverbirds drooped over the front door of this place, and inside (smooth concrete floor, painted stucco walls, minimal furniture) we were shown the living room and kitchen and various bedrooms whereupon, after a quick discussion, we all dropped our things onto various beds and then made our way over to the main house to meet the missionary in charge.

Her name was Wendy, and although we all exchanged greetings with sober handshakes rather than slobbery hugs, it felt to me as if I was coming home to the old farmhouse, pushing through the old screen door where mom—or maybe grandma—was ready and welcoming with open arms. Or maybe I was just hungry. Or maybe I was dreaming. But in any case, I was irrationally glad to be back on steady earth and also to be greeted by a friendly and kind and honorable presence in a safe environment in the middle of what seemed like, probably, an unfriendly wilderness from the back of nowhere. OK, I was hungry.

Wendy wore round, thick glasses. She was in her fifties, short, with short-cut graying hair and a pleasant, polite manner underlain, so I thought, with a latent tension. Further assessments and speculations were postponed by the immediate drama occurring in a very small room off to the side of the small living room. The very small room was the dog den, where a slow-moving, heavy-teated bitch and three little puppies were being confronted by a meowing cat. The cat had moved into the dog den, displaced the mother, and was now licking the puppies and lying down next to them, purring and trying to play mommy. The real mommy, meanwhile, seemed relieved to get away.

＊

Wendy offered us tea and biscuits, and, after she declared that dinner would be ready in about an hour, Karl, Reas, Ron, and I took our teas and biscuits onto the back porch of this house and sat down to look off in the distance, not so far, over the river—which was low enough to be invisible from where we sat—across to the seething green edge of the Democratic Republic of Congo. A cooling afternoon breeze seemed to be rising up from the invisible river, while the late afternoon sun plastering a patch of tin roof with its farewell blast made the roof go *tick tick tick tick tick*.

Ron said that there used to be a problem with mambas coming into the main house and, sometimes, pythons eating the mission dogs. Once, he said, he and his brother were going hunting with their father. They had a tracker ahead of them and were walking along a trail when a python leapt—or sprang, or whatever pythons do—at the tracker, wrapping himself quickly around the guy's leg and biting into his kneecap. Pythons, Ron paused to explain, have four rows of very sharp teeth and jaws that open like a hinge, and the python had bitten the tracker's knee. The guy grabbed the snake's head and pulled the toothy mouth back open, ripping off his kneecap in the process. Someone shot the python in the head, killing him. They put the tracker's kneecap back in place, wrapped it, put him on a stretcher, and hauled him back to camp for medical attention. They hauled the python back too, as evidence, and when they got back there, his dad hung the python up in a tree by his head, letting the tail dangle. Then his dad posed for a photograph with that giant, eighteen-foot snake dramatically wrapped around his neck.

As the photograph was being taken, Ron could see that his dad was really getting into the mood, really hamming it up, grimacing, making faces, puffing up his face, really getting into it—until he realized that his dad wasn't acting at all. The dead python's muscles were reflexively tightening and strangling his dad. They all had to grab and pull the snake off. "And when I tell this story to kids in the States," Ron concluded, "I say, 'And that's just what drugs are like. You start out thinking they're a joke. Fun thing to do with friends. A way to get in with the crowd. And then before you know it, they're wrapped around your neck, strangling you, and they won't let go.' And then I roll out the snakeskin. That really gets their attention!"

Ron had been thinking quite a bit about the States lately, since he was anticipating a few months' leave very soon, during which he would be required to speak before all the supporting churches back home and explain how their money was still needed to save souls. Ron didn't like that part of the job—going back to the States to ask for money—and in fact it was fair to say he hated it. In his hometown, some of the parishioners would say, "But Ron, your grandfather went to Africa almost a hundred years ago, so when will this job be done?" Ron found it hard to tell people that things were probably worse today, for the local people, than when his grandfather arrived.

He also had trouble understanding Americans' interests in shopping and material goods, and their lack of understanding about the rest of the world. Africa, for instance. He found them to be too often isolated and self-centered, and it was thus very difficult to go there and talk about raising mission funds. People didn't want to give without having a receipt for their tax write-offs, and they don't know even the first thing about Africa. Americans seemed more concerned about things like whether or not a ball was kicked from one side of a barrier to another side, and that was just something Ron had a lot of trouble relating to: sports. So he found it very hard to talk to strangers in America, which he would be doing soon. But sports! He would want to say, "Look, people, thirteen million people died in the Congo civil war, eight million in Sudan, five million in Darfur. There are large, large problems, huge problems in Africa that could be helped."

Americans have the power and resources to do something about them, and yet when you go there to the United States the power and the resources are used for such fickle, self-serving entertainments. You just look at this project or that project, and you say to yourself, "So much could be done." So Ron just dreaded going back to the States and living among strangers, day after day, and having to stand in front of strangers while wearing a suit and tie, and explain what was happening in Africa and why they should give money to the missions. He would rather be up in a plane in a thunderstorm, with the engine on fire and some missionary kid's snake loose in the cabin.

✳

Wendy called us in to dinner, and in passing through the sparsely furnished living room, I had a moment to appreciate the only real art in the house—a nice collection of African musical instruments.

Seated at the table in their small dining room, we all bowed our heads and held hands while Wendy prayed.

For dinner, we had stewed waterbuck—and, after it became known that I was trying to become a vegetarian, cheese quickly followed—plus some kind of green vegetable paste as well as peanut butter with bread. The meal was perfectly satisfying, and during it I asked Wendy about her fascinating collection of indigenous musical instruments: harps, pipes, and drums. Wendy was a musician, she explained, and her task at the mission was to record the Azande music for posterity and also, of course, to be a witness for the glory of God. And since I had been admiring one particular drum made out of a hollowed log with an animal skin pegged across the wood, she also told me the story of that special drum.

She had given a music seminar to a mission group in the Congo and bought the drum at a market for around ten dollars. She was very pleased with it, until after she brought it home and heard that the woman who sold it to her was the biggest witch doctor in the entire region. She began to worry that the drum was suffused with evil magic. She had been disturbed. Should she keep the drum? Would it bring evil? Was it all right? Oh! But then she spoke to one of her workers who said it would be all right. They took it home, and they all joined together and held hands around it, and prayed to remove the evil magic. So that was all right. And, as it turned out, one of this woman witch doctor's sons became interested in Christianity and started coming to church. So that was an unexpected blessing.

✴

But it had been, for Ron, a sobering, distressing experience: flying us from Entebbe, in East Africa, out to the Zemio mission in Central Africa. And after dinner—once we were back in our guest bungalow—he tried to explain why he was upset.

Ron had been born in Africa, a missionary kid. He went to college in the States, studying engineering before going to Bible School, followed by flight training. He worked in Chicago flying overnight freight, then went to Alaska to get the bush pilot experience. Finally, he came back to Africa as a missionary pilot in 1983. The route we took out of Uganda: He used to fly that route all the time, and in the first years, he'd seen elephants in enormous herds and hundreds of buffalo. You couldn't make a flight without seeing animals. Twenty would be the norm for an elephant herd, but there were herds of up to fifty and even eighty back then. These days, though, he'll see elephants only once in every five trips—and this last time, with us, he saw nothing. No animals. No elephants. No buffalo. Nothing.

Upon my encouragement, Ron explained a little more about his life. His grandfather had been called by the Lord to join the African mission in 1922. He was a very interesting man. He was a good teacher, an artist. He painted pictures and had a good grasp on colors and things like that. He was not mechanical at all. He was a good diplomat. The mission used him a lot to liaise with the government officials because he spoke Flemish, which a lot of the Belgian officials spoke as well. So he did the relationship work between the government and the mission, and he was just a very calm and peaceful man with a very loving heart. Ron respected him a lot, never saw him angry.

Ron's father was a little different: very good mechanic, builder, and, definitely unlike Ron's grandfather, an avid hunter and a lover of wildlife. Having been born in Africa, he knew the African people very well, and he knew many, many African languages. And he loved to hunt. He would hunt elephants to provide meat for the schools, and he also shot meat—often buffalo—for church conferences. But, Ron continued, his father just loved wildlife and being outdoors.

As for himself, Ron felt that he was very lucky to grow up in a time in the Congo when the animals were plentiful. They were everywhere, and a lot of his growing up was with African kids. They would head out into the bush all day long and wander around and see animals. Actually, a big part of his life growing up was animals. He had pets. Had a bush pig. Had monkeys. Had antelope. Their lives and animals were just so intertwined, and the bush was their life. And it was also the life of his father. He loved to get out and just walk. He and Ron one time took a saltshaker and a rifle, and said, "We're going to be gone for three days." And that was just wonderful. He wouldn't have to shoot a thing, but just go out there and walk, and watch these herds of animals moving around. It was just heaven. They ate plants, shot a bushpig, cooked it, and just lived out there in the bush for three days. Just for total enjoyment. It was a sort of heaven. No headaches. People weren't asking you for this and that, and just to get away and just be out in nature for three days: That's what they would choose for a holiday, his dad and Ron. They loved that. It was incredible to be out there in the bush and see all of that nature. It was just so incredible. And that doesn't exist anymore. It's gone. Ron's children, when they were here in Zemio, they had a chimp. And they could go down here and watch the hippos in the river. But in their short little childhoods, the animals disappeared. Vanished. They're gone.

And it's something Ron tries to relate to others, tell them what it was like growing up in Africa. But it's gone. That Africa, with all the animals, and the sense of limitless game and wilderness and great freedom, doesn't exist anymore. Growing up in that situation was very, very important to him, and it's gone. His kids got a little glimpse of it, but no more. It won't happen anymore. That's been very hurtful to Ron. A lot of the kids he grew up with in Congo and went to school with in Kenya, they express the same thing. The world as they knew it doesn't exist anymore. The joy and just the awesomeness of this world that they got to grow up in and experience is not there. It all happened so fast. A blink of the eye in God's sight . . . or in evolutionary terms.

Ron strongly believed that God, when He created this earth, put us in charge. He is going to be very upset if we don't take care of it. It's our responsibility. Of all the species in the world, He chose us and gave us intelligence, so that we could take care of his garden, and what have we done? We've devastated it. It's not right, what we've done. It is absolutely wrong.

✳

The next morning, a woman, a bushmeat trader, showed up at the mission door, offering for sale a big dishpan full of hippo and bush pig. Wendy bought some of her meat, while Ron gave the trader a long lecture in Azande: as she sat there—a pained look on her face, half hiding her face with her hand—keeping in her lap that big dishpan full of meat, flies swarming. Ron later paraphrased and seriously abridged for my benefit the lecture he gave: "I told her, 'God has put us in charge of all the animals, and he's going to be pretty upset with us when all the animals are gone.'"

Later on that day, a young woman and her small daughter showed up, apparently just to say hello to Ron, who had once saved the mother's life, evacuating her to a hospital and doctor as she was dying from a pregnancy gone bad. The woman, maybe eighteen years old or so, her manner tentative and shy, had wrapped herself in an attractive kanga, green, with yellow-and-orange speckled and ribboned floating umbrellas. Her hair was woven into five snaky tails that stood directly up from her head.

Karl, meanwhile, had been keeping records of the smuggling of tusks and elephant meat that passed through Zemio, registering amounts and prices. Across the river from the mission was, according to Karl, one of the biggest protected areas in Africa, and it was all being hunted out. "The last elephants and hippos are now being shot and brought out."

A well-traveled track in the Congo led up to a river crossing at Zemio and then the long road—or whatever you might call it—across the Central African Republic to the capital city of Bangui. Karl's spy, a local person from Congo whom he had hired to monitor the traffic in elephant parts as they moved from A to B, visited us at the mission and brought us out to meet and chat with one of the transporters.

Karl's spy had a classically handsome African face, chiseled and angled, with blue highlights reflecting off the black skin of his face. The transporter was a very young man with a very old bicycle, who, as Karl quizzed him about prices and quantities, quietly stood to one side of his wicker baskets full of smuggled goods. The goods consisted of a couple of small, sad tusks sawn off an immature elephant and a good deal of meat, the latter serving as a silent planet inhabited by obscurely undulating maggots and orbited by the noisy satellites of boldly buzzing flies. Tusks and meat, maggots and flies, would soon be put on the road to Bangui.

※

Road? I spent a few hours riding on the back bench seat of a mission Toyota Range Rover over that thing called the "road," and I can say it would not be identified as such in happier places. Most of the bridges were out, which meant that one drove the vehicle down a steep bank, crossed a rocky and sometimes muddy riverbed, then climbed steeply up the other side. But even where there weren't dried-up rivers and disintegrated bridges, the "road" itself was imperfectly distinguishable from a riverbed.

It was a long drive past a few shops, a couple of parked and rusting trucks, some racing pigs, and then we were out of town and bouncing or churning along past villages of mud brick houses, people sitting in front of their mud brick houses, women gathered in cooking pavilions, women walking along with bundles and basins on their heads, men pushing vastly overloaded bicycles. Sitting in the front seat of our vehicle was the driver and also a man from the mission church named Jean-Baptiste Mbolihoundole: a small man with regular features and a bright smile who wore dressy brown pants, a tan cotton short-sleeved shirt, and a baseball cap with NEW YORK embroidered on it. We were headed out on mission business, Jean-Baptiste explained, off to visit the Mbororo, a people who were in the process of becoming Christian, hopefully, and so now they were maybe half Christian and half Muslim.

The Mbororo were cattle herders who had come down from the north, bringing along their cattle. But having come this far south, into this southern bush land of the Central African Republic, they were experiencing a good deal of cultural and social conflict with the local Azande people. Mistrust. Hostility. Et cetera. The Azande thought this was their land, but the Mbororo intended to use a bit of it, too. The Mbororo had tried moving into the area before, but they had never before been able to settle down because their cattle were vulnerable to drought and the diseases caused by tsetse flies. Thus, the Christian church sponsored by the mission was helping them drill wells and bringing in volunteer veterinary and cattle experts from other parts of the world, Australia, for example, and vaccinating the Mbororo cattle. Once the cattle were all fixed up, the Mbororo would no longer have to leave, and that was a good thing. It was Christian charity at work.

The Mbororo village was called Gbondi. The chief, an impressive man dressed in a green ankle-length shirt and wearing on his head a white turban wrapped around an embroidered Muslim bowl cap, was named Arda Umaru. He was lean and tall, and he had a high-bridged nose and a chin that terminated with a white tuft of beard. He was decidedly light-skinned. In fact, all the men in this village were light-skinned, and many or most of them were also lean and tall and had high-bridged noses. The women, too—or at least what I saw of the women, who were sequestered away and thus could only be observed in fleeting glimpses as disappearing figures in the distance or faces occasionally gazing out from inside the village houses.

Jean-Baptiste Mbolihoundole made all the introductions and all the translations—from Mbororo and some Swahili to French and back again—while Karl, Reas, and I were treated as a delegation of some very big gents from somewhere very far away and altogether very important indeed. Wherever we traipsed, we were surrounded by Mbororo men and boys, all eager to shake our hands and listen attentively to our incomprehensible gibberish, and in this fashion, we were led out to the village mosque, a small but daring Frank Gehry edifice of bundled straw, and introduced to the imam, whose name was Ammadou Adamou. Next we were taken out to appreciate and say hello to the Mbororo cattle, who were huge, lyre-horned, and dangerously aggressive. And finally, we were led over to the village meeting hall, which was an open-air, center-poled, raised-cone thatch pavilion, also designed by Frank Gehry.

Five chairs of various provenance, all handmade, were brought out for the chief, the imam, and the three visiting dignitaries.

We sat down, and soon the pavilion was filling up with Mbororo men, dressed in long flowing shirts, some of them ankle-length, with baggy trousers underneath. Nearly all the men had elaborately patterned or single-color scarves draped across their shoulders and wrapped around their ornately embroidered, inverted-bowl caps. A thin mustache and small tufted beard seemed more or less standard, and the men all sat on mats that had been spread across the ground, shaded from the sun by the thatch overhead. All around the pavilion, meanwhile, a seething cotillion of curious young boys stood blinking in the sunlight and peering into the shadows of this meeting of olders and elders and dignitaries.

The meeting began with a communal prayer, the men sitting with their hands open, mumbling and mumbling, and after they had done enough mumbling, in unison they passed their open hands across their faces, thereby washing themselves, so it seemed, with the invisible water of a great blessing. I heard the sound of wood being chopped, of cocks crowing, of a baby whining in the background—or rather a bawling goat. And I appreciated being in the shade, felt a breeze pass through, rippling the grassy fringe of the pavilion roof and cooling my face simultaneously.

Then the palavers began, with the chief and imam opening their hearts and minds and welcoming us with their greatest something or other, and with us opening our hearts and minds and accepting their welcome with our greatest something or other. This was followed by a few questions about animals in French, spoken by Karl, then translated by Jean-Baptiste into Mbororo, with the answers gradually coming back in the opposite direction. In this fashion, we passed half the afternoon exchanging appreciative glances and poetically generous phrases, and, I suppose, making sure no one had any bad intentions or hidden knives, until eventually it was over, whereupon we climbed back into the Toyota and navigated our way back.

✳

The next morning, back at the mission, Ron gave his blunt assessment of the situation with the Mbororo: "Well, they're taking over this land, and when they do it'll be the end of the wild animals. It's all because of drugs—antibiotics—that allow them to move into these southern bush lands. They keep the grass low, and they do it by burning. Normally, the grass burns once, but they don't allow the grass to grow to seed, so that eventually the bush land turns into grassland and then desert." Ron considered them to be part of a much larger movement: Islamists steadily moving south and slowly taking over. "They buy up all the businesses in town, then take over the schools."

But Ron, just then, was getting ready to fly: a fact made apparent because he was wearing the shirt with the epaulettes. And so we packed our bags and, directly after breakfast, we walked over to the hangar and hauled out the plane, turned it about until it was facing a long stretch of grassy runway. Ron did the usual checking and reviewing, after which we tossed in our luggage and then ourselves.

Sitting in the pilot's seat, Ron bowed his head, and said, "Let's pray." We all went silent as he followed through: "Dear Lord, thank you for a beautiful day. Thank you for. . . ." He thought of a couple of other things to be thankful for before moving on to the subtle, two-part request. "With your blessings, we will have a good time and see lots of animals. In Jesus's name, amen."

He looked down around the prop and said, since we were now in Francophone Africa, a French word with the properly adenoidal enunciation: "*Attention!*"

He pressed the starter button.

10: BANGUI INTERLUDE

We flew over Zemio: a long, red-dirt road with red, mud-brick buildings on either side, the buildings thatched or roofed with red and rusty tin. We rose higher, and I could see the greens of the forest and the grasses, and still make out the scratch of red, the dendritic stretch of ferrous-soiled road that ran from Zemio to Bangui. It was iron versus chlorophyll, a competition we more or less followed for the next 450 miles.

"I hate Bangui," was Ron's succinct assessment of our next destination, spoken through the headphones. He told a story about flying a very ill woman there. The ill woman died during the flight, but her family in Bangui refused to take the body. The local hospital refused to get involved. Then the police decided to arrest him for murder. Once they got that straightened out, the airport authorities forbade him from removing the body and gave him until a 10 p.m. deadline to leave, to fly back to Zemio with a by-then grotesquely ripening corpse. Finally, he hired a gang of underemployed soldiers with AK-47s to take the corpse off the airplane, out of the airport, and off to a funeral home in town.

In Bangui, we waded through the usual mob scene while getting out of the airport but quickly found our fixer, a local guy named Alexis. Alexis wore a beautiful yellow-and-black spotted shirt with leopards on it, and an orange-and-black baseball cap. His face was distressed by deep furrows in the forehead, and his eyes looked swollen, with a scarred area around his right eye, possibly caused by someone's fist.

We found a taxi and driver. The taxi was a tiny Nissan with a spidery crack in the windshield, possibly made by someone's head, that was held in place by a green-and-white circular bumper sticker that said, blissfully, *Je me confie à Dieu*. Our driver, a bulky man in blue shirt and shorts and pink flip-flops, turned out to be a perfectly patient sort of guy, and so he became our driver for the entire time we stayed in Bangui: two days spent on errands and meat.

The driver took us past the new stadium, recently built by the Chinese, then past the old stadium where in 1977 Jean-Bédel Bokassa, erstwhile head of state, seated himself on a gold throne and had himself crowned Emperor of the Empire of the Central African Republic—the throne now stripped of gold and gone, the stadium now collapsing and undergoing a vegetative overcoming. We found a small, rough downtown with a couple of decent cafés, the Phonecia and the Grand, both protected by private security guards at the door, and an Internet café, a gambling place, a bank, plus a few modern buildings apparently dedicated to serious commerce. We passed the Witness Chapel and the Ministère des Affaires Étrangers, a few burnt-out buildings, and then the town devolved into long rows of commercial shanties, some built of shipping containers, others of stick and tin, places with names like Elvira Coiffure, Chicago Coiffure, Bla Bla Boutique, the Chez Papi bar, Cave Oceanna bar, Sylvia Froid, Paradis le Cinéma, and Lovely Phone.

Errands. Filmmaker Reas had to pay a lot of money for a filming permit from the Ministry of Tourism, and then he had to pay a lot more money for another filming permit from the Ministry of Communication, Arts, and Culture. The rest of that first afternoon was spent checking into our hotel and trying to locate a doctor for Karl, who was suddenly experiencing some kind of severe pain.

Meanwhile, I was never sure what Alex, our fixer, fixed, but it soon became obvious who Junior, our minder, minded. Junior met us at our hotel. He was a member of the Presidential Guard, an elite force of soldiers who dressed sharply in red berets and camouflage khakis, and covered their left shoulders with a gorgeously embroidered red scorpion on a yellow patch. They carried AK-47s and in general looked ferocious and probably were, since they served as the president's private bodyguard in a place where the presidency was always precarious. They also moonlighted when the price was right. Junior was a big guy with a sweet baby face. His full name and rank were Sergeant Junior Ngaerosset, but he sometimes went by the nickname Bokassa, in honor of the country's former Emperor.

That sweet baby face was possibly a disguise for a coolly brutal person, I thought, but just as I was getting used to Junior, I began to understand that he, for some reason, couldn't be our bodyguard. He introduced us to his replacement, another member of the Presidential Guard named Juvenal.

※

Juvenal reappeared early the next morning: a young man, very lean and somber, dressed in the beret, khakis, and red scorpion on yellow patch, and carrying the AK-47, ready to assist us in a little elephant meat research. The day began with a quick survey of a couple of smaller markets, followed, around midday, by a longer look at a much bigger one.

The latter, located in the dirt alongside the dirt road twelve kilometers outside of town, was called P. K. Douze (Kilometer Twelve), and it seemed to ramble on for a considerable distance and to include a few or several thousand sellers and buyers, all of them black Africans.

I said to Karl, "Let's try to blend in."

But as Karl and Reas began sweeping down beside the tables and tables of bushmeat with their video cameras running, and as crowds of market women rose up in waves beyond the cameras and began shouting "*Ce n'est pas bon! Ce n'est pas bon! Ce n'est pas bon!*" and other angry things, I began to understand the logic of a bodyguard. A touchy situation, I thought, and I did my best to act like it was just one more boring day at the market. But then appeared a drunk man wearing a black-and-white striped shirt, like a comic-book jailhouse shirt, who made an aggressively dramatic show of photographing the white guys with his cell phone. A big crowd began to gather, mostly quiet but with some of the market ladies yelling nastily, in French, "You think we're stupid!"

The situation seemed to be getting tense, but Reas turned to make a dramatic show of videotaping the drunk man with the cell phone. It quickly became two guys with their equipment aimed at each other, and Reas milked the minor comic element for all it was worth. It was crossed swords, leveled pistols, a mock duel, a high noon showdown at the OK Corral. People started laughing. Reas moved in closer, closer, still a duel, but pretty soon he started talking to the drunk guy, and then the latter was giving the former a lecture about bushmeat. Together Reas and the drunk guy walked up and down the market, Reas filming the meat, the guy holding up various pieces of monkey, duiker, sections of buffalo, and who knows what else, drunkenly lecturing about how this or that is cooked, what's good, what's bad, and so on.

We didn't see any obvious elephant meat then, though there were thousands of different pieces of meat there, most of it obscured and blackened by smoking. And when we inquired about elephant meat, we were told that it was illegal to sell, so there was nothing in the market—but if we wanted some, a phone call could be made.

Karl was by then nearly crippled by pain, so off he went to see a doctor for what would turn out to be a stubborn kidney stone, while Reas and I returned, late in afternoon, to the P.K. Douze, where we met two girls who had agreed, as a result of a phone call, to show us their elephant meat.

The two girls were teenagers, very shy, giggly, and pretty, named Josiane Dwili and Stephanie Magba. They said selling elephant meat was not allowed, which was why they kept it in a storehouse just behind the meat tables.

The storehouse was a dark, mud-brick and tin-roofed shed with a corrugated tin door, and inside we saw many bags and cardboard boxes of meat. Reas videotaped Stephanie emerging from the doorway of that dark hut, emerging into the afternoon light and carrying one of the boxes. After she brought it over to one of the plank market tables, he taped her pulling the meat out of the box, piece by piece. It looked like just random bits of blackened and dried meat to me, could have been from any sort of animal, but everyone in the gathering crowd of onlookers confirmed it was elephant meat. The two girls handled the pieces deftly, as together they eagerly explained the many good things about such meat, while several older market women added their considered opinions. And Reas, with his closed-mouth smile, a crease appearing in his cheeks, a pleasant if slightly bemused and clownish expression in his eyes, got it all on camera.

It had rained hard earlier in the afternoon, incidentally, and so the market was now situated in a long stretch of red mud. But Josiane and Stephanie, as they contributed to Reas's documentary, moving here, walking there, standing this way and that, stepped bravely through the mud in their sandaled feet, and they still managed to look fresh, pretty, and altogether charming, with Stephanie wearing a beautiful print dress with a design featuring elephants.

✳

Our hotel in Bangui had seen better days, but it was in a nice location: right next to the Oubangui River, where the muddy water flattened and pooled, was smoky olive when you looked into it, gray when you looked across a wind-ruffled expanse, with a bank of high grass down to a sandy flat shore and sandbars—and a dozen fishing pirogues being paddled here and there.

Our first evening at the hotel, while Reas and I were meeting baby-faced Junior and appreciating the river, we also met a British guy by the name of Anthony Mitchell (rectangular glasses, pale skin, severe haircut on a nearly bald head), who stepped up and, by way of introduction, said, "I'm looking for Karl Ammann."

Anthony, a reporter for the Associated Press, happened to be based in Nairobi, so he might theoretically have flown out with us, but in truth our little plane couldn't hold sufficient fuel and another body simultaneously for such a long flight. Thus, he had taken a commercial flight from Nairobi to Douala, in Cameroon—where he was badly harassed and unreasonably delayed by an immigration official looking for money—before eventually catching another commercial flight to Bangui. Karl had briefly mentioned this guy, the Associated Press reporter rendezvousing with us in Bangui, only Karl had mostly described him as the reporter who had recently been kicked out of Ethiopia, which did, we all agreed, seem like an impressive thing to have on your résumé.

In any case, Anthony was now joining our group, and the first thing he planned was an interview with the president of the Central African Republic: something that Alexis, our fixer, thought he could fix. So while, the next day, Reas and I did the market rounds, and as Karl was off finding a doctor to diagnose his kidney stone, Anthony was out with Alexis and looking for the president with the intent of getting an interview.

The day after that, after we all crammed our several selves and all our luggage like a circus clown act into the tiny taxi, and began the drive to the airport, I learned that Karl had successfully located a doctor, had an X-ray, and been given some medicine that would probably enable him to survive the next few days. I also learned that Anthony had spent some time not interviewing the president, which seemed to surprise as well as frustrate him. As he put it: "I mean, Associated Press—pretty much you can always get an interview with the president of some godforsaken place that no one's ever heard of."

As we passed through the airport, through the narrow rats' maze of corridors leading from the outside, through immigration, and onto the airfield, we came face to face with an unhappy young man being escorted off in the opposite direction by a much bigger man who was gripping him tightly by the shirt collar and lifting up—so that his shirt served as a temporary noose, as he was pushed and pulled and hauled away from the airfield and back out to the street and, presumably, the nearest gutter. And we, having passed this dramatic vignette, were now out on the airfield, where great flocks of snowy white egrets hid in the tall grass alongside the runway. We walked over to Ron's plane, which was, as he noted with some relief, still filled with fuel. ("This is the first time I've come back after two nights in Bangui, and the fuel hasn't been siphoned out of the plane.")

We climbed in, strapped ourselves down.

Anthony sighed, settled in next to me, and said, ironically, "Bangui: Now that's my idea of a charming town. It has that intriguing air of brutality." And then, wryly, "Where's the stewardess?"

Ron said the prayer. Then, head raised, eyes scanning the airfield ahead and below, he shouted in French out the window, "*Attention!*"

11: THE ELEPHANTS OF DZANGA-SANGHA

Soon after we landed at the dirt airstrip a mile or so outside Bayanga village, a murmuring crowd appeared—children, mostly, including Bantus from Bayanga and some Ba'Aka Pygmy girls and women. One Ba'Aka woman, dressed gloriously in a wraparound print, shaded herself with a red, blue, and orange umbrella and carried a baby. The Ba'Aka were notably smaller and seeming subtly to keep themselves apart from the Bantus; and when Karl passed out candy and balloons to all the clamoring children, the Ba'Aka were pushed back by the other children and thus were last to get their share. When they finally did get some candy and balloons, I noticed, the prizes were often snatched out of their hands by the others.

We rolled the plane over to a concrete pad, and Ron tied it down. Then, having given away all our candy and balloons, and having unloaded our packs and piled them beside the plane, we stood there next to the pile and waited. A short while passed, and Karl said: "Where are they? They know we're coming. If this is a tourist operation, they should be here to pick us up."

Another short while passed, and Karl said: "This is not much of a tourist operation if they can't pick us up when we fly in. They knew we were coming. We flew over before we landed—they would have heard it. Where are they? They'll never get tourists coming if they treat them like this."

An additional short while passed before Karl added: "This is no way to run a tourist setup. We got a good reception last time."

At last a pleasant-mannered African man in a light, cream-colored business suit, shiny shoes, and a blue necktie, drove up on a motorbike, talked quietly to Karl, and drove off again. Ten minutes later, the man returned driving a brand new Toyota Land Cruiser with the air-conditioner turned up high. We put our luggage into the back, and the man—Jean-Baptiste Gomina, the tourism manager—drove us out to the Doli Lodge, explaining in his French-accented English some things about the place: "Zis is ze way to Doli Lodge. Doli. It's ze Sangha word for 'elephant.' Doli Lodge." We drove past a turnoff and a sign that said GARAGE, and he said, "And zis is where ze garage is. For when your car breaks."

The road rolled down past the Doli offices and into a riverside clearing that included a cooking pavilion, some communal showers and latrine, a number of huts and cabins, and a restaurant-and-bar pavilion balanced on stilts and cast over the river's edge. We paid our fees, threw our packs inside some sleeping huts, and rendezvoused a few minutes later at the restaurant-bar pavilion.

It was made out of rough-sawn lumber, with a thatched roof on sawn posts, kerosene lanterns fitted with electric light bulbs, a couple of electric ceiling fans, five tables set for meals, a dozen padded arm chairs around a couple of coffee tables, with the bar at one end holding a medium-sized elephant jawbone as a conversation piece. We ordered cold beer and gazed lazily over the Sangha River and the haze-screened forest on the far side.

It was a peaceful scene, and I was soon hypnotized by the heat, the humidity, the droning of insects, and the compelling beauty of that particular time and place: a wild, mirrored and wind-ruffled river, a long yellow sandbar, two pirogues beached on the bar, four African boys shouting and playing splashily on the bar and in the water, their happy voices drifting in our direction. It was a nearly perfect moment, I thought, and when I noticed them again, the four boys were in one of the pirogues, laughing, with three of them paddling and the fourth in front jumping up and down to rock the boat. I listened to the contented warbling of birds and, in the background, Karl's voice: ". . . that's what it is. The laws are extremely good. But no one follows the laws. You have to enforce the laws. Don't just keep saying, 'It's all about food security' and all that crap. . . ."

But it really was a lovely sweep of river, with a flat, slow current; pieces of leafy green vegetation drifting along and looking like potted greenhouse plants; a rivulet cutting through the yellow sandbar; a wide pebbled surface in which olive green and bluish gray were continuously battling each other along some uneasy, rippling seams. And above: a hazy blue sky with circling and then landing white egrets. Were those egrets without regrets?

Then Ron's voice: ". . . all depends on what you've grown up with. I grew up eating bushmeat as a child, and it's better. Tastier. . . ."

Then Karl's: "It's a nice setting for an African scenic shot."

※

Karl and I, now sitting in the dining pavilion and holding our respective glasses of chilled beer, had arrived in this remote part of the world with a pair of perspectives that might crudely be summarized as glass-half-empty versus glass-half-full. Let me tell you the half-full version.

First, we had come to the only place in the world, just about, where an outsider can hope to see forest elephants: Dzanga-Sangha.

Second, the Dzanga-Sangha Forest Reserve, established in 1990, officially covers a very large piece of species-rich real estate in the forested southwestern point of the Central African Republic. The forest reserve is part of a larger collection of protected areas in CAR (including the Dzanga Park and the Ndoki Park) that, in turn, are contiguous with two large national parks located in neighboring Cameroon to the southwest (the Lobéké National Park) and neighboring

Congo-Brazzaville to the southeast (the Nouabalé-Ndoki National Park). The full conglomeration, known as the Sangha River Tri-national Protected Area, represents the second biggest piece of delimited forest in the world. It's owned and operated by an African entity called the Central African Forest Commission, and it's monitored and funded by the World Wildlife Fund, the German Cooperation of Technical Collaboration (GTZ), and the Wildlife Conservation Society (WCS) . . . and being considered as a UNESCO World Heritage Site.

You can say all kinds of bad things about this part of the world. Poaching—all species, including elephants. Illegal logging somewhere. Probably shifty deals and shady transfers of money. Probably corruption high and corruption low. All the rest. That's the glass half-empty version, I believe. But elephants! I share some of Karl's doubts about the WWF, which in my opinion has gone off the deep end with its official attachment to the lie of "sustainable" development and has gotten too cozy with tropical forest loggers and logging. But for the moment (still sitting dreamily on the bar-restaurant pavilion settled over the edge of the river), I was thinking some distinctly positive thoughts.

I was also aware of some of the more personal history behind all those new boundaries and pronouncements and collaborations, in which the Dzanga-Sangha *baï*—a swampy hole in the forest where the elephants congregate—serves as a significant centerpiece for much of the rest. I was additionally aware that the Dzanga-Sangha baï was made known and then essential largely because of one person, Andrea Turkalo, an American originally from . . . New York, I think. She first began going to Dzanga-Sangha in order to watch the forest elephants. She built an observation platform at the edge of the baï. She studied the elephants as a scientist, then opened up the place to other researchers; and by the time we arrived, she had spent enough time with the elephants to be able to recognize several hundred individuals on sight. I've long admired Andrea as one of these unaccountably tough and stubborn individuals who do heroic things and inspire others.

I had met her about ten years earlier while traveling in northern Congo, and so I could now call upon my memory of a quiet, steady, warmly sympathetic woman, who also happened to be physically very attractive. Or was my memory playing tricks there? No, it wasn't! Here she was, walking into the pavilion, then rushing over to greet me with a quick hug.

"Hello, Dale! Nice to see you. I remember you from Bomassa."

"Yeah, a while ago!" I said, adding, "My beard has turned gray since then."

"Well, thanks to modern chemistry, my hair hasn't," she said, brightly.

She was slender and beautiful with a very direct manner, as well as gray eyes or green eyes, or maybe they were light-hazel eyes, beneath arched eyebrows, an oval face, brown hair tied into a small knot at the back. She wore olive-green Levi's and a woven leather belt, a white cotton blouse, a watch on the left wrist and silver bracelet on the right. After we talked a bit more and agreed to meet at seven o'clock the next morning for an interview about her and the elephants, she disappeared on behalf of some pressing obligation, while I turned back to continue working on my beer while staring dreamily at the river.

Late afternoon heat.

A silvered, flashing surface.

A flat, shimmering, moving world.

A world of flickering light and ball-peened shadows, with three pirogues and four piroguists, one of them singing as he stood and paddled slowly downriver.

※

The pressing obligation Andrea rushed off to that afternoon was a meeting with some bigwigs from Germany. These were mainly folks associated with the German version of the World Wildlife Fund, and I was soon listening to speculative gossip about this group from Karl, Reas, and Anthony, all of whom were trying to line up interviews with some of them, particularly the one who was CEO of the NGO known as WWF, who may or may not have been an OK sort of VIP.

As it happened, Reas got there first, landing a videotaped interview with the WWF NGO CEO OK VIP near the end of the day. A handsome man with wavy, light-brown hair, he spent nearly an hour in front of Reas's tripoded camera, standing inside a hemisphere of artificial light in front of one of the more-rustic looking staff buildings. I saw this interview from a distance, was only told later the following version of what happened: that after the German head of the WWF said on camera that some twenty thousand elephants were being protected in the area, Reas pulled out a recent report that placed the elephant population down to around eight thousand, whereupon the WWF guy said, "If you know everything better than I do, why interview me?"—and then walked away. He also declared that he would not give permission for Reas to use anything that had just been recorded.

We all discussed this unhappy turn of events over our late dinner that evening. Not surprisingly, Reas was upset, while Karl added his perspective, saying things like: He can't do that. He's a public figure. Reas should use the material anyway. And so on. Anthony, meanwhile, who had requested an interview with the same guy, was now being put off.

Since the Germans, as I understood it, were responsible for much of the financing behind the tourist camp at Doli, they were important to the people running Doli Lodge, while at the same time our group had just arrived from Bangui, apparently dragging along our own little cloud of inchoate ill-will and mistrust.

Mattias—the stocky, ruddy, round-faced German who served as an assistant tourism manager at Doli, or something similar—later explained to me his own thinking about the tension generated by our arrival. He said, with his distinctive German accent: "Karl has been here before. I do not dislike him. And then, he said he vas coming. OK. Fine. OK. Good. He can come. But then he said he vas bringing a writer. OK. And then he wrote again and said he vas bringing a journalist, too. Good. And he wrote again and said he vas bringing another journalist from AP. So ve vere not sure vat to expect. Ve vere not certain vat vas going on, you know?"

But dinner that evening was an interesting situation if only because, while our group was sitting there and leisurely consuming our late repast, Reas upset, Karl displeased, some of the Germans had come into the dining pavilion for their own leisurely consumptions. There seemed to be an international tension in the air. At one point, I spoke to one of the Germans—an intellectual-looking bloke with short hair and glasses, who, after I quietly tried to coax him over to our table, said, "I've never met Karl Ammann. I'm not sure I want to."

"You really should," I said. "I'll introduce you."

"Maybe. . . ."

Eventually he did come over, and we all engaged in a neutral blab about some meaningless thing before Anthony, Reas, and Karl nailed him down for interviews the next day.

✳

I went to bed early, while Reas and Anthony stayed out late talking and drinking beer. Reas and I shared the same low-rent hut: a gloomy shack of wood-slab walls, concrete-slab floor, one faint and dangling lightbulb, no furniture to sit on, a single cheap mosquito net strung up to cover two side-by-side beds. It was stuffy and dark in there, but I soon turned in with the expectation of quickly passing out.

It didn't happen.

At last I heard Reas and Anthony trippingly wander back—Anthony headed for the hut next door—both of them pausing to urinate noisily into the ground between the two huts. Then I heard some thumping, after which Reas opened the door, shined his bright flashlight around the room, here, there, here again. He shut the door heavily, and then, after a good deal of rustling and knocking about, he climbed under the mosquito netting onto his bed and soon had slipped into a slow and steady suspiration suggesting a soft and sweet state of suspended animation.

I was feeling displaced and uncomfortable, and had begun listening to the night chorus, which was an infinite ticking conversation of insects punctuated by the tooting commentary of frogs. Some of the insects went: *ting-ting ti-ti-ting ti-ti-ting*, and *ting-ting ti-ting ti-ting*. Other insects went: *chip-chip-chip chrrrrrrrrr*. And still others were going: *zi-zi-zi-zi-zi-zi-zi*. The frogs just went *toot-toot, toot-toot-*

toot, toot-toot. But who else was out there not making sounds? Poisonous snakes, probably, who were slipping and slithering about, looking for stupid insects and frogs to swallow while simultaneously keeping an eye open for an opportunity to puncture the bare foot of a naive American gone out with an urge to urinate during the darkest part of the night. Meanwhile, the hut was becoming stuffy and gloomy. The mosquito netting around the two beds was irritatingly inadequate. And all the gritty grime once settled neatly onto the concrete slab floor was now, working through the adhesive medium of bare foot-bottoms, rising up to settle within the sweaty sheets of my bed.

I drifted into a filmy simulacrum of sleep and passed into a series of absurd if occasionally erotic dreams. Next morning, I made it over to the restaurant in time to have a coffee, a decent breakfast, more coffee, and be prepared for my seven o'clock interview with Andrea, but at around 6:30 a note arrived that said she would have to postpone it until later in the morning, maybe around 11:00. She was sorry. She would let me know more particularly.

I hung around the Doli lodge, waiting for the next note that finally appeared around 10:30, telling me she would have to delay our meeting until late in the afternoon. She hoped that would work out. She would let me know.

I understood that Andrea was busy, not stupidly putting me off in a weakly adolescent fashion, but then I had Anthony's case to consider. Anthony had yesterday been promised an interview with the WWF CEO, an event that had been postponed last night and again this morning, so he was hanging around as well. Then, at lunchtime, the object of his desire appeared at the restaurant pavilion to say goodbye to a few of the Germans sitting there. He was all packed. He looked fresh and bright. He was headed back to Germany. So Anthony walked up, shook the young man's hand, and said clearly enough for everyone around to hear: "Thank you for the non-interview. It's always nice to meet a man with vision." He paused, then added: "It's really inspiring to see someone in a position of power exhibit leadership, courage, and candor."

The German, meanwhile, appeared to take it all in . . . though slowly, pausing momentarily to untwist the linen before discovering, too late, the dagger inside.

Yes, Anthony was a master of Irony, which he could deliver either cold or cool: the sort of skill Brits learn in school the way Americans used to learn Shop and Home Economics.

✳

Not long after that episode, the tourism manager of Doli Lodge, Jean-Baptiste Gomina, appeared at the restaurant and suggested some non-elephant touristic possibilities for the day, speaking mainly to Anthony.

Gomina: "If you want to see hippos, we can take you downriver. There is a family of four hippos two kilometers downriver."

Anthony: "Ah, hippos. . . ."

Gomina: "And if you want to try some local palm wine. . . ."

Anthony: "Ah, local wine. My favorite kind of wine."

After lunch, in fact, we all decided to make our own little tour of the area, starting with the village of Bayanga.

Bayanga village was surely more prosperous than most African villages in the region, apparently because of a European logging operation. The loggers had disappeared by the time we got there, though, so whatever benefits the people of Bayanga acquired while some Europeans made off with the big money were rapidly receding. Still, an after-image of that bright blip of prosperity was easily discerned—not only in the layout of the village, which was clearly organized into a grid pattern, with a sandy passage between houses big enough to drive a car through, but also with the houses themselves, most of them, which were made of sawn wood. They were shacks, actually, about the size of an American garage, with thatched roof, a door, a couple of windows, but wooden shacks—and friendly people occasionally peered out the windows and spontaneously tossed out their *bonjours* and *ça vas* as we passed by.

We stopped at the market to watch some beef being chopped up, also to observe a small collection of bushmeat, looking like pieces of duiker and monkey, and then passed out the other end of town, where a barrier in the road forbid trespassing, but it did so in French, while a man in a guard shack just waved us on.

So we entered the former leased property of a European logging company that had spent a few years raping the African forest before very suddenly making themselves disappear. The evidence for "very suddenly" was that they had left a lot of valuable things behind, which instead of being sold or recycled were now being guarded indefinitely by a few men wearing Eaux et Forêts uniforms and carrying AK-47s.

We first came to the maintenance garage, which was surrounded by some enormous and expensive-looking Caterpillar machines and decorated, inside, with the disintegrating remnants of a Land Rover or two. Then we walked over to the sawmill, which covered maybe an acre of land and consisted of a giant shed and a two-story, broken-windowed block of offices, with more expensive-looking Caterpillar machines sitting around outside and being painted white by birds and red by air and water. A section of the sawmill roof had collapsed. Bird shit was accumulating in heaps on the concrete floor and across some great stacks of sawn boards and giant beams. Vines were beginning to embrace the boards and beams and the heaps of bird shit.

As we wandered around the abandoned sawmill, one of the AK-47-toting Eaux et Forêts guards wandered over to us, asked sternly what we were doing, instructed us emphatically not to take photographs, and then began talking. He said that the loggers had arrived in 1987 and disappeared about four years ago, having been kicked out for not paying their taxes, so that may have explained something.

✹

I missed Andrea again that evening and spent the next couple of days with Karl, Anthony, and Reas watching elephants in the Dzanga-Sangha baï.

From Doli, it was a forty-minute drive along a rough forest road, followed by a forty-minute wait for our Pygmy guides, followed by a forty-minute walk along a windy forest trail: through a sandy-bottomed stream or a moving swamp, clear water running to mid-thigh, through a passage of mud and elephant dung, past elephant footprints, and back on the trail through the forest, a beautiful shady forest with dapples of light, obscure birdsong, some dangling looped vines and lianas, until after forty minutes or so we heard a groan, a roar, a trumpet. Elephants! And again, another groan and roar and trumpet.

Then we emerged onto a wooden walkway through the muddy mush and finally out to some wooden stairs leading up to the viewing platform. The platform: about forty-five feet across, fifteen to twenty feet deep, some thirty feet high, with a four-foot high railing to lean on and avoid falling off with—well-built with a thatched roof, sawn timber uprights, anchored on concrete blocks and stabilized with cables. Up there on the platform were some high, wooden chairs to sit on, as well as three wooden benches.

It was nice to sit down and look across the baï: an open, swampy meadow of maybe three acres. It was bathed in a wavering sunlight, crossed by a single complex stream flowing right to left that spread out into the series of pools and puddles over sandy and sometimes muddy earth . . . with a lot of animals enjoying themselves in the grass and sand and mud and water. At first, I counted thirty-three elephants, one red river hog, and then one sitatunga (forest antelope) who was folded neatly into the grass and flicking away insects with a pair of nervous, leaf-shaped ears. The elephants included one big male with a dangling penis as thick as a fire hose. Also several babies, maybe half a dozen, and around a dozen young.

Some of the elephants were drinking, it seemed, while using their trunks to blow bubbles and make bathtub noises in the water. I watched one big tusker, caked with a cream-colored coating of mud, digging digging digging with his feet into the mud at the bottom of a stream. Then, having dug deeply enough, he submerged his trunk into the water, at last so far down that his mouth was almost touching the water. He stayed that way for a minute or two at a time, tail swinging back and forth, ears slowly wavering, sometimes still, as if concentrating blissfully. Then he drew back, pulled his trunk out, and sprayed thick mud into his mouth. He reminded me of a child in a soda fountain who, having sucked deeply into a big chocolate milkshake through a straw, then pulls up the straw and places its dripping end right into his mouth in order to slurp the chocolaty sludge more directly.

But the place felt more like an elephant social club or spa: a great watery wallow known far and wide for its magnificent sauna and mud baths, its refreshing sweet drinks and salubrious mineral stews, and the one hundred-and-one public and private Jacuzzis. The elephants and other animals would silently appear through a vibrating green door somewhere and then, minutes or hours later, dreamily vanish through another vibrating green door. Animals came and went, in other words: not only elephants but buffalo, bushpigs, red river hogs, sitatungas, waterbuck, as well as birds of all sorts and insects of even more sorts.

The insects included butterflies who arrived in white, iridescent clouds, sometimes tornados, as well as sweat bees and a kind of very persistent and very evil fly. A devil fly, I guess. If you're going to spend time in a tropical forest, it's important to be stoic about insects, but I found those flies, whatever they're called, rising up in the day's heat to swarm the platform and the eyes and ears and noses and hair of its innocent denizens, close to overwhelming ... although Anthony and Reas bravely continued to work on the right attitude.

Anthony: "These flies make it much more enjoyable, don't you think?"

Reas: "Yeah. Nice bonus."

I watched a pair of elephants in a high, dry glade who, having found a patch of golden dirt, were quietly dusting themselves gold.

Two big females stood face to face, standing together in a single pool and gently touching, then intertwining trunks before one stepped aside and the other passed by.

A trunk was dipped into a small, circular pool, concentric circles rippling away from it.

Ears were folded back against a head like a pair of shells, then pressed forward like a set of circular wings.

A big golden male with large tusks, maybe two- and-a-half feet long, appeared in the two-toned style, caused when a mud-plastered animal walks through water: black socks up to the knees.

A group of three adults and three young including a tiny, wobbly thing moved with some spritely eagerness over to a large pool at the far left, joining another group to become a congregation of fourteen. Why?

Twelve moved in unison, including the young. Then seven gold sitatungas with flickery tails, flickery ears, moved in and out, finally passing through a soft green door that closed behind them with a silent, leafy vibration.

A big elephant would do something: such as roar and bellow and chase a younger one, who would squeal and scamper out of the way. But aside from those occasional moments of dramatic excitement, the dash and chase, the scamper or determined trot, these animals' movements seemed profoundly slow and deeply deliberate. They were solemn, giant beasts or spirit beings passing through a more viscous medium of truth. They walked on gray, columnar legs: rear leg moving forward and seeming to kick the front one into motion with a similar procedure in an alternate phase on the other side—yet so slowly, so deliberately, all the while swaying, shifting, swaying, shifting, sometimes pausing in mid-stride as if to think for a moment, or to spread the ears or turn the head or lift the trunk and sniff the air before continuing on that slow, slow, slow journey.

It was like watching a foreign drama unfold in slow motion on a vast and brightly lit stage. A melodrama, actually, accompanied by a forest orchestra arranged in three dimensions and softly if endlessly tuning up: strong on the percussion and woodwinds, with a thousand hidden castanets, with whistlers, pipers, warblers, a hollow flute-bell playing in the rhythm of a bouncing ball.

Reas and Anthony spent the next day on interviews and other journalistic endeavors and investigations having to do with ivory, meat, and elephant poaching in the area, while Karl and I returned to the baï. This time the parrots showed up: about a hundred gray-and-scarlet-tailed birds in a big flock overhead, moving this way with a *craawk craawk craawk*, their wings whipping the air. Then another flock, maybe two or three or four dozen altogether, crossed overhead in another way with a *craawk craawk craawk*. Then a third flock of about four dozen parrots crossed, *craawk craawk craawk*, at yet a third angle, flitting and filtering into the trees at the baï's edge to hold a brief but noisy conference before slowly, one by one, filtering out.

Karl was all the while taking pictures, I should mention, although by around 9:30 in the morning he announced, "The light is getting flat," and stopped taking pictures. The light was good before then and after around three o'clock in the afternoon, but between those times the sun blasted down brightness and hammered out blobs and blurs.

The Pygmy trackers who had led us out to the baï that morning were named Clement Balambi and Gilbert Tanchiko, and after putting his camera down, Karl had a long talk with them about poaching in the area. They said there was quite a bit, and they talked about the poachers who killed an elephant last November at around five o'clock in the afternoon. It was getting dark and raining hard, so they took refuge on the platform. The ecoguards arrived at nine o'clock, beat up the poachers—five men from Bayanga—badly. The poachers were then brought before a magistrate who let them go.

There was also the dead elephant in the clearing—over there, to the left. The trackers said he had arrived with bullet wounds and died in the clearing. Anthony and Reas later interviewed some well-known poachers in the area, who said that the elephants they killed were for big-shot officials and they didn't care how WWF felt about it.

※

I had my interview with Andrea late in the afternoon of our last full day at Doli, and during the next morning, as we flew from Bayanga back to Bangui, I asked Anthony about his real life back in Nairobi, thus discovering that he had two beautiful children, a daughter six months old, a son of one-and-a-half years. And I started to recognize that Anthony's irony was just one manifestation of a clear mind and subtle wit. He was funny and could be fun to be around. This mental shift was gradual, but when we landed at the Bangui airfield and Anthony said to Ron, "Thanks for the flight. Nice landing. You seem to have really picked up, you know, the flying stuff," I laughed out loud.

Anthony hadn't shaved during the last few days, and thus a beard had begun to form, dark and stubbly around his bald head and full, squarish face, and I suddenly thought he looked like a friendly Homer Simpson. That was funny, too. I laughed a second time—and since we were parting ways there at the Bangui airfield, I shook his hand warmly and said, sincerely, "Take care of yourself!"

"Yeah. You, too," he said, without a hint of irony. Then he turned to leave while a 1,200-liter can of fuel mounted on wheels was towed onto the tarmac by the gas guy driving a Massey Ferguson farm tractor. The gas guy parked the can in front of our plane, dismounted the tractor, uncoiled the hose, handed the nozzle to Ron, and began turning a crank: *ahoo, ahow, ahoo, ahow.*

Ron stood with the nozzle poked into a hole in one wing, and when the gas spilled over, he moved to the other wing.

Anthony left us at Bangui for the same reason he had joined us there a week or so earlier—body weight versus fuel weight in a small plane going a long distance—and I now watched him disappear back into the airport building and on his way to catch the commercial flight to Douala, Cameroon, where he would catch a Kenya Airways big bird all the way back to Nairobi.

I was vaguely envious for a moment, thinking to myself how much faster, simpler, and more comfortable a commercial fight in a giant plane could be. And how much safer. Big planes are tough, stable, hard to break. And the care, the training, the professionalism, the backup systems in big planes. Well, simple economic sense, if nothing else—the bald fact that 120 passengers on a big plane are worth about thirty times the lives of four passengers in a dinky plane like the one just now being gassed up by the gas guy turning the crank with an *ahoo* and an *ahow* on the tarmac at Bangui—means that everything about the former is going to be safer, more obsessive-compulsively designed and built and flown.

Having thought such thoughts, and with the plane now gassed up, I climbed in—riding shotgun again, with Karl and Reas seated behind. Ron said the prayers and pressed the button.

Then, once we were successfully back in the sky again, I asked Ron to describe how a non-pilot such as myself might land the plane, in case a pilot such as himself should suddenly lose consciousness. He patiently explained and demonstrated the process, which I immediately forgot, and then he identified the many arcane instruments on the instrument panel, including a weather radar system that showed storm clouds with dark splotches and marked electrical storms with little flashes of imitation lightning. The plane also included a GPS that automatically radioed our position to the headquarters in Nairobi once every half hour. "If they haven't heard from us in an hour," he said, "they send out the search and rescue mission."

As if to ladle on the reassurance, he went on to describe some of his experiences repairing and building plane engines before adding, "I never like to fly a plane I don't know how to fix." Then he told me about some of his early career as a bush pilot in Alaska. He would fly people, fish, and equipment back and forth between a fishing operation on the coast and a town inland. When he started, people asked him, "How many times have you crashed?" When he said, "Never," at first no one would fly with him. They didn't want to fly with someone who didn't know how to crash. But after a while people saw that he didn't get drunk, and they said, "You don't drink?"

He said, "No."

"You don't take amphetamines?"

"No."

"Well, how do you stay awake?"

"I sleep when I'm tired."

This was during the summer, when most of the pilots were flying all the time they could, even if it was twenty or twenty-four hours a day. Ron didn't push himself that way, and by the end of that first summer, everyone wanted to fly with him. They realized he was the only sane pilot around.

I liked that story, and I thought all was going swimmingly up there in the sky, except for, about two or three hours out of Bangui, a sudden *thunk* that sounded like a bullet had hit the plane.

I saw Ron look over the plane with an expression of professional concern.

"What was that?" Karl shouted from the back seat. "Did we hit a bird?" But Ron said nothing. He leaned over to the right, looked at the wing, then the strut, then the wing again, and he did the same thing on the left. Meanwhile, I was looking at the ground, which was an endless scatter of trees and rocks, rough grass and bush, and wondering where someone might land the plane safely while waiting for the search and rescue.

Then we dropped down to the mission in Zemio. Before rolling the plane into the hangar, I watched Ron inspect the outside of the plane with great care, at one point saying, quietly, "It sounded like a bullet. . . ."

A couple of days later, we took off again and set our sights for Entebbe. We flew for more than an hour before seeing any signs of people. Then we saw smoke. A footpath. Maybe two or three tiny villages. And that's when the weather started to go bad. I could watch it on the weather radar or out the window, and I did both alternately. To our left appeared an ominous bank of clouds, a great wall of darkness. To our right it was still clear, with some occasional dark clouds carrying their own private storms underneath. On the weather radar, meanwhile, I was watching all the storms ahead, several with their own ominous flashes of lightning.

We began dodging the storms, moving higher, moving lower, banking to the right, to the left. At one point we actually reversed course—a tactical retreat in order to find a special secret passage between storms.

We had been flying at around 5,500 feet, and then we went lower and banked right to avoid a huge city of evil weather, then banked again and descended down to 3,000 feet. There was a full ceiling of clouds overhead now, but at least we could see some of the ground, and we followed the occasional vision of a long, straight road on the ground, beneath the haze and clouds: the road to Arua—147 miles ahead, according to the instrument panel.

And then we began fighting the weather in all seriousness, climbing up and swimming around several dark, heavy rainclouds, going right into some—water chopped by our prop and plastered onto the windscreen—until at last we landed at Arua. A couple of hours later, we reached Entebbe.

At Entebbe, we said goodbye to Reas, who was flying back to Switzerland, and to Ron, who was doing something in Uganda; and Karl and I boarded a regular flight to Nairobi, landing there by the end of the afternoon, and finally—after immigration, bags, and so forth—finding a taxi.

Our driver, a tall and slender young man, eager, hard to understand, wearing a black shirt covered with some white geometrics, said, as we drove away, "It was a bad thing today, with Kenya Air. Did you hear? The plane from Abijan crashed into the Congo rain forest. This morning."

"Oh, that is bad," I said.

"Yes, it's very bad for Kenya Airways. That's the second plane from Abijan that's crashed. Another one did two years ago. It's a good plane, the 737. Computer systems. It shouldn't crash. It was a new plane. One hundred and fifteen passengers."

"Oh, that's bad," I said again, adding, "You know, I flew to Nairobi from Abijan once, and we had a terrible thunderstorm during that flight. I mean, we were struck by lightning. It was like an explosion."

"Yes. It could be."

Karl joined in here, mentioning that we had just flown through thunderstorms over the Congo rain forest, then thinking to ask, "Was it direct from Abijan . . . or . . . ?"

"No, it stopped in Douala. Left there at midnight, Nairobi time. Supposed to get here at six a.m. And when it didn't arrive, they started to wonder. No one knows where it is."

"Douala? It stopped in Douala?"

"Yes."

I said to Karl, "That couldn't be Anthony's flight."

"It could. Let's see. We left him off in Bangui on Thursday morning. He was going back to Douala, then either going to leave from there on Friday night or wait until Monday."

Karl pulled out his cell phone, eventually finding a number for the Associated Press office in Nairobi and speaking to Anthony's boss. What I remember now of Karl's side of the conversation went like this: "Oh, shit."

The driver dropped us off at the Muthaiga Club, where I spent the night in solitude and colonial solidity: private room, old-fashioned bathtub, tropical hardwoods around the tub and sink, old-fashioned brass fittings, and, hung above the big bed, a mosquito net filmy and white like a luxurious sleeping cloud.

After learning nothing of interest on television—the place where the plane crashed had yet to be identified, the plane's fragments were yet to be located, the crushed and broken bodies (no survivors, surely) yet to be retrieved—I had a drink and went to bed. But I couldn't get the image out of my mind: Kenya Airways Flight 507 leaving Douala in a heavy tropical thunderstorm, rising into the fist of the force of that storm, the plane heaving, dropping. And what would a passenger be feeling and thinking? Fear. Disbelief. Always hope, a small flame of hope, a flicker of disbelief. How can this be happening? How is it possible? How can life part from life, existence leave existence? A brief passage through terror, heat, light, pain, followed by a film of unconsciousness slipping down softly like a white mosquito net from above, and then you sleep.

12: BETRAYAL

We rallied for about a week at Karl's house in Nanyuki, a few hours north of Nairobi. There were hyraxes on the roof, monkeys in the trees, backyard screams from the chimp Mzee—sometimes the other chimp, Bili—followed by four or five dogs barking crazily.

The living room was a cathedral-ceiling affair with a giant stone fireplace. The walls and tables and fireplace mantle were laden with masks, spears, carvings, a complete reed boat, about fifty carved-wood-handle knives and whangers, a pygmy crossbow or two, a lion's skull, a tusk fragment, hippo teeth, authentic log drums hauled out of a place where people still bang on log drums, and so on. Karl had parked an office desk in the living room, and he worked there more or less all day long: bent over his computer and teetering squeakily in a broken and off-kilter, wood-and-leather office chair. Had Karl ever unbent his body and raised his eyes, he would have experienced, through the living room windows, a stirring vision of light rains and glowering sky and, in the far distance, the toothy projections of Mount Kenya. It might have cheered him up. He was in a black mood.

When he spoke, he did so in a weary monotone, grimacing in frustration as he recalled, again and again, the failure of conservation, the disappearance of wilderness, the vanishing world of animals. He was tired, and no doubt he was depressed by Anthony's death. He just sat at his desk and assaulted his computer keyboard, hardly talking, not saying hello in the morning.

At 4:30 p.m. came the day's end. Karl would pass through the door to the other side of the house: the isolated side, where Mzee was. "OK, see you tomorrow," he might mutter on the way out. Thus began his private time, for dinner and television and relaxing and who-knows-what-else with Mzee and Kathy before the three of them turned in for the night. Not wanting my face ripped off, I've never been comfortable in the presence of other people's favorite chimps, so I was content to eat dinner (served by the house staff, enjoyed by candlelight) every night on the safe side of the house, accompanied by Andy, Karl's volunteer.

Andy got free room and board, plus spending money, to help take care of Mzee and Bili when Karl traveled. Andy had also worked with Karl on the Elephant Coffee project in the Congo, and he now made himself useful in other ways: keeping records, handling correspondence, maintaining records and files, carrying out the occasional spy operation, performing arcane miracles with computers, and so on. Andy was important.

He was also young, with long brown hair that fell into his face and required the occasional brushing back with a flick of the hand. He wore sandals, shorts, and T-shirt. He was shy and evasive. He avoided looking at me. When he talked, he ended each sentence tentatively, in that adolescent way, fading in volume and rising in pitch: as if to speak an ordinary declarative sentence would produce some kind of unbearable anxiety? Better to speak in questions?

Andy was from the Midwest, a big family, and he said his father used to spank him after church for misbehaving? They'd get home every Sunday after church and be spanked for making noise? So now he didn't talk much, Andy admitted, and he believed he would prefer to continue in his current line of work? Dealing with the two chimps, Mzee and Bili, and doing the occasional spy mission while following through on Karl's documentary on the illegal trade in apes?

One of those spy missions first brought him out to Lebanon, where he discovered a sweet little captive chimp, a male who was kept in a cage at a gas station, serving as an attraction for customers. The cage was right next to the pump. "He's a very nice chimp?" Andy said. "Never tries to bite? Never gets mad? And he recognizes me when I come near. He recognized me this last time I went to see him, after I had seen him earlier?" But the chimp was illegal and being kept in a tiny cage, with constant gasoline fumes all around, so Andy had plans to steal him. He told me this while carefully monitoring my reaction, as if wondering: *Will he disapprove? Will he betray my plans?*

Andy had originally worked with the legal authorities in Lebanon and gotten a formal confiscation order. It was—had been—all set. Andy had been financed by some South Africans, and so they were going to confiscate the chimp. They had even written a new ownership document in Andy's name, all official and legal. They had the police all ready to confiscate. But someone from the police must have warned the owner, so when they showed up at the gas station, the chimp was gone. The owner said the chimp had died. Andy knew that was not true, because he went back later and saw the chimp again, and the chimp recognized him. Andy said he had friends in Hezbollah, and now they were going to help him steal the chimp and smuggle him across the border. This time it would be without the police, so obviously the whole thing would be a little more risky?

That was the sort of thing I heard from Andy over dinner, and then after dinner, with the house by then dark and late evening settling in, I would quietly retire to my room, dizzy from too much wine. I would climb into bed and listen to the rasping splats and screams of a hyrax on the roof: a regular, rhythmic call that sounded like an evil devil with a terminally sore throat: *Splattt. Shereeeum. Shreeeeee-um. Shreeee. Splattt. Shreeeee. Shreeeee. Shreeeee.*

✺

After about three or four gloomy days, Kathy lit out for Nairobi, and a few days later Karl and I stuffed our things into the family Land Rover and headed for Samburu, looking to find and photograph more elephants for our book. Andy stayed behind to look after the chimps and maintain Karl's various systems and projects.

We drove out of Nanyuki on a rough road, past the Gender Equity Bar and through the rough little town of Timal: concrete buildings, tin roofs, muddy rubble. A truck in front of us, spewing enormous purple-black clouds, made sure we moved slowly through the foothills of Mount Kenya, past a bare wooden shack with a single-word promise, Hotel, sloppily painted in white over the doorway. There were big vegetable farms that served European markets followed by a random scattering of cattle and sheep and people on bikes lining the dirt edge of the road. We passed the Sun Set Butchery in a wooden shack, followed by scrap wood fences, followed by long stretches of tilled green fields and a whiff of eucalyptus and, in the far distance to the left, a hazy gray ragged edge of mountain range. That was the Matthews Range. "There are meant to be some rhinos up there," Karl said. We passed curving slopes of cultivation, green and pale yellow, then yet another little cluster of shacks and shops, including the Solstice Hotel.

Two or three hours later, and we were rattling over a bad road into the Northern Frontier.

Karl: "The guy exaggerates. *Dark Stars*. What is his name? That book?"

"Oh, Paul Theroux."

"He went through here and talked about how dangerous it all was, and how he got shot up by bandits. He made that all up. His imagination must have taken over. I mean this is the same road which he traveled on. I'm sure it happens once or twice a year. Bandits, yeah. I do this five or six times a year for the last twenty years, and it's never happened to me. What are the chances it would happen to him on the very first time he travels on the road? I mean: Bloody hell, I think he's exaggerating!"

Bicyclists transported enormous white sacks full of potatoes and other vegetables balanced precariously on their black bikes as they rolled down the hill, while Karl talked about a Congolese minister named Enerunga: "Everyone accepts that he's probably the most corrupt minister who ever held that portfolio"—and then he talked about corruption in Kenya, the need for carrots and sticks in Africa, the selling of false hope and feel-good conservation by the outside conservationists. By then, we had entered a drier country, with dust and acacia and thorn bush, a strong wind blowing, a dusty taste in the air, people walking along the road with the wind whipping against their clothes and hair. We came to the town of Isiolo, where according to Karl, a Kalishnikov could be bought for around fifty dollars. Drove past the Maximum Miracle Centre, past the Bomen Hotel Tourist Class, past cattle crouched in the dust and competing with each other for the twisted shadows of twisted thorn trees. We fell in bumpily on a bumpy road behind a yellow Mazda pickup with a dozen people bouncing in back and *Try Jesus* on the bumper.

A carpet of steel spikes had been tossed into the road and some uniformed police were squatting inside a dark shed, but Karl drove right around the spikes, not looking at the police or slowing down, and then we entered a flat, dusty, scrubby land with rotting plastic bags scattered in an endless dirty garden of plastic alongside the road. Karl: "This is supposedly the trans-African highway, going from north to south." Finally, we turned away from the rocky road onto a sandy road, and stopped at the giraffe-patterned entry gates to Samburu.

There was a strong wind, swooping swallows, sword-bladed cacti, and a clean sweet smell in the air. There was a sign with a painting of a lion next to a young domestic calf—lion lies down with lamb concept, I suppose—and the caption, *Samburu National Reserve, Where Nature Defies Itself.*

Three elephant skulls were bleaching in the sun beneath the sign.

After registering and paying our fees, we drove on a sandy, wandering track until we came to our camp, called Larsen's, and registered at the desk. "You are Shrikes and Herons," someone said, whereupon two staff members grabbed our bags and escorted us to our tents: Shrikes for Karl, Herons for me. My escort unzipped the mosquito-net entry, and we both stepped inside. "Just remember when you go outside to zeep your tent because of mangie," he said.

"Because of. . . ?"

"Because of mangie."

"Oh. Monkeys! OK. Thank you."

The tent was big enough to hold about a half dozen elephants, albeit small ones roped together tightly. It had a slab floor, two plump clouds made to look like beds, a giant ceiling fan, and a fully tiled bathroom plus an enormous shower. Aside from the beds, there was a chair, desk, floor lamp, full-length mirror, even a safe to put my jewelry in, just in case I had some.

After rendezvousing on the camp deck overlooking the river—and consuming lunch, a wonderful meal, as I recall—we climbed into the Land Rover and went out to find elephants.

✳

We drove through a curlicue of dusty tracks in the grass and through the thickets, and, after a lot of back and forth, up and down, in and out, this and that, we stopped at the edge of the Ewaso Nyiro and watched a herd of elephants on the other side moving slowly into the water, with more elephants behind them gradually emerging into the light from a screen of darkly shadowed trees. Karl pulled out his camera, rolled down his window, and screwed on a bazooka lens for the long shots.

He aimed the bazooka out the window and attached the camera base onto a mount that locked on top of the rolled-down window glass. The river was shallow there, with sandbars, pools, and channels. In the channels, the brown water glistened and shivered. But the elephants were in no hurry, and once they reached the river, they just started enjoying a big bath and playtime. I watched all this through binoculars, while Karl looked through his bazooka lens, regularly snapping pictures and making comments.

"Little guy just rolling on top of the bigger guy," he said.

It looked like a big celebration over there, with a nice breeze and a half dozen gray monsters frolicking around like fat cherubs. The elephants were cavorting, rolling joyfully in the swirling water, their skin darkened by the wetness.

"Good light. . . . No complaints. . . . I mean, you can sense the pleasure and joy they get out of this rolling around and having a good bath," Karl said. He was clicking away, madly taking pictures.

Sometimes I saw nothing but a haunch or a back. Sometimes I heard a roar and trumpet and then the distant splashing produced by big bodies. A massive body rose like a whale and then rolled playfully back into the water, the trunk snaking up, the feet gaily kicking, splashing, kicking. An elephant stood upright and, shaking ears and head, launched a shower of diamonds flashing in the sun.

A very big female with big tusks advanced—the matriarch, apparently— leading the way, with the rest of the gang now gradually queuing up. I counted almost thirty elephants; and they began their leisurely procession across the river, yet pausing here and there to drink, to cavort, to raise a trunk up high and splash it down like a fist into the water. The group included several youngsters and a couple of small babies: perfect miniatures with floppy trunks, a bouncy walk, and heads held high as they daintily tried to follow the moving tree trunk that was mom's leg. The grown-ups waded knee-deep into the swirling channels, the water snapping at their feet—and I watched a baby step into a deeper place where she seemed, suddenly, overwhelmed, on the verge of being washed away. But this tiny elephant was surrounded by many big others, and soon they had all made it back into the flowing shallows and then, eventually to dry land on the other side, which was where Karl and I sat in the parked car, windows open, watching the lumbering giants as they slowly climbed out of the water and proceeded up the bank, dusting themselves with the river bank sand before stopping to rub themselves against a standing tree. Slowly they walked right around us—babies, juveniles, adult females—some of them pausing to push at another tree, to strip away ribbons of bark, to treat themselves to yet another long, refreshing side rub.

A young adolescent male suddenly appeared right in front of us, shook his head once, shook his head again, flapped his ears, then trumpeted—at us. "You're too close, my friend, for my lens," Karl said, and he unscrewed the bazooka, tossed it in the back, and pulled out a second, smaller lens, which he quickly screwed in. But nearly all the elephants were dusting themselves as they came out of the water, and now as they continued walking, around us and past us, they continued dusting themselves, the fine brown blossoming clouds spreading into the air, lifting, shifting, and drifting through the open windows of the car and into our faces.

Over the next several days, we watched, and Karl photographed, elephants and elephants and more elephants.

We watched them taking a long time to cross the river, wrestling and drinking and splashing and cavorting—as before. This time I counted about thirteen adults, including a big old female with a damaged leg (moving laboriously with the remaining three yet still keeping up), and maybe eight youngsters. It was a very splashy crossing, this one, with some babies just tossing themselves into the water—and with two big males in the group engaged in a slow and splashy kind of showdown: wrestling with their trunks intertwined, their ears out and flapping. They had huge ears, like giant beach umbrellas, and they wrestled and clanked their tusks. There was a rushing of wind, a shifting of bodies, and then a shake of the head, ears flying up, water splattering off into a sudden halo that turned, with the wind and sun, into a bright, driven mist.

We watched others meditating in the midday heat: a family group of them, standing in one quiet clump in the shade of a sausage tree.

We drove a little farther and saw another family standing quietly in the shade, standing in a star formation as they meditated, their heads out—their tails, so I could imagine, all knotted together. Karl, speaking sweetly: "Can we come into the shade with you guys? Is that OK?" And so we just sat there next to the elephants, the car engine turned off, absorbed by the midday quiet, unmoving—us and the elephants—except for an occasionally flicking trunk quietly tossing a cloud of dust onto a head, a back, a head. So still and meditative, the elephants standing inside a slowly swaying Rorschach chiaroscuro of shade on a hot day, eyes open and not seeing, ears slowly rising and falling but not hearing . . . the animals thinking deeply about life or, more likely, just enjoying the cool air on a hot day.

We watched still other elephants, about twenty of them, being boring: crossing a grassy plain away from the river—moving, eating, moving, eating, moving, eating, moving, eating—amid a shuddering, whipping wind. The trees were swaying, the grass kow-towing.

And we watched two elephants fucking. Or, rather, one elephant trying to. He was about the same size as the female, which means he was still young, had not yet reached his gargantuan prime, but he still harbored big ambitions. He had the female in his sights and was trying to mount her, his fire-hose erection purple, S-shaped, and waving about like an engorged python. Unfortunately for him, the object of his desire kept walking away. Unfortunately for us, by the time all this began happening, Karl and I no longer had the luxury of watching from the serene perspective of our isolated vehicle. We had been joined by three tourist vans filled with tourists hanging out the windows, leaning out the open tops, and doing their best to destroy the romance: recording every loving detail with cameras that looked like grenade launchers. "Jesus Christ, I hate this!" Karl said. "I just hate this!" And as the hapless male with the purple penis continued his hopeless pursuit of the reluctant female, I was suddenly distracted by the sight, from inside one of the vans, of two Japanese girls, teenagers, dressed in white tennis outfits, or maybe light-khaki safari outfits, giggling, squealing, and jumping up and down at the sight of such a mean and mighty member.

✳

We'd get up before dawn, go out in the darkness, and head for the hills, Karl driving around and around while saying things like: "Come on, elephants, where are you?" And: "Maybe those blobs on the plains are elephants."

We might be driving to the top edge of the plain: an area of sweet-smelling grass and thorny bushes and small trees, rising into a woodsy steep hill filled no doubt with hidden elephants. And, one day, giraffes. We counted five with four of them gathered about a single tree that they were nibbling on as if it were a giant ice cream cone.

Then it was back to camp for breakfast and out again in mid-morning to get some gas at the Samburu Game Lodge. By then the sun was high, the morning coolness burned away, and Karl said, "OK. Sun is here, so the elephants should be feeling hot, so they may come down to the river."

We drove down to the river and watched eight marabou storks, white-legged with black feathered bodies, looking like sour-pussed old gents in formal evening attire.

We continued driving along the river and stopped at a tree-lined stretch, where we could look down into the water, which was churning, boiling, opaque, its brown and silver surface animated by an endless undercurrent of writhing snakes. I was imagining the snakes. Then I saw the croc: long snout, two raised and blinking eyes, a jagged ridge along the spine: an armored body drifting innocently, like a drifting log, but aimed murderously upstream.

Karl's earlier mood, meanwhile, had leavened considerably. He was behind the camera and happy to be there, enjoying the serenity and beauty of nature, the abundance of a natural world protected. I thought the natural world looked pretty good, too; and in the evening, sitting on the porch of my tent, it seemed close to perfect.

Yes, there was the occasional simian explosion on the tent roof, followed by the sound of monkeys galloping maniacally across; but it was beautiful there, just cool enough, with a wavering wind of dry air, the background whine of cicadas, the chirp and twitter of late-day birds, the flapping tent canvas, the auto-ecstatic rubbing of vegetation—leaf against leaf—that rose and fell in intensity with the wind. A shivering, flickering light passed through wavering leaves . . . and not a single mosquito to spoil the show. The meals were delicious, too, with always a vegetarian option, beautifully presented, no oppressively large portions, just excellent food. There was a wandering Samburu minstrel who would occasionally play the flute; and once the side nets of the dining tent had been drawn up, we were surrounded by sweet and eager birds: bright, red-breasted, blue-backed starlings—superb starlings (*Lamprotonis superbus*), as it happened—and one or two small hornbills waiting expectantly at the patio's edge.

On Sunday afternoon, down by the river, we found three giraffes made of brown stones held together by white mortar. At first, they seemed like a family— big papa, middle-sized mama, just-right adolescent—all being affectionate with one another, the young one licking the neck of the middle-sized one. "Real love going on," Karl said. "I've never seen that." He took pictures. On closer inspection, though, all three seemed to be males. The smaller two began moving their necks in unison, twisting and stroking each other with their necks, bumping each other gently with their necks. . . .

We left them, finally, and drove in the direction of the mountains, getting away from the river and moving into the high plains: yellow grass, green acacia clumps, and fourteen giraffes browsing right in the middle of things. A couple of the males were interested in one of the females. Karl: "She seems to be a female, and he's after her. Come on, big fellow." She, after walking slowly and swishily in front of him, paused. He lowered his head and nosed her pudenda. A second male approached. He did the same—and then lifted his head, drew his lips back into a professorial grimace, and then quietly reflected on the chemical composition of her pheromones.

Late in the day, we stopped to watch a herd of gazelles, all females, their ears thin and erect and looking like several pairs of fragile, tremulous leaves. And then we saw the lion. Or lioness. She was lean and alone, passing through the bushes, looking intent, pacing, moving in silence: mouth open, teeth exposed, sun illuminating her face and yellow eyes.

Karl: "She's looking for her pride."

We drove slowly, following alongside. She ignored us, continued pacing slowly. I could have reached outside the car and touched her, almost. But where were the others? There was an edge of white to her short and tawny fur; she was lean, with muscles rippling in her back and shoulders, with a rolling, steady, quiet walk, pausing every ten or twenty steps to listen and look around, then resuming her rolling, steady, pacing progress.

Early the next morning, we saw her again: right on the road, completely in the open. Karl: "She's still looking for the rest of her pride. A little disturbing. Where are they?" Speaking out the window, to the lion: "I don't know where the rest are, my friend. . . ." Then, back inside the car, to me: "It would be bad if there's only one lion left. . . . It's the same story. Millions of dollars pouring into the park, but the people living around it are still poisoning the lions."

Iain Douglas-Hamilton, the famous pioneering elephant scientist, maintained his research site at Samburu, and Karl and I stopped in to find out what he thought about the solitary lion and maybe to get an interview for the elephant book. We located the hidden entrance to his camp and came upon a cluster of small buildings and four cars, including one marked SAVE THE ELEPHANTS on its side. Another car was sitting in its own little thatched carport, shielded from the elements and resting on a bed of broken brown grass: crushed, battered, and shattered, pretty obviously, from a close encounter with an aggrieved elephant.

Several elephant jaw bones were bleaching in the sun in front of one of the shacks, from which one of Iain's assistants or associates soon emerged to tell us that he was elsewhere. Actually, the assistant or associate went on, Iain was in the process of being kicked out permanently from Samburu: return payment for his public complaints about the overcrowding of the reserve with new tourists and a giant new tourist lodge.

We found elephants later in the day, splashing and dashing and trumpeting on the far side of the river, and while we watched them, Karl paused to haul out his satellite phone and dial up Iain, still hoping for the interview. Iain was in Naivasha, it turned out, and he had business in Nairobi. I could hear the buzz of his voice at the ether's other end, as Karl said things like, "So you're going to the Hague as well?"

Buzz.

Karl: "Vice president, oh yeah."

Buzz.

Karl: "The problem with this park is that the county council wants money money money, so they keep putting in new lodges, but they can't keep the cattle people from poisoning the lions."

Buzz.

That was followed by a short pause in the conversation, long enough for Karl to cover the mouthpiece and say to me: "He says it's on the front page of the *East African*: 'Elephant Man Expelled from Samburu.'"

✴

Karl showed up at breakfast the next morning shivering, sweating, and complaining about a very bad headache. It was malaria, probably, so we hit the road—with Karl insisting he would drive. It seemed like a much longer and rougher road south than it had been north, and, in the meantime, Karl's cell phone rang: a call from Julius, his housekeeper in Nanyuki, who said that Andy had disappeared.

Andy was gone. Vanished. He went out late last night, Julius added, without telling anyone.

Karl's hands were shaky, and so was his driving, which became shakier as he continued to drive with one hand while punching Andy's number into the phone with the other. "Watch the road, Karl!" I blurted out—as he just about ran off the road while failing to get Andy on the line. "This is why we have cell phones!" he said, "to reach people when you need to reach them." And then: "You hire people so they will take care of problems, not make ones. It's a total choke!"

Karl called Julius again, but he now had trouble making sense out of the garble at the far end. "Julius, will you please speak up? You speak too softly. I can't hear you! What's that? Andy's things are gone? Is that what you said? *Speak up!!!!*"

Half an hour later and another call from Julius: informing us that the car Andy had been using was found parked in town. Andy had paid someone to keep an eye on it.

We finally reached Nanyuki and stopped at the hospital, where Karl got some treatment and medicine for his malaria, after which we returned home to confirm that Andy had done a runner, having emptied out his room of most clothes and personal supplies. To complete the betrayal, he had also erased some of Karl's files on the desktop and destroyed some of the backup disks for a film on the ape trade Karl had been working on. I then mentioned my dinner-time discussions with Andy about the sweet little chimp at the gas station in Lebanon; and Kathy called in from Nairobi to say that Andy had phoned her travel agent a couple of days ago to ask about the price of a ticket from Nairobi to Beirut.

13: ILL IN AMBOSELI

Karl's malaria got worse, so now—back at the house—he was trying to get his computer back in shape, yelling at his computer nerd over the phone, and stationed at his desk in front of the recalcitrant machine while wearing a thick jacket to keep warm, sitting on that broken chair and being periodically seized by the shakes. "Ooooooh," he would say, "it's one of those shakes again." And his skewed chair would rattle and creak wildly as he shook. "Ooooooh," he would add, "can't even type."

Meanwhile, Iain Douglas-Hamilton stopped by, buzzing the house in his plane before landing at a nearby strip. Someone drove out to fetch him. He showed up in khaki shorts and a blue canvas shirt, with a handsome, angular face, longish gray hair, glasses, and a scholar's potent reserve. He was still in the process of being kicked out of Samburu, though, and not in a good mood. "Do you think you'll get this all straightened out?" I asked.

"No," was the simple answer.

I then asked him a couple of general questions about elephants, and he said, curtly, "I've written all this in my book. Honestly, I've been asked these questions so many times over the years, I can't do it anymore. I thought we were going to talk about the conservation situation."

In short, he had come solely to get some information and opinions from Karl about the forest elephant ivory situation in Central Africa. Karl provided that, and then, after a bit of tea, we drove him back to the airstrip: his plane painted cream with red trim and SAVE THE ELEPHANTS in red on the door, on the rudder, across the wing. He shook hands, climbed in, slipped on the headphones, began talking to someone on the radio. The engine chugged into action, prop spinning, but even before he had taken off, Karl and I were back in the car and driving back to the house.

✶

The plan was to head for Amboseli, which could be the world's most spectacular elephant environment. Since Karl still had a malarial fever, however, we decided I would make the trip by myself. Fine! So the next day I took a Kenya Air flight from Nanyuki to Nairobi, arriving around noon, and, after the usual headaches and chaos, finally dropped my pack onto a lumpy bed in an anonymous room at a standard hotel called the Panafric. I would catch a plane to Amboseli the next morning at seven.

My room had no clock, and since I had no personal timepiece, I began to wonder about the time. What time was it? I spent the afternoon and evening watching television in my room, bored and headachy and hoping for some chronological clues, but all I found were events on CNN taking place in a seriously different time zone: Las Vegas, with boxing followed by the World Poker Championship (overweight players with bad skin and bland faces wearing sexy sunglasses: secret wankers all), and then, when CNN lost its edge, I slept for about four hours. Or was it two? I never had a clock at Karl's house either, but I would be put to sleep by darkness and the hyrax and awakened by light and the birds. Here, with the city lights always on and reflecting into a continuous fog or smog or low clouds, I had no idea what time it was—only, generically, as in, *middle of the night*. Awake and sweating in a puddle and a muddle in the middle of the night, I opened the glass door to my balcony for some fresh air, but then the traffic was too noisy, so I closed it again and lay awake, wondering what time it was. I turned on the TV and watched an entire movie, wondering what time it was.

I was showered, packed, and downstairs at the check-out desk by, according to the man at the desk, 4:30 a.m. Too early. As it happened, my taxi driver appeared not much later, which was also too early, so we headed out to the Wilson Airport, arriving there before it was open. Some people eventually showed up, turned on the lights. A baggage handler took pity and let me into the waiting room so I could sit down, saying, "Better too early than too late."

The plane was a Twin Otter, according to a little note next to the cockpit, and the pilot inside turned around and offered me some hard candy. He said that if it was clear in front of Mount Kilimanjaro we could pass our cameras up to the cockpit and he'd take pictures. It was. We did. He did. *We*: myself and one other passenger on the flight, an American woman approximately my age, maybe a little younger, with a full head of rich, dark hair. She wore a sleeveless white cotton shirt unbuttoned about two buttons lower than I might have suggested had I been her mother, olive-colored nylon camping pants with zippers on the legs that could turn them into shorts, and leather sandals on her feet. Her name was Tereza.

We flew over pale red dirt dotted with pea green pustules and pimples, a Martian desert with a dark gray lumpy horizon that then turned into brown desert followed by salty-white desert crisscrossed with trails—and, down below, a landing strip. Our first attempt at landing was aborted at the last minute, since some wildebeests were dancing wildly on the airstrip, but we buzzed them away and came around for a second try.

Someone from the hotel had driven out in a minibus to pick us up at the landing strip. His name was Cephas ole Sipanta. Cephas was very reserved, or maybe very shy, and he herded us onto the minibus and drove us on to our destination, the Ol

Tukai Lodge, which had been designed by the same architect who consulted on Noah's Ark: grand and airy, made of stone and stripped-bark timber and decorated with rough brass chandeliers, banners, African art, and baronial high-backed chairs. Tereza and I entered the lobby, where we were the only tourists visible, and stood together at the check-in counter. We explained to the person there that we weren't a couple, and so were given separate cottages (the cottages sweeping out in a series of curved extensions beyond the main lodge), but in spite of that initial explanation we somehow got stuck with each other for the next several days. It started with a late breakfast that morning, when we simultaneously walked into the empty dining hall and were immediately shown to the same table.

Over coffee and waiting for our food, Tereza explained that she had recently finished divorcing her "boring banker husband," as she called him, then came out to Africa as part of a volunteer project studying vultures in the Virungas or something. Now she was on vacation from that vacation, forgetting about life back home and also, she added, losing any lingering regrets about the divorce. She was free! At those words, a small muscular tension at the far edges of her mouth registered as a minor quiver that turned into a smile that proceeded smoothly from shy to thoughtful.

It was the start of a beautiful relationship.

Tereza was a vegan, she went on to say, and at first I was delighted to be eating with someone who would not be mystified by my recently acquired vegetarianism, but then I was mystified by her veganism. I made the mistake of asking: Why vegan? She muttered something about reducing animal suffering, and I countered: Not drinking milk? Not eating butter? No eggs? "The animals who produce eggs and dairy products," I said, "are alive and are given a place in this world entirely because they produce such things." Tereza didn't respond. I knew I was skating on thin ice, but I proceeded onto the thinner part: "If we asked any of these animals to vote about whether they wanted to be alive and producing eggs and milk for humans, I bet they'd all vote for life." She still didn't respond. I had somehow hoped to open a conversation here, but instead I had just shut it down. I could see now that she was irritated; and, after considering the mild flush and sullen expression on her face for a few more moments, I felt irritated in return.

It was the end of a beautiful relationship.

✳

It was still a relationship, however, and Cephas soon showed up and herded the two of us out to a lodge Land Rover, and so we went out for our first real look at the place. Amboseli! There must be grander places in the world, but at the moment I couldn't think of any: great barren plains and grassy savannas, ancient salt flats, green-edged swamps, and looming like a madman's impossible hallucination in the distance—or maybe not so far away, who could tell?—Mount Kilimanjaro, which was huge and pale-white and strangely triangular, as if a giant wedge had broken away from the moon and landed right in the middle of an African plain.

The grassy savanna, green and brown and gold, stretching away perpetually, was echoed perpetually overhead by a plain of puffy gray-and-white clouds, and covered by an endless stretch of grass-eating animals: buffalos, wildebeests, gazelles, and ten thousand zebras dressed casually in their escaped prisoners' outfits.

We were stopped by a herd of twenty-one elephants, walking single-file and dragging themselves slowly, slowly across the road in front of us—with a monstrous old bull elephant watching both them and us from a distance. The old guy, three white herons riding on his back, moved slowly, keeping track of the herd, slowly and ponderously moving with a heavy rocking motion, like a big gray ship on a wavering sea. The elephants moved and stopped, moved and stopped, pausing whenever they came across a nice stretch of green grass.

Cephas turned off the engine, and glanced back at us—Tereza and me— through his rearview mirror as we watched the bright brave world through our open windows and listened to the wind winnowing through the grass. We listened to the elephants, who were periodically emitting pachydermic borborygmi. Then we listened to the sounds of grass being torn out of the ground and ground again between about eighty giant teeth. The elephants were surrounded by dozens of bright-white egrets, looking like dozens of tossed and sometimes flapping handkerchiefs, who feasted on all the insects trying to escape from the grass all the elephants were eating. Cephas said: "This morning they are going to the swamp. Then about four o'clock they are going to dry land." So the elephants proceeded slowly in the direction of the swamp, which consisted of bright green grass surrounding pea green water. Zebras were moving in the direction of the swamp, too, along with a scattering of wildebeests, who sometimes galloped, sometimes paced steadily, lowing and mooing, while a bawling wildebeest baby—*maaaaa maaaaa maaaaaaaa*—was lost among the zebras and calling for his mama among the wildebeests.

Out again for another game drive that afternoon, we passed more crowds of wildebeests and zebras, with Tereza providing a running commentary for, I think, my benefit: "Oh, that's a tiny baby in there. Look at that one." And: "Oh, my gosh! Fight. Wildebeest. He was goin' at 'im pretty harsh."

Two zebras stood side by side, facing opposite directions and resting their heads on each other's rumps. Cephas commented: "Sometimes they scratch each other's backs."

Three spotted hyenas lolled languidly on their sides, a fourth emerging from a den, with two whimpering babies now peering out at the world above. One climbed out. The second climbed out. The hyenas looked like a cross between dogs and bears, brown with somewhat bearlike brown faces and round, bearlike ears, and they were being very lazy. Cephas: "Sometimes you can see them really overfeeded. Their stomach too big. And you find their head in the water, the rest of them out! Very funny. They are too big. I think they want to cool the stomach. And dropping of the mouth, like a dog." To clarify the latter point, he imitated a dog panting.

Some time after that, we came across a pair of lions, about eighty yards away, a male and female, next to a small waterhole. The dark-maned male looked at first like a tan blanket tossed onto the ground. Peering through binocs now, I saw them lying side by side. Then the male stood up, squatted on the female, made a few thrusts, got off, and lay back down while she rolled onto her back as if in pleasure, exposing a white belly, rolling, rolling, with all four feet up for maybe twenty or thirty seconds. Then she lay back on her side, her tail twitching once, twice, thrice.

Tereza: "They have black spots on them. Are they ticks?"

Cephas: "What they have, they have another type of flies, yeah."

Tereza: "Oh, flies. Yeah. There's a lot of flies."

Cephas: "It's normally one male and one female. And normally they can stay, they don't eat anything, they can stay for about a week. No hunting. No water."

About two minutes later, they were doing it again. This time he roared briefly as he thrust—or maybe she did. Again she rolled on her back after, as if in pleasure.

Tereza: "Do you have any idea how old they are?"

Cephas: "No. No. I don't. And I don't want to cheat. Elephant we can estimate because the age and size and also the more they live they become bigger. Mostly the lion in Amboseli don't have the man."

We watched them do it a third time, accompanied by roaring, purring, coughing. It seemed like both were making those noises—and she rolled onto her back afterwards. "They've counted that they do it up to a hundred times a day," Cephas said, and then Tereza added another angle: "It's interesting that the female started. She got up and seemed to get in position. It wasn't him that started it."

Next thing we knew, a hyena was creeping forward to watch the lions having sex.

Cephas: "The hyenas are coming. You know when they smell the lion, they sense there is meat. They must sense there is a carcass around."

Tereza: "Doesn't want to get too close. Just close enough to see, not close enough to get into trouble." And then, out of nowhere: "Hyenas have both genitalia, yes?"

Cephas: "No. But they look same. That is why there is confusion, because they look almost same."

And now the hyena, having seen enough of fucking lions, began wandering away, sniffing the air, looking back from a distance. But then he turned around, began approaching again. Approaching, then moving away, then approaching. Couldn't make up his mind. At last he moved off.

Tereza was barefoot and squatting next to me in the back seat, her legs folded up, her bare, smooth arms wrapped around her legs. Cephas, meanwhile, quiet and acting patient from the front seat, was, I thought, actually bored out of his skull. And Tereza, having seen enough of the lions and bored herself, turned her attention to a wisp of smoke on the slope of Mount Kilimanjaro: "Where that smoke is coming from: Is that a village somewhere?"

But I was still interested in the lions, who were still interested in sex. Now a fourth time, this one longer, maybe thirty or forty seconds. He seemed to purr deeply. She cough-roared rhythmically, as if in pleasure. Then again she rolled on her back after it was over—and Cephas, after looking in the mirror to determine whether we had yet fallen asleep, started the car.

※

A nagging devil of loneliness sat on my shoulder each night and made me eat dinner with Tereza, although we quickly ran out of things to say. It was like a bad marriage. And after dinner I would retire to my cottage, which consisted of a bedroom, washroom, closet, and a combined toilet and shower. It was nice, actually, and the door opened onto a porch with a couple of chairs, in case I wanted to take in the sultry evening air. Cottage? It shared a wall with a second unit, so it was actually one of those things the English call semi-detached. The main difference from an actual English semi-detached was the view, which was always splendid and usually spectacular.

The semi-detached cottage units ran in aesthetically curved rows out from the main lodge building, and everything was surrounded by green and mowed grass, actual suburban grass, which ended at the edge of the property, which was marked by lights and a high chain-link security fence. The fence was there not so much to keep out human thieves and riff-raff but rather to keep out all the non-human ones: lions and elephants and such. Still, in the early evenings you could walk across the grass out to the fence, raise your binocs to peer through the holes in the chain links, and watch animals and animals and animals or consider, at the far horizon, a dozen meteorological dramas going on simultaneously: purple columns of rain with their own self-generating clouds above, dark and flickering on and off with lightning inside. Tightening up the focus and looking a little closer, you might follow the evening stroll of elephants in two big herds, eating grass and headed to bed in the same direction, side by side, as dusk descends and the evening breeze blows in. It was wonderful. Amazing. There was a primordial quality to the scene, as if one were watching the world before the start of human agriculture. Before writing and books, roads and rifles, swords and cities, empires and rockets, before the collective destructive power gathered so ferociously by the human ape.

Such a grand setting makes you think grand thoughts.

At least it did for me. At least at first. It had been quiet at Ol Tukai when Tereza and I arrived, only a relatively few other guests coming and going. But I never appreciated how quiet until, a couple of days later, the buses pulled up and the tourists poured in. The hordes had arrived, dressed in Ernest Hemingway safari outfits for some and for others, especially the young men, baseball caps and shapeless T-shirts with strange things written on the front and pedal pushers that rose halfway up their calves. The tourists were significantly overweight, some of them with extra flesh waggling under their clothes like squabbling cats. While the graceful, slender Africans quietly hauled in their luggage, the noisy tourists flapped and waddled behind, their shorts and pedal pushers exposing legs as round and featureless as sausages.

After dinner now, as I sat on my porch and contemplated moving up to the fence to look out at the animals and the grand vista, the tourists would get there first, gathering in gregarious gangs and shouting out to each other while trying out their binoculars, shouting things like:

"I want to see some hippos."

"Yeah, I'm just gonna look to see what I can see."

"I cain't keep still long enough to look. I cain't keep still. I don't have a steady hand."

"I see what he's talkin' about. I cain't tell what it is either."

"I'm not real good with these things. I'm not steady enough."

"Well, the wind blows it, too."

"Yeah, the wind blows it."

"Hey, where were those hippos? Did you actually see some?"

"You can see a group there. And a group over there. And a group over there. And another way, way, way over there."

"Did you see the zebra fightin'? *Poooze!* Up on their hind legs. This is crazy. What did you want, Annie? I'd put some shoes on if I was walkin' around in Africa."

"Yeah. There's a lot of zebras. They just look like black-and-white horses to me."

Tourists! Not only Americans, but Japanese tourists with giant metal suitcases, German tourists with big cameras and bigger tattoos, Indian tourists with beautiful children and scowling mothers-in-law who were dotted red on their foreheads, British tourists with bad teeth and awkward table manners, Dutch tourists with Che Guevara thinking revolutionary thoughts on T-shirts covering their bourgeois chests. Suddenly, there were people, people, and people: overweight, over-dressed, over-packed, over-equipped, over-protected, coming for the experience of African animals separated from them by fences, by car doors, by discreet distances, watching nature as if it were just another very good program on television with only the mild illusion of nature as something wild, coming to Amboseli and turning it into a high-priced zoo. Next stop, Las Vegas.

✴

I had none of those sour impressions about the Africans who ran Ol Tokai. They were all perfectly fine . . . starting with the omelet chef: a big, beaming, round-faced man, genuinely friendly, who wore a chef's hat that looked like a long-stemmed white mushroom. We'd have a little chat each morning as he cooked my vegetarian omelet, a simple but sincere conversation usually having to do with good food, good sleep, and good mornings.

It's true that Cephas, our driver and guide, was more of an acquired taste. Short and compact with small ears and a regular face with a fine trace of a mustache on the upper lip, he was always neatly dressed in a ranger-style uniform: forest green shirt (frayed at the edges but freshly ironed), khaki pants, tan bush vest, brown shoes. He was smart and obviously well informed but always terribly reserved, as if he were in fact sick to death of carting around tourists—and who wouldn't be? He would drive us to a spot where there were animals, turn off the engine, then lean his shoulder on the car window, rest his head on his shoulder, and, sometimes lolling sleepily, would occasionally glance back at us in the mirror to determine when we were bored enough with the latest animal sighting to require starting the car again. Me: I was never, ever bored with the animals.

Then there was Joseph. Joseph ole Ntalamia. Dressed in the full Masai regalia—beautiful red robes with brightly beaded bracelets and anklets and necklets and waistlets, clutching a beaded walking stick in his hand—he was, you might imagine, merely a living anthropological exhibit. Not at all. He worked as a greeter and porter at the hotel, and while it was true that the hotel seemed to employ lots of Masai while only Joseph (and his brother Sapota Serengeti) dressed that way, Joseph did his job with tremendous grace and dignity.

He was young, quiet, unassuming, with a sweet smile and a fine-featured face. He had a small round scar on each cheek, and his smile would reveal two missing lower front teeth—physical aspects that he explained late one afternoon to a handful of interested guests at the lodge, including Tereza and me.

"The Masai people have marks," he said, simply.

After a long, dramatic pause, he began to elaborate. "First," he said, "they have the elimination of the lower two front teeth. This is done," he went on, "because some time in the past some children had locked jaws from disease and were unable eat or drink, so the elders broke away two of their lower teeth in order to feed them, and so now all Masai have to have their two lower teeth taken away. To remind them of the children."

He smiled to show us his teeth.

"The same applies to the mark on our cheek," he said—as I freshly considered the pair of scars, small and circular, at the center of each cheek. "In a village there is a lot of cows, and with the cows there is a lot of cow dung. And with the cow dung, comes a lot of flies, and the flies bring disease. So we make burn our children when they are four years old. This confuses the flies. Instead of landing on the children's eyes, and bringing disease to their eyes, the flies land on the wound, and this reminds the child to chase the flies away."

Joseph explained such things with deep seriousness, pausing every few moments to look deeply into the eyes of his listeners to confirm that he was serious, that they were paying attention to serious things.

"The third mark of a Masai are the pierced ears," he continued. Masai men pierce their ears, and they put in plugs to make the holes in their ears become bigger and bigger. Masai women think this is very attractive, and although Joseph did not, in fact, have the big holes in his ears, Joseph was not troubled, because he was able to attract women with his cleverness, so it evened out.

"These marks are how you can tell a true Masai from those people who dress up like Masai and pretend," he concluded.

Joseph was fine, in my estimation—and so was the clerk at the desk. He was a mere clerk, mind you, not a manager. Nothing special. No big deal. His name was Shadrack, as I reminded myself every time I saw him by glancing surreptitiously at the name tag on his shirt, but he knew my name from the first day without looking at anything but my face. That was impressive when there were maybe a couple dozen people in the lodge, on the day I arrived, but how much more impressive it was, now that there were a hundred and fifty or two hundred guests at the lodge and he still remembered my name.

I went to Shadrack in the morning of my penultimate day at Amboseli to say that I was feeling ill and to wonder whether there was a doctor anywhere in the lodge.

"No doctor," he said.

I then asked if I could catch a flight to Nairobi that same day, one day before my scheduled flight.

"No. No flight today."

Since there was nothing to do, I decided not to worry. That was the right decision, and when I passed through late in the afternoon, when Shadrack was no longer at the desk, the night manager, a very attractive woman, called me over and spoke to me.

"How are you feeling?" she asked.

"Better, thank you."

"We were praying for you," she said.

Praying! How thoughtful.

※

But, yes, I was feeling ill. In fact, I had not been feeling my best the entire time I was there. It had begun in Samburu, not long after Karl came down with the malaria. I was feeling hot and headachy myself and began at first to wonder if the same mosquito who bit Karl had bitten me, but my symptoms turned out to be less shakes and more swells: a subtle thickening of the thin parts. That was worrisome. I had a few years earlier experienced two or three episodes of what my doctor called analeptic shock: an allergic reaction to something causing lips and face and throat to balloon, leading to death by auto-asphyxiation—except, as in my case, for the benefit of skilled medical intervention.

Now, as I felt that peculiar swelling in my face, my lips, around my eyes, I had begun to wonder whether I was about to repeat the same experience without the benefit of skilled et cetera. To stave off death, I began dosing myself with the only logical thing I could find in a Kenyan drugstore: Benedryl. But Benedryl, of course, was no substitute for an actual doctor and emergency room treatment, and, as the days rolled by in Amboseli, the medicine was no longer working very well. I still went out morning and afternoon, driven and guided by Cephas and accompanied and irritated by Tereza, to look at elephants and all the other animals, but at the same time I had begun to notice a ringing in the ears, then a spotting before the eyes. My face still felt thick in the thin parts. I began to lose my appetite, and my stomach felt raw. I became restless at nights, then severely insomniacal. In fact, I slept only a couple of hours on my last couple of nights at Amboseli. The rest of the night was spent staring at the ceiling, killing mosquitoes, and thinking crazy thoughts while waiting for dawn and breakfast and my next salubrious dose of Benedryl.

Two or three years later I would conclude that the Benedryl itself had caused most of those symptoms, but for now—on my last day at Amboseli, as a yellowish hint of dawn began nibbling at the horizon—I was pathetically pleased to be still myself and headed back to civilization in the form of Nairobi. I washed and organized and hauled myself and my pack down to the dining hall, only to find it was not open. I wandered over to the desk, rang a little bell, and soon Shadrack appeared and began to check me out. After completing the process, I sat down in an uncomfortable chair not far from the desk in order to wait for the dining hall to open.

Tereza was due to leave that same day, and, as it happened, she showed up at the desk not so long after I had finished checking out. As I sat groggily in the uncomfortable chair, however, I began to notice a commotion at the desk. It was Tereza, speaking in an unpleasant voice to Shadrack. "I'm not happy with this, Shadrack," I heard her say, and I approached the desk to see if I could help sort things out.

It was an argument over the bill. Tereza said she had been told the game drives were twenty-five dollars each and now she was being charged with fifty dollars— and as she was elaborating on the problem, I was already thinking: *Who cares? You're a rich American. If you can afford to be here, you can afford the extra few dollars. . . . Moreover,* my thoughts continued, *no one here is unprofessional enough to cheat you—least of all Shadrack.*

She showed me the bill. Yes, they were billing her fifty dollars for each of the game drives, but, really, I had never wondered about the cost. It seemed to me fair enough. Weren't there standard charges for such things, written down somewhere? As it turned out, we couldn't find the standard charges in printed form, so the logic of her argument depended on who said what when. I didn't care.

I looked over to Shadrack, saw the unhappy, deflated expression on his face. He was troubled. He was chagrined. I said, "Sounds like a communication problem to me." But Tereza wouldn't stop: "I spoke to the lady behind the counter when I came in. She said it was twenty-five dollars. I asked again to make sure. This is not a communication problem! I am not happy."

I walked away, soon discovering that the dining room was open at last. I found a table, put down my pack, and poured myself a cup of coffee. Then I went up to the omelet table, where my friend the omelet chef had just taken up his station.

"Good morning," he said.

"Good morning."

I ordered the usual, which he began cooking up in the usual way.

"You slept well?" he asked.

"Yes," I lied. "And you?"

"Yes. . . . You're leaving today?"

"Yes!"

"I'm going to miss you," he said quietly, then added, "going to miss your company." This was stated simply and sincerely: no seething irony here.

"Thank you!" I said, and then I looked up at his hat, his chef's hat, which I had seen every morning before, of course, but had never fully appreciated. Now, looking at it once more and up close, I saw it freshly. It was white, bright white, brilliantly white and clean, a gorgeous piece of newly ironed linen, a crisp and fluted cylinder rising up like a perfect column of white smoke from his head for about fourteen inches before blossoming into a white and rounded cloud at the top.

"I am just admiring your hat!" I said.

"Oh!" he said, and his face opened into a beatific smile that, for just a moment, felt like the rising sun.

✳ PART III

14: WHERE HAVE ALL THE ANIMALS GONE?

Last time I saw Karl, he was shivering with malaria hard enough to rattle his chair. That was how many years ago? Three? Two? I don't want to think about time, but now—at the start of our photographic and research work on a book about giraffes—meeting him in the entrance to the Muthaiga Club, I see that he looks a little older, a little heavier than I remember, although his hair is still sandy. There is still the dark chopped mustache. Still the mild squint.

Early in the evening, we head out for a curry and to catch up on things. Karl spends half the meal talking about his latest project: an exposé for television on how endangered snakes in Southeast Asia become expensive snakeskins for the European high fashion industry. He's just come back from an investigatory trip to Indonesia, Thailand, Vietnam, filming snake catchers and the snakeskin processing factories. "They keep pythons in boxes without water or food for weeks, awaiting the slaughter day. Killing takes about two hours for some of them. They are hit over the head with an iron bar, which in many cases just knocks them out. Then they're hung up for about ninety minutes, while the skin stretches, and many of them are still twisting and clearly alive. Then the skin is removed, with many still alive, until the head is cut off," he says. "I am convinced that if I am able to film this, I will show reptiles feeling pain."

But the real audience for this film would be the Swiss, who, because of the watch industry, are the biggest importers. "We're really trying to nail the Swiss guys. These reptiles become Swiss watch bands, handbags, and shoes. I mean, what is going on here? Do we really need to make these animals go extinct so the Swiss can have their watch bands?"

A lot of undercover work was required to get to the exporters and their way of business, he says, hidden cameras and such, and of course there is always the organized crime element, which makes it more interesting. But the complicated part has to do with CITES. The Convention on International Trade in Endangered Species is headquartered in Geneva and supposed to be in charge of regularizing the international comings and goings of endangered animals and their body parts, including certain snakes and snake skins. But what is the point of all the regularizing that CITES supposedly does? Is their job to protect the snakes who are skinned or the sharks who do the skinning?

Karl, dramatically punching right fist into left palm, summarizes his perspective on CITES: "I would really like to hit them hard."

The other part of our dinner conversation concerns tomorrow's trip to the

Congo. "Hey, let's cancel that," I say, but, of course, it's too late.

Karl understands my reluctance. "It's no picnic going into the Congo," he says, smiling eagerly, "but that's a good thing! Everybody else is doing all the tourist things. You can't go anywhere in Africa without seeing backpackers from Holland in flip-flops. You can't get away—except the Congo."

We've been planning this trip for a while. True, there are no giraffes in the Congo, but there are okapis, who happen to be the only living relatives of giraffes. Meanwhile, however, I in my reluctance had put off applying for a visa to the Congo until about eight weeks ago—time enough, maybe, but I only got it about two days before I left the States. My application kept being rejected by an embassy person who said he didn't recognize the proposed itinerary. I rechecked, added more documentation, only finally realizing that I had been applying to visit the Republic of the Congo when I actually intended to visit the Democratic Republic of the Congo. The DRC. Not the RC. I had been applying to the wrong country. Meanwhile, I was secretly hoping the visa application would fall through anyway.

The big war—many millions of people shot, tortured, raped, robbed, displaced, and starved to death by twenty-five different criminal gangs calling themselves revolutionary militias—is supposedly over by now, but then, just last week, my wife handed me the news story about a young Danish tourist who showed up in the DRC with an imperfect visa or something and was arrested as a spy and sentenced to death. That was a total choke, obviously, because: *Who would want to spy on the Democratic Republic of the Congo?*

As we make final arrangements that evening for our trip, packing our bags, checking our money, papers, and so on, Karl shows me his spy cameras. They're charming devices disguised as ballpoint pens with little holes at the top. The hole is the lens. Press a button, then clip the pen into your shirt pocket, lens aimed out, and it starts to film in digital. You can download all onto a computer. Karl has brought extras, he says, since Dan will also want one or two.

Dan? Oh, right, Dan. The ivory guy.

✳

We meet Dan at the Entebbe airport, in Uganda, and soon Ron the missionary pilot shows up, too, wearing his blue shirt with the epaulettes. Ron won't be our pilot this time. He's come now just to catch up. We all four buy cappuccinos and cookies and sit down at a little table in the airport's transit café for a drifting conversation about depressing things.

Ron: "Years ago, when I first started flying, I'd pass over this vast open area—Garamba National Park—and see huge herds of elephants. Now I fly over and see nothing. Or maybe one or two or a half dozen—and they're running. The Janjaweed have come down. They take everything."

Dan tells about how, when he was in the Peace Corps in the old days in West Africa, he tried to introduce a sustainable harvest of bark as part of a community conservation program. "If you can harvest this bark, I'll pay you for it," he told people. He showed them exactly how to harvest it. They didn't care.

Karl: "In this part of the world, ninety percent of the community-based conservation turns into blackmail-based conservation. The local people think that we"—conservationists, Euro-Americans, daft blancs—"have too much money to waste on silly issues like wildlife and habitat protection. So out come the lists of what they need and want: airstrips, schools, dispensaries, water wells, employment for sons and friends. And suddenly all the chimps or gorillas or elephants become *yours*. 'If we do not get what we expect, we see no reason to protect *your* elephants or chimps!'"

So this desultory review of bad news goes, in between sips of cappuccino, nibbles on cookies, a cigarette break for Dan. But the worst news has to do with where we're going, give or take a few hundred miles. The Fulani are moving south and into that part of the world, and then a children's army is wandering around in the woods out there somewhere, the LRA, or Lord's Resistance Army—a potent mix of Christian fundamentalists and African mystics led by a charismatic wacko named Joseph Kony and using tens of thousands of boy soldiers to carve out a God-fearing nation based on rape, murder, and mutilation.

Karl: "Kony: I mean, why can't we just get rid of that fruitcake?"

Before anyone can seriously consider answering that question, however, the purse-lipped bursar for the missionary plane shows up, holding a clipboard with our names on it and asking for perfect money. We have to pay for the charter. Perfect money: unfolded, unmarked, unused US dollars printed by 2002 or later. Nothing earlier. Nobody in the Congo will take credit or checks. It's all cash out there, and nobody except local shopkeepers or isolated villagers will take Congolese francs or any other form of cash except perfect US bills printed by 2002.

✳

In the spring of 1900, almost a hundred and ten years before the four of us are sitting in Uganda's airport transit lounge at Entebbe, moaning about the state of the world and squeezing our wallets for perfect money, the British Governor of the Ugandan Protectorate, Harry Johnston, was sitting in his house at Entebbe and listening to some Mbuti Pygmies from the Ituri Forest. They could have been moaning about the state of the world, too, although I will imagine they were far more concerned about their own personal condition, since they had recently been kidnapped by a German entrepreneur who planned to exhibit them in Paris at the World's Fair. Once the entrepreneur traveled with his human cargo into the lands of the Ugandan Protectorate, headed for the coast and a boat, however, Governor Johnston put an end to all that nonsense. He freed the Pygmies and sent the evil-doer back to Germany.

Governor Johnston encouraged the Pygmies to recuperate in Entebbe that spring as he made the preparations for their difficult journey back to the Congo. But the Governor was an amateur cryptozoologist—interested in mythical or mysterious or undiscovered species—and since Europeans had yet to explore most of Africa's forested middle, he began quizzing his guests about their home in the Ituri. What did they hunt? What kinds of unusual animals did they know about?

The Mbuti may have been familiar with the Central African trading language known as Lingala. Perhaps they knew a bit of French, too, picked up while dealing with traders and government officials. I imagine that Johnston also brought in a translator. So now, the conversation between the Pygmies and the Governor could have included a little spoken language and a lot of pantomime. But the Governor also had a good idea of what to ask about, since he was familiar with an account published in 1890 by the American journalist and explorer Henry Morton Stanley about a strange animal of the Ituri. Stanley had never seen this animal, but he had spoken to some Mbuti who described the elusive "Atti," a kind of forest-dwelling donkey, Stanley thought, whom the Pygmies occasionally captured with pit traps. They weren't donkeys, of course. They were some other kind of quadruped, adapted to live in the dark and leafy world of the rain forest. "What they can find to eat is a wonder," Stanley wrote. "They eat leaves."

Based on Stanley's brief account, Governor Johnston held up before his guests the picture of a donkey, and they confirmed that, yes, they were familiar with an animal like that. When Johnston pulled out a zebra skin, the Pygmies again confirmed a resemblance. They called this animal an "o'api," Johnston would later write. The word soon became anglicized to *okapi*.

Johnston knew enough to be excited. Such an animal, never heard of by a European before Stanley's brief mention, never seen by a zoologist anywhere, never written about in any of the world's zoological literature, could amount to a great discovery for some enterprising person like himself. He therefore organized a full expedition out to the eastern Congo and placed himself at the head of it.

By July of 1900, they had made it as far as the Belgian outpost of Fort Mbeni, on the edge of the great Ituri. The Pygmies left the expedition at that point, returning to their village, while Lieutenant Meura, the commander of Fort Mbeni, declared that he too believed there was a donkey-like creature in the forest, although perhaps more horse than donkey. In any case, Meura provided Johnston with several trackers and some extra supplies, enough for a several-day journey right into the hot heart of the oppressive place. At least Johnston thought it was oppressive.

Johnston's negative impressions may have been intensified by malaria. He was soon stupefied enough that when his Pygmy trackers showed him what they claimed to be o'api or okapi tracks, Johnston refused to follow—thinking, apparently, that he was about to be tricked by devious natives. Donkeys and horses, the Governor knew very well, did not have cloven hooves. The tracks being pointed out to him were of a cloven-hoofed animal. Couldn't be an okapi. He was wrong, of course, but by then everyone in the expedition was too wracked by malaria to think about it. They returned to Fort Mbeni, and from there back to Entebbe. Too bad for Harry Johnston.

Luckily, Lieutenant Meura was a generous sort who rummaged about and found two small pieces of okapi skin that had been sewn into a pair of bandoliers. He presented those to Johnston as a parting gift, and he promised to send more okapi pieces as soon as he could. Meura then died of blackwater fever, whatever that is, but his faithful second-in-command eventually sent to Johnston a full shipment of okapi pieces, including a complete skin and a couple of skulls along with, it seems, a jawbone. Cloven hooves also in the package, according to an accompanying note, disappeared in transit.

Still, there was enough specimen material to justify Governor Johnston's mailing it to an expert at the British Museum in London, who, after a quick examination announced in 1903 the discovery of an entirely new mammal, a new genus and species, actually, which was named *Okapi johnstoni*. In that way, Harry Johnston acquired his own mote of immortality, but the important part of this story—and the reason why Karl and I are now strapped into a missionary plane and being bumped across the green and misty sea of the Ituri Forest—is that the expert at the British Museum also announced that okapis are the only living relatives of giraffes.

✳

How can that be? you ask yourself. When you first look at an okapi you don't see anything like a giraffe. You see a strange and ghostly beast, shy, with a bony face and a body that reminds you of a horse with a beautiful chestnut-brown coat that, in a filtered forest light, glows and turns dark chocolate with orange highlights. A horse with, when you examine him or her more fully, horizontal zebra stripes wrapping the forelegs and, at the rear, zebra stripes emerging from the rump, fanning out and spreading forward in a feathering of wavery horizontal lines. The stripes look like strips of sunlight reflecting off a fan of rain-wet leaf layers. Ghostly? Especially the face, which is bony with black circling around the eyes and nose, with a dusting of white or gray cast gently over the rest of the face. It's a gray mask, making this animal look like a horse dressed up for Halloween and wearing a horse-skull mask topped absurdly by a pair of moth-eaten donkey ears. Donkey? Horse? But then you look down at the cloven hooves.

I forgot to mention the tongue, which is bluish-black and long enough to wrap halfway around the animal's snout—in fact, a lot like a giraffe's tongue, which is one unlikely clue to the okapi's obscure ancestry. It's true that okapis don't have long necks, but neither did the direct ancestors of giraffes until only a few million years ago, so the fossils say. It was, in any case, a generally hidden anatomy that convinced the expert in the British Museum back at the start of the twentieth century that he was looking at pieces of a giraffe relative: particularly a specialized set of lower canines that are notched in the middle and flattened into a couple of spoon-shaped lobes on either side of that notch. It's an odd feature but useful for both giraffes and okapis as a specialized tool for stripping leaves off branches and twigs.

Then there are the okapi horns, which, like a giraffe's horns, are actually what experts call *ossicones*, meaning they began life as pieces of cartilage that eventually turned into bone. Okapi horns are a lot smaller than the horns of giraffes, though, and they're pointy at the ends. Also, only okapi males have horns, unlike giraffes, while the females are just left out . . . even though, again unlike giraffes, *la femme est plus gros.*

※

The French I'll let you figure out. It's being spoken right now by a lean and vigorous man named Jean-Prince M'Bayaa at the Okapi Breeding and Research Station, which is where Karl and Dan and I happen to be, having just, with the help of the missionaries, magically dropped out of the sky and landed in the middle of the Ituri Forest. We're actually inside a 13,700 square-kilometer patch of the Ituri called the Okapi Faunal Reserve, not far from the village of Epulu and right next to the rushing, roaring, cool-watered Epulu River.

Here at the Okapi Breeding and Research Station near Epulu, thirteen okapis are living inside fenced pens, but the pens are very large, with plenty of giant trees and other vegetation inside, so it's possible to look through the chain-link fence and at least imagine you're looking at wild animals in the forest, rather than ones who have just been suckered into pit traps and put in prison. Anyway, it's a nice prison. The okapis don't seem frustrated or unhappy, and they appear to have plenty to eat and, possibly, enough to keep them mentally occupied if mental occupation is what they desire.

Jean-Prince has just brought out a green-painted wooden wheelbarrow full of bundled leaves and personalized in white lettering with the name Tatu, and now he opens a gate to the pen for a female named Tatu. He enters the pen and starts tying the leaf bundles onto an outstretched rope. It looks like he's putting green laundry on a clothesline, which seems a silly way to feed wild animals, but it probably reproduces the okapis' usual feeding posture in the wild. Tatu seems satisfied with the deal.

In the wild, Jean-Prince tells us, okapis eat the leaves of a hundred fifty species (or maybe it's fifty species, and I misheard the French), while here at the Station they're fed leaves from about forty-five different species. The Pygmies—Mbuti Pygmies—go into the forest every day, harvest the leaves from those species, and bring them into the Station. . . .

Three days later, Karl and I, followed by our minder, follow a couple of the Mbuti workers on their morning route into the forest to harvest leaves. The minder, a young, quiet, and rather sweet-looking African named Michel Moyakeso, wears green military-style fatigues and carries an old rifle. He works for the Institut Congolais pour la Conservation de la Nature (or ICCN), which officially runs the Reserve from a headquarters based next to the Okapi Station. For some reason, someone at the ICCN has assigned Michel to follow us with his gun whenever we leave the Station grounds.

The two workers, Bernard Mtongani and Abeli Doki, are both wearing black rubber boots, standard issue for the project, and carrying machetes. Bernard is older, with a ski-jump nose in a small face beneath a big wool watch cap. When he talks, his face lights up with the pleasure of communication. He's the talker. Abeli, not so much. Abeli is dressed nicely in an Okapi Center T-shirt and fancy jeans with zippered back pockets and the name Obama embroidered in bright yellow letters going down the front of his right leg.

In the wild, Bernard tells us (his unfamiliar words translated into French by our minder Michel), okapis eat leaves from over a hundred species, while his and Abeli's daily job is to collect the leaves from thirty to thirty-five different kinds.

We follow these two as they wander through the forest, locating the various species of plants, and then—maybe it requires shinnying up a pole-like tree or scrambling into a difficult, thickety branch somewhere over our heads—harvesting the leaves and packing them into little bundles tied with vine. Later on, Bernard and Abeli assemble the bundles into fuller packets, and at the end of the morning's harvest, which has taken altogether about three hours, bind the fuller packets into big, clumsy bunches that they then skillfully balance on their heads and tote off to the Okapi Station.

※

Once our rented car complete with driver shows up from Kisangani, Karl and I, with Dan now coming along (and, of course, the minder Michel), visit the Mbuti village of Lembongo.

The driver takes us for a short while down the main mud road from Epulu and the Okapi Station and then off the road through a series of twisty ruts until we can go no farther. He stays with the car. On foot, then, the four of us walk until we reach the edge of the village: greeted there by a few sickly people and an old woman, her bare breasts flat and hanging like banana leaves, who sits before a blackened boiling pot resting on three or four logs hotly welded into a small fire.

The full village includes some beehive huts made of palm fronds and several cube-shaped, mud-and-stick huts: maybe four or five dozen dwellings altogether, casually spread out around three or four dusty, flattened centers, along with a few subdued, smoky fires, and one central pavilion made of poles and thatch. We sit down in the shade of the pavilion, and soon half the villagers have turned out for the occasion. We shake many people's hands, the men dressed in rags, some of the women wrapped in colorful cloth. Someone brings out a yellow-enameled bowl containing a treat of fresh, dripping honey straight from the hive, and the bowl is placed on the ground near where we're sitting. Several eagerly orbiting bees have already started drowning in the honey, and there's a reason why: It's delicious.

The village "chief," in Karl's assessment—But do Mbuti have "chiefs"? Maybe he's just the oldest bloke around—comes out of his hut to sit down and chat with the visitors. He's wearing pants printed with a portrait of Jean-Pierre Bemba, the rebel commander from a few years back who was given a vice presidency as his reward for quitting the war. The old man's wife stays back inside the doorway of the hut, watching us quietly from the shadows.

His name is Myanamenge, he says, and he has a small, rounded face and a quiet reserve. He speaks in a language that Michel translates into French and then, since I'm missing a lot of the French, is occasionally turned into an explanatory bone of English tossed my way by Karl. Myanamenge says he doesn't know how old he is. His life has always been hard. He doesn't eat elephant meat. Sometimes hunting is good, sometimes not—and here Karl inserts his own opinion: "He's not going to say that in the old days there was a lot more game."

Meanwhile, as we're slurping the honey and exchanging words with Myanamenge, a hunting party from the village shows up and seems to confirm Karl's assessment about the game. We see only a small part of this returning parade, starting with a giant net rolled up like a household rug and looped around someone's head and shoulders, followed by a solemn-faced hunter with a thin goatee carrying a spear and knife. The hunter slips into his hut and then slips out again to greet us and show us the blue duiker he's just killed: tiny, about the size of a Chihuahua, with gray fur, tiny feet, no head. The hunter holds up the duiker. Karl takes a picture. The hunter, dressed in cutoff shorts, a dirty gray polo shirt, and a faded red baseball cap, now slips back into his hut and brings out the duiker's head, tongue lolling out, which he holds up. Karl photographs that.

Karl now photographs me standing next to the red-capped hunter, whom he calls "the chief's son," and the miraculous image at the back of his camera provides an interesting contrast between tall and short in one way and soft and hard in another. Then, after a good deal more random socializing and chitchat, we leave—having arranged to join the village on another hunt for another day.

✴

And so, early one morning, we return to Lembongo as the hunters are fixing and straightening out their nets. The nets are fed and looped around the heads and shoulders of five sturdy men. A partner does the feeding and looping in the style of someone looping a hose or rope, pulling arm-lengths of rolled netting, tossing it skillfully over the head and about the shoulders of the carrier, forming at last a large thick loop of netting that settles onto the head and hangs about the face and drops back across the shoulders and down the back to the buttocks. From the front, the net carriers are half hidden by the nets, their faces solemnly peering out, the nets brown and piled high enough to make the carriers look like forest trolls with impossibly spectacular hairdos.

We all leave the village led by the red-capped chief's son: a party of (not counting Karl, Dan, Michel dressed in green and carrying his rifle, and me) about a dozen men (net carriers and hunters gripping iron-tipped spears), a dozen women (including one or two adolescent girls and a mother carrying a baby), and four small brown-and-white hunting dogs. Both men and women are short and small and, at least some of them, rather delicate-looking. The women have cut their hair short or fixed it into cornrows and snaky plaits. The men have given themselves more severe cuts, although, as if to make up for that severity, many have left a scattering of delicate growth on chin and lip. The women are wrapped in colorful print cloths, some of them with wicker baskets strapped to their backs, and the men are dressed in T-shirts and shorts. The men are all flip-flopped. Some of the women are barefoot, others flip-flopped. And one of the women carries the fire: glowing embers inside a log small enough that she can carry it in one hand.

After a long walk through the village gardens and other areas that look recently slashed-and-burned, at last we get into the tall forest. After another hour or so of walking we come to a small, cavern-like clearing at the base of a giant tree. An old man stacks some small pieces of wood below some outreaching branches of the giant tree and borrows the transported embers. With a leaf, he fans the embers into a flame—which he then stifles with green leaves, creating at last a steady column of uprising white smoke.

Most everyone is sitting down now, and there's a good deal of relaxed conversation, some laughing, the women always grouped together tightly and focused on their own society, the men more spread out, several people smoking rolled up cigarettes and luxuriating in this lovely moment before the hunt.

Now people are getting up and, one by one, bathing themselves in the smoke, walking over to the smoky column and reaching with their hands into the writhing immaterial substance, splashing it back like water into their faces and hair. Next the net carriers step one by one into the smoke, thus smoking out the nets for some reason or other, maybe the practical one of neutralizing organic smells in order to confuse the game.

And then, quickly now, all are up and laying out the nets. A net carrier moves quickly along a game trail, unlooping his long, long net, drawing out a netted line that stretches away along the trail until he's reached the end of his piece, whereupon another net carrier takes up the task, unlooping his long net, and drawing it out into a continuance of the netted line. The women, meanwhile, follow this unreeling act, expertly joining the nets together at the ends, while spreading them out at the sides and raising them up: deftly attaching one lengthwise side to bits of vegetation on the forest floor, raising up the other side and attaching it to any standing vegetation—bush, vine, small tree—at a height of maybe three feet. The net, which was a rolled line reeled off by the men and stretching along the forest floor for a mile or so, has now become a netted fence, and because the fence is woven from oily brown twine or liana-fibers, and vibrating softly in resonance with the secret filtering of air, and the breeze-quivering greens and browns of the forest, it turns invisible—as do, suddenly, the Pygmies.

Karl, Dan, Michel, and I are left standing in a sleepy daze near the invisible net somewhere around its midpoint, I believe, and everyone else has vanished. Dan smokes a cigarette, and as he does I can picture as in a dream that long net drawn out into a long crescent in the forest, with the Pygmies quietly slipping through the forest and over to the open face at the far side; and now I can hear, in the distance but gradually moving closer, a series of strange, dreamlike high-pitched whoops and barks that sound like the faint cries of birds and dogs that after a while sound like whistles and flutes that after another while sound like women's voices. As this ethereal chorus approaches and gathers, closer, closer, I understand that the Pygmies must be chasing or driving or calling out for the game. The Pygmies could be saying to the animals: *Where are you hiding, our sweet little friends? Where have you gone, our dear little ones?* And the animals, at first alert and drawn in by the mysterious whoops and barks but now anxious or afraid, might be saying to one another: *This is not good. We should run.* Some might say: *Let's go this way!* Others will say: *No, this way!* Another says: *Quick. Down this hole.* Yet another says: *No, not that hole! That one leads into the other world!* And so the animals are altogether scared and confused but generally headed, one can imagine, towards our part of the net at the closed bottom or pocket of the crescent. After a time, however, the disembodied chorus fades and dies out, and the four of us are left listening to silence, which isn't silence of course but more the in-and-out breathing of a sleeping forest, the eternal susurrus of insects, the turning clockwork of burps and chirps from small birds and hidden frogs. Silence for all practical purposes, though, and it is in this whispering silence that the Pygmies at last materialize to take down and roll up the nets as deftly as they had earlier rolled out and hung them up.

With the nets rolled up once more and looped over the net carriers, we continue walking and walking until we come to another place that someone—who knows how these decisions are made?—determines is right, and the nets are again laid down rapidly by the men, raised and fixed in place by the women, with the four of us again left standing near the bottom of the crescent. Again we hear the high-pitched whoops and barks in the distance and coming closer, and again at last the Pygmies silently materialize from inside the forest—but again, this second time, no animals: no nervous leaping monkeys, no ragged zigzagged duikers, nothing. Nada.

A third time as well the Pygmies spread out their great nets, fix them in place, whoop and bark, singing thus to push and drive the game into the pocket of the crescent—but the calls die out, and the Pygmies appear while the animals do not. This hunt has become a tedious vegetarian's exercise, and so the question one is provoked to ask is this: Where have all the animals gone?

✳

We return to the village as the sunlight turns yellow and angled. The four of us say good-bye and shake many hands, walk out of the village and back to the car, climb in. The driver, who has been napping inside the car, blinks his eyes, shakes himself awake, but just as he's about to the start the car, the chief's son appears: aggrieved, I can see from his face, and wondering, I can detect from his gesturing hands, where the money is. Money?

Our driver starts the car, but I tell him to turn off the engine. "We should give him something!" I say. But what? How much? Karl has no idea. Michel has no idea.

"We should pay him something," I repeat, adding: "What's appropriate?"

I happen to have a roll of Congolese francs, the imperfect money we've been using for small, local purchases. I pull out my oily bundle, begin leafing through it. Dan names a figure, and I double that and hand out the window the resulting wad.

The driver starts the car. I roll up the window. And as we drive away, I observe the chief's son, whose face—as he quickly counts through the wad of francs and then determines the sum to be inadequate—turns into a bulging-eyed mask of fury. Too late. We're off, and soon moving down the road, but now I'm left with the unpleasant image of his furious face pressed into my mind.

It's nearly dusk, and we stop at a place a couple of miles down the road called Eden, which is a concrete-and-wood building with a tin roof, including a larger bar-restaurant section out front and close to the road, and a little store to one side and back from the road. The glory of Eden is its mural, facing the road and showing, among other Edenic scenes, a life-sized okapi to one side and, to another, a dreamy African in an Adidas shirt, reclining and listening to an animal rock band, with members of the band including a crocodile, a chimp, a rhino.

A sign over the door to the little shop says ALIMENTATION, and we go inside to find a wooden counter, a shelf on the rear wall holding a modest sampling of a few supplies, and a refrigerator with cold beer and soft drinks. A dozen plastic chairs are arranged on the concrete floor of the shop. A single bulb has been screwed into a dangling socket overhead. And on a rickety wooden table near the door is a blaring television set with, in full color, the World Cup from South Africa. Karl, Dan, and I order Cokes, buy one for the minder, one for the driver, and sit down to watch. It's Germany versus Argentina, with Angela Merkel ostentatiously standing up and cheering on the Germans—and always the raging, droning, ten-thousand-hornet sounds of vuvuzelas in the stadium. I hear thunder outside. The light dissolves from twilight into night, while African faces appear at the door and more and more people move in, standing, sitting down, crowding in—a bluish glow highlighting sweaty faces—and we all gasp and roar and cheer as the play proceeds. One goal is based on a spectacularly well-aimed header . . . and then I see the chief's son walk in, grim and gloomy. He pulls out the oily wad of bills I recently gave him, pays for his first beer, drinks silently by himself in a dark corner.

The Argentinians look at first abstracted, then dazed, then despairing, and the score is 4 to 0 at the end. Their coach, a young man with a full head of long dark hair and a diamond stud in each ear, looks as if he would like to cry. But the Germans play well, the Argentinians don't, and that's that.

15: BULLET HOLES IN THE CEILING

Dawn.

I'm lying beneath the mosquito netting in my bed in my bedroom in our cottage beside the Epulu River at the Okapi Station. I open my eyes to look up through a cloud of netting overhead to consider the bullet holes in the ceiling. Still half asleep. Being awakened by an alarm clock, which is the temperature bird, a repetitive little fellow who hangs around outside the window and every morning wakes me up at the same time with the same monotonous query: *Temperature. What's the temperature? Temperature. Temperature. Temperature. What's the temperature?*

It's warm now and going to be hot soon.

I open my eyes again and once again size up the bullet holes in the ceiling, which seem now like a dangerous form of punctuation, like a stream of ellipses screwing the syntax of the synapse in the middle of a dream, like . . . and . . . and . . . that make one pause to wonder again: Where have all the animals gone? They've gone, I think, into a black hole made by the soldiers who shot the bullets that made the bullet holes. Or maybe they've gone into a deep hole dug in the ground by the meat merchants and the ivory traders and timber thieves, the butchers, bankers, bosses, and bumblers. Or maybe they've just dropped into the giant hole being screwed into the earth by the mighty march of modern progress.

Temperature. Temperature. What's the temperature?

It's our last day at Epulu, and now, as I scribble these words into my little notebook, I hear a series of clinks, clanks, and clunks in the kitchen, a discordant concert conducted carelessly by Samuel, our cook, as he rummages about. He's early this morning, maybe because he's eagerly anticipating final payment for services rendered.

The Epulu River rushes past the Okapi Station and our little cottage in the Station, creating a surf-like roar day and night, nature's white-noise machine that I find mostly comforting, as it masks most of the rumbling of the trucks moving past the Okapi Breeding Station and the headquarters of the Institut Congolais pour la Conservation de la Nature (ICCN) on Route Nationale 4 (RN4). That's the main clay track connecting east with west, in the process slashing open an orange gash right through the Ituri Forest and, as well, directly through the Okapi Wildlife Reserve. A brief pause in the rumbling, as a truck stops momentarily at the security barrier in front of the ICCN barracks. Then the driver revs the engine, shifting gears, getting underway—although still carefully, one hopes, across the wood planks bolted onto the steel girders of the new bridge over the rushing Epulu River—headed, as he would be, west, on the way to places like Nia Nia and beyond, as far perhaps as the big city of Kisangani. . . .

Or maybe the driver is pointed in the other direction, in which case he has already crossed the bridge before stopping at the barrier. It's still a momentary pause at the barrier (no inspections here) before he revs the engine, shifts the gears, and heads east to places like Mombasa and Irumu and on, perhaps to Bunia and out to Uganda and beyond.

✳

I sometimes think of Africa as the center of the world. It is, in any case, a center of life, and the Congo—the great warm, wet, and all-embracing Congo—is the forested center of the center. In 1989, the Democratic Republic of the Congo held more elephants than any other nation in the world, with an estimated population of 112,000 individuals. Surveys published in 2007, less than two decades later, concluded that only between ten and twenty thousand elephants were left. If those figures are reliable, one can conclude that somewhere between eighty and ninety percent of the elephants alive in the center of Africa were, during the last couple of decades, wiped out, erased, extinguished, exterminated, killed, or just shot full of holes and cut up into a hundred thousand pieces.

Such is the elephant holocaust: the sad, sad circus of Pleistocene refugees all lined up and marching trunk to tail in their grimly organized program of extermination. What drives this bloody parade is the Great I-Want, the mysterious matrix of human desire, the unaccountable human passion for the peculiar luster and texture of the elongated front teeth of elephants.

Elephants have those teeth.

People want the teeth.

Too bad for the elephants.

Until recent times, ivory was sold openly and legally in the Congo, carved as it often was in dozens of workshops located in the urban centers of Kinshasa, Kisangani, and elsewhere. A ban in 1989 pushed Congo's ivory trade underground, while the war, beginning in 1996, brought it back into the open with a vengeance. Thugs temporarily employed as soldiers looted the forests for meat and ivory, and they looted all the settlements along the road, including the village of Epulu and the offices and barracks of the ICCN and the various buildings and guest cottages of the Okapi Breeding Station.

Aside from that dozen or so okapis cared for at the Okapi Station, Rosmarie and Karl Ruf (the Swiss couple who ran the place) also took in chimpanzee babies who had been orphaned by hunters, keeping the growing apes on two islands in the middle of the river. The thugs employed as soldiers killed and ate all those chimps but somehow were persuaded—Who knows how? A promise, a deal, an appeal?—to leave the okapis alone.

Meanwhile, thousands of amateur miners had been moving into the Ituri Forest, scratching holes into the earth in search of gold, diamonds, coltan (critical for the manufacture of electronic gadgets), and cassiterite (for tin), while other extraction entrepreneurs moved in to mine the trees, the meat, and again the ivory. Mining ivory was easy enough. No shovels required. Mining ivory required little more than pointing an AK-47 in a certain direction and pulling the trigger, then hacking away an elephant's front teeth and getting those teeth out to market. But what market, where, how?

The dirt highway, the RN4 could help. On the RN4, elephants' teeth could be taken either west to Kisangani and from there on to the north or west. Or one could take the ivory on the RN4 east to Bunia and from there out of the country and on, ultimately, to China, where a rising middle-class has become the big market for big teeth these days.

The end of the war came after all the deals were finalized in Kinshasa, whereupon the various rebel chiefs signed papers, were given rewards, and the national army and police drove out the last of the thugs employed as soldiers. With the end of the war, a number of outside organizations—the World Bank, for example—moved in to make things even better. The RN4, the link between east and west, the red-clay cut through the Ituri Forest, and the Okapi Reserve inside the Ituri, had gotten bad. It was rutted, washed out in places, muddy, seriously unreliable. The World Bank financed the improvement work, hiring Chinese crews to do it right and even to build a beautiful new steel bridge across the Epulu River right in front of the Okapi Station and the ICCN headquarters.

That's the World Bank. That's development. That's progress. After the World Bank refurbishment, traffic on the RN4 went from a small trickle to a major rush: hundreds of trucks a month rumbling along the road. But the question the World Bank officers, teetering in their ergonomically engineered chairs inside their high-rise offices at the very tippy-tops of cities in the First World, may not have addressed fully enough is this: What might be inside those trucks?

✸

A good X-ray machine would help, since official barriers on the road are run by soldiers and police among whom many are not altogether averse to closing their eyes. The RN4 has become a major conduit for illegal timber, bushmeat, and ivory. A few weeks after the bridge at Epulu was finished, a giant double truck carrying twice the legal load, all of it illegally harvested timber bound for markets in Kenya, tested the tensile strength of the bridge girders and found it wanting. A 200-meter span of the bridge buckled and dropped into the river, along with the truck and its driver and the wood. Of course, the World Bank was quick to refinance the building of that bridge by a Chinese crew. The trucks soon returned.

Along with the illegal timber goes illegal bushmeat. There is legal bushmeat, too, but in truth all animals of all kinds, including elephants and okapis, are chopped up and sent piece by piece on this road in both directions and sold as meat at the various village and town and city markets outside the Okapi Reserve.

Ivory also moves in both directions on the RN4, and occasionally a truck is popped open to show us more particularly what it looks like. By "popped open," I'm referring to cases like the truck bound for Kisangani recently that crashed into another vehicle, whereupon 116 tusks stored in jerry cans flew off the back. The ICCN rangers who monitor the barrier at Epulu are unusual in that they do not take bribes, so I have been told, but they have an additional motivation not to look closely into the trucks. A lot of the criminal traffic in ivory moving past their checkpoint is run at the direction of the general commanding the 13th Brigade of the Congolese army, based not very far away in the town of Mambasa.

The general is a Big Man, as are most of the people at the free enterprise heart of the ivory mafia. These are the *commanditaires*: men of money and power who will organize the hunting expeditions at the start and take care of the ivory sales at the end. The commanditaires are military officers, government officials, well-established businessmen, and they hire the hunters and provide them with all the necessities: food and marijuana, guns and ammo. Guns are usually military AK-47s, owned by the Congolese military, but sometimes also 12-gauge shotguns with the lead shot melted down and reconfigured to make elephant-stopper slugs. A hunting expedition might include a couple of hunters going out for a couple of days or perhaps a dozen and a half men headed into the woods for a few weeks. The principal goal of the expedition is ivory, which is the shiny prize that motivates the commanditaire, but the hunters may be rewarded with meat for themselves and their families or to sell or give away. Meat will come from antelopes, apes, buffalo, bushpigs, monkeys, okapis . . . any unlucky animal will do, including, of course, elephants.

Sold in the city markets at Kisangani, elephant meat goes for around five to six dollars per kilogram. By comparison, antelope fetches between $3.60 and $4.80 per kilo, while monkey goes for $3.22 to $3.50 per kilo. Yes, elephant meat is more expensive than other meats, and apparently more desired, especially the succulent steak from trunk or feet. The skin of an ear makes a good drum head, while the hairs of the tail can be sold to make bracelets that are said to protect a person from lightning. The dung is used as a medicine to treat malarial convulsions among small children. But all that—dung, ears, feet, trunk, basketfuls of other body parts—is for the hunters and the traders and transporters to think about. The meat and byproducts: That's their take. The commanditaire is just hoping to sell his cleaner and more portable ivory for his own nice profit. Right now, as I listen to the temperature bird outside my window and to the clinking, clanking, and clunking of Samuel in the kitchen working on breakfast, raw ivory sells for around $160 for a pair of five-kilogram tusks, $580 for two ten-kilogram tusks, and $1,680 for a pair of fifteen-kilogram tusks.

Temperature. Temperature. What's the temperature? Temperature.

Those price figures are based on the report Dan the ivory guy is just now working on, so they must be up to date. Before the trip, Dan had hired through some regular connection a couple of professional ivory spies—make that professional researchers—named Richard and André, two young Africans, cool and self-confident, dressed well and wearing shades, who day before yesterday rode their motorcycle all the way up from Kisangani for 460 kilometers, in order conduct their own interviews.

Dan gave them some money as a down payment, lent them a video camera, and sent them on their investigative journey up and down the RN4, west to Mombasa and east back to Kisangani, to meet and interview elephant hunters, transporters, marketers, and, if possible, a few middlemen or commanditaires. Richard and André are local guys, have good connections in the area. They will do their job, while today—this morning, just as soon as we finish our breakfast and pay Samuel the cook for his services—Karl, Dan, and I will hit the RN4 on our own little spy mission that will include stopping in markets and making ourselves as inconspicuous as three daft blancs in the middle of the DR Congo can be, while checking meats and prices. . . .

✳

But first, as I say, we must pay the cook, Samuel, who, as a worker contracted through the ICCN, has his own official prices that are carefully summarized on an official bill that he now—now that the breakfast dishes are cleared and left to soak in the sink—hands us.

We do the math and assemble the money: a small fistful of clean, crisp American fives, tens, and a couple of twenties. Samuel looks tentatively grateful, but he wants to make sure the money is good. He counts the bills once, twice, thrice, turning them all in the same direction, and then carefully, one by one, he goes through them once more to examine the dates. One five dollar bill has a bad date. Luckily, though, Dan has a five that's better. Then, having satisfied himself about the dates, Samuel presses them up, one by one, against the glass at the window, using sunlight to check for any imperfections.

Ah! One of the tens has a crease that looks like it could be the beginning of a slow tear. He hands that back. Karl fishes around in his wallet to find a replacement.

But now, as Samuel examines the bills even more closely, he finds three of the bills—two fives and a ten—have actual holes in them. Pinpricks. He shows us, shaking his head with sincere concern. They won't do.

Dan, dripping with a sly sarcasm, comments quietly: "This is unbelievable. I can't fucking believe it. Somebody has put pinpricks into our money!"

But patiently, patiently, we go back to our wallets, and with a good deal of backing-and-forthing, leafing through bills, considering the dates and holding them up for new examinations, we finally come up with sufficient replacement money, making Samuel at last satisfied. Then we jam our bags into the car and hit the road.

Good-bye, Samuel.

Good-bye, Michel.

Good-bye, Jean-Prince.

Good-bye, Bernard, Abeli, and Myanamenge.

Good-bye, Tatu, and all the other okapis.[1]

---

1 Two years later, an armed gang of poachers and illegal miners stormed the ranger station and the Okapi Breeding Center, looted and burned the physical structures, and killed six people. I can only hope these generous individuals were not among the victims. The criminal raiders also killed all the okapis.

16: SPY VERSUS SPY

The RN4 was a ribbon of dirt with stretches of forest on either side followed by patches of dirt and a few huts—mud plastered on sticks, leaves splashed onto a roof—and here and there people sitting on stick chairs, women cooking over smoldering fires, children playing, a few chickens scratching at the dirt, maybe a goat or two, and in one place a man relaxing in the dirt, lying on his side and watching the road, head propped onto a hand, elbow on the ground. From the driver's boom box player came a stream of clicking percussion and joyous voices weaving a tight harmony.

When we saw the big container truck parked alongside the road, Karl told the driver—Edmond Malemo was his name—to pull over, and we quickly piled out, Karl already pointing his video camera at the truck, the plank gangway leading up to the open back of the truck and the scene playing away inside it. Four perfectly muscled young men were inside the truck, bare-chested, black-skinned, dressed in rags and drunk on palm wine, and they started to laugh as Karl rushed their way, his video camera turned on, racing right up the gangway and into the truck. The four men, sweat pouring off their faces, a bright sun bouncing around outside the truck dully reflecting from their chins and cheeks, broke into a dance. They danced, laughed, and sang: a spontaneous Vaudeville act for the camera's benefit. Then they walked down the plank and into the thickets beside the road, waving the three of us on, beckoning us to follow.

We followed. Back into the thickets, we stumbled over a large stash of timber, an entire lumberyard of it, off-the-books timber cut by chainsaw into enormous, dark-colored planks, maybe four-by-tens or four-by-twelves, about twelve to fourteen feet long. Karl swept across the piles and piles of illicit timber with his video camera before turning the shiny eye back on the four workers who, divided into pairs now, were taking both ends of single planks, raising them up high, balancing the heavy planks on their heads, and toting them thus out to the road and up the ramp into the back of the truck—as Karl followed, camera still running. It was strangely hilarious. They laughed. We laughed. They chattered in French. We responded cheerfully back, then climbed back into the car and drove on.

We crossed the boundary of the Okapi Reserve some time before noon, and not so long after noon we rolled into the town of Nia Nia, where we stopped to check out the market and meat, which included about fifteen monkeys, maybe eight duikers, but no elephant or okapi meat. We stopped at the mission in Nia Nia, a nice building with Catholic imagery painted on the walls and some Catholic priests and nuns inside. We passed by the city hall, a wonderful colonial-style building with a rusty tin roof and a giant, grass-lined hole in the roof.

Outside Nia Nia, we passed through one then two police barriers, were stopped and finally released at the second by an official in a blue Adidas track suit. Listening to Congolese pop on the machine—bouncy rhythms, chorusing harmonies, cymbals, woodblock—we sailed past places with names like Badambu, Bagwanza, Bofwagbouma, past mud-and-stick huts, sun-cracked walls, a man sprawled in a chair, a woman holding a multicolored umbrella against the sun, other women walking along the road with heavy-laden wicker baskets strapped to their foreheads, others with cloth packets or plastic jugs balanced on their heads, one with a single large yam on her head.

Coming to the edge of Bafwasende, we halted dutifully at yet another barrier, which was a lowered stick that could be raised by the two armed officers sprawled in plastic chairs next to it. I saw the handoff from a truck ahead of us at the barrier: wad of cash shifting from one hand to another, owner of second hand, policeman in blue uniform, giving the nod and the stick is lifted. The policeman, cradling his AK-47, turns back to consider the next customers in line: us.

It was late afternoon by the time we rolled into the center of Bafwasende, and we found the best hotel in town and took rooms. It may also have been the only hotel in town. It was fronted by a bamboo fence, isolating it from the mud street outside, and it had no name that I could see, but if you happen to visit Bafwasende someday and wish to find this establishment, it's off the main drag and wedged between a night club to the left and the Ibra Forest Diamond Merchant to the right.

The guy at the hotel desk, tall with a bulging forehead, showed us a selection of rooms while pointing out the general direction of the showers and toilet in a mud yard at the rear of the hotel, and I chose Chambre No. 2, which seemed to be the only one with a window to the outside. I dropped my pack in the room, went out back to investigate the toilet and shower. The toilet was a hole in the ground. The shower was a faucet above the ground.

Back in Chambre No. 2, I found my room to be the interior of a concrete cube, with geckos on the walls. There was a pink rubber mattress for a bed, a dirty sheet covering the mattress, a pinkish mosquito net strung over the sheet and mattress. Since there was no electricity in the hotel yet, the single light bulb dangling at the end of a couple of wires dribbling out of the ceiling wasn't working. I was grateful for the window, a rectangular hole in the wall nailed over by a sheet of corrugated tin bent back at one corner to let in a triangle of light and air and, as I soon discerned, a triangular view of the mud passageway outside and a wall of the night club next door.

The light was fading into a grainy gray, and I pulled a flashlight out of my pack to consider the room more thoroughly: plastic chair, wood table, wood desk with one drawer, inside of which was a Gideon Bible. The concrete floor was cool. The air was hot. The room was stifling.

I sat on the plastic chair, sweating and scratching nonsense into my notebook, and listened, dreamily, to fragile, early evening sounds coming in through the open triangle: voices, babbling baby, sound of a cock crowing. I could smell wood smoke, a faint, sweet, pleasant odor. The voices and babbling and crowing were pleasant, too, friendly, familiar, reassuring . . . and suddenly bludgeoned into oblivion by an enormous blast, followed by another and another and another and another, a shuddering series of explosions that spun into the rumbling of a giant diesel generator somewhere just outside the triangular hole of my window.

The generator belonged to the night club next door. I saw the night club's lights go on. I heard a thumping and some voices that turned into a crooning kind of repetitive dance music—the evening dance program had begun—and then I smelled and saw the diesel fumes, a bluish cloud emanating from the generator and rising in a Brownian arabesque of curls and coils that oozed through the triangular hole and into my room.

✳

By the time I had persuaded the guy at the desk to give me a room without a window—Chambre No. 4—it was dark. I left my new room in darkness, met up with Karl and Dan in the darkness, and the three of us wandered tentatively out of the hotel and onto the mud streets of Bafwasende, looking for a restaurant or at least a bar with some food. I soon realized that we three presented the only white faces in town. People floated out of the dark and stared at the oddity of our ghostly apparition until, embarrassed by their staring, they looked determinedly away and, moving purposefully along, sank back into the oily night. Still, there were some lonely spots of artificial light along the main drag, where we found a small shop and bar with a patio out front.

The patio was floored with pebbles spread over mud. It included three baby-blue plastic tables surrounded by baby-blue plastic chairs and was separated from the road by a miniature picket fence. The bar, up three concrete steps from the patio, was a baby-blue cave beneath a high stucco façade painted cream with blue pennants hung gaily over the entry, a line of ten bullet pocks in the stucco, and a painted slogan that said, *Pour la Paix et le Développement*.

Inside the baby-blue cave were two more plastic tables and several plastic chairs, a counter, a small television set with World Cup scenes spinning out of it, long rows of beer for sale, and some shelves and racks with minor essentials and snack items, along with sticks of Obama brand strawberry-flavored chewing gum.

A picture of President Laurent Kabila was hanging on the wall.

Congolese music played from a CD player behind the counter, and the woman running the place—tall and young and pleasant-mannered, with narrow hips and light streaks in her hair—told us, in French, to take a seat in the patio. She'd be out to take our orders soon. Meanwhile, however, sitting with several others at a table inside the bar, like a troll on a bridge, was a drunk, clown-faced soldier dressed in a green uniform with epaulettes on the shoulders and brass stars on the epaulettes, who told us to buy him a beer. Pretending not to understand, we proceeded out of the bar, down the three steps, and onto the patio. We sat down at one of the tables, pulling up a fourth chair for Edmond, who was off doing something or other but was supposed to join us soon.

Soon the drunken soldier walked out of the bar and stepped down to the patio, pulling out the chair we had saved for Edmond. At that point, I stood up, said, "I'm headed back to the hotel. Anyone else interested?" and walked away. "See you later," I added.

Dan soon followed. It was not a nice thing to do, leaving Karl there by himself, but I knew he could handle it and figured that reducing the number of people involved in this irritating contretemps would reduce the amount of time wasted by it. Karl, I thought, would soon join us back at the hotel.

Instead, we were summoned back to the patio by a messenger sent by the drunken soldier, instructing us to return with passports in hand. We did, finding Karl sitting quietly alone at the table and drinking a beer. Our inebriated antagonist had returned to his own table inside the bar, pulling on a beer and surrounded by a half dozen drinking comrades. As he saw us walk onto the patio, he smiled and grandly motioned us over. A subordinate took our passports and passed them over to El Borracho, who was already sloppily thumbing his way through Karl's.

I sat back down at the table on the patio with Karl and ordered a beer from the woman, while Dan walked down the street a short distance to order some food from a street vendor camped out there. Dan returned. Dinner, he said, was on the way. Then El Borracho staggered down to our table, all three passports in hand. He stood before the fourth chair at the table in a mock imitation of politeness, his eyes a pair of glassy marbles, grasping the back of the chair with one hand as if waiting to pull it out while graciously anticipating our concurrence. Karl said, in French, "No, that chair is for our chauffeur."

The soldier smiled, mimed his mocking plea a second time.

"No," Karl said.

Dan and I said, "Go ahead. Sit down." He sat down.

So began the negotiations, which soon landed onto a single theme sloppily articulated in English by the soldier: "Beer ees passport." He paused to let the profound significance of those three words sink in, then repeated himself: "Beer ees passport."

Karl laughed. "That's a good one," he said in French. "That could be the title of a book: *Beer is Passport.*"

But the guy merely continued repeating himself, smiling in his stupidly alcoholic sort of way, shaking the passports at each word for emphasis: "Beer ees passport. Beer ees passport."

Karl: "OK. You give me my passport, and I'll give you a beer."

"Beer ees passport."

"OK. OK. Beer is passport! You give me passport. I give you beer."

The lightbulb turned on. The soldier opened Karl's passport, looked at the picture, read the name: "Karl Ammann." Then he slapped the red booklet onto the table in the style of someone playing a trump card in a hot game of bridge. He made the call: "Beer ees passport."

Karl picked up the passport, and the soldier turned and shouted at the woman standing back in the bar, ordering a beer. She ignored him. He repeated himself more loudly and aggressively. She ignored him. Finally, Karl went into the bar, quietly bought a beer, and brought it back to the table.

The soldier took a noisy swig from the bottle—but, not to be distracted from his mission, still holding two passports, he now opened the next one. He examined the photo, looked at Dan, then said (cleverly reversing his equation), "Dan, passport ees beer."

"But you already have a beer," Dan said, in French. "What do you want another one for?"

Edmond, our driver, meanwhile, had appeared. He pulled up a chair from one of the other tables, sat down, and shared a superficially friendly exchange with El Borracho for a moment before the latter turned back to continue squeezing Dan: "Dan, passport ees beer."

Dan finally handed over enough money to buy another beer, then took his passport, whereupon the drunk turned to my passport. "Peter," he said to me, "passport ees beer."

"My name isn't Peter."

Just then our food came—three paper plates with rice, beans, and sardines— and El Borracho, suddenly looking inspired, took another sloppy swig of beer. He thumbed through my passport again, got the name straight.

"*Dale, nous sommes une famille, oui? Une famille.*" He smiled sweetly, looked at me deeply with a mocking imitation of great sincerity, folding his hands together in a prayerful gesture, then translated his French into English, "We are family, yes?"

"OK, we're family."

"Passport ees beer."

"No!" We all started arguing with him now. But finally I offered him the plate of rice, beans, and sardines. He handed over my passport, slobbered hastily over half my dinner, and then, laughing at us and at the stupid drama created by his own pathetic power, he at last retreated back into the bar to join his gang of soldiers at the table. Half an hour later, the drunken soldier triangulated away with a couple of buddies—but not before introducing us to another drunk, this one not in uniform. The guy sat down at our table and within a few minutes had begun demanding his own beer. But we had our passports now, and this fellow, drunk as he was, simply did not have the bold authority that comes with epaulettes and stars.

"We've already done that," I explained patiently, and finally the man gave up and stumbled off into the darkness.

But it was hot, hot, hot. I was tired, soaked through with sweat, and now the humid heat and the dark streets of Bafwasende had begun to seem seriously oppressive. I was drinking my beer and starting to think a string of negative thoughts, such as, *Why did we ever come to this hell hole?* Dan must have been thinking more or less the same thing, because when Karl said, quietly, "Some people only get to go to Hawaii or Bali . . . ," Dan and I both burst out laughing.

❉

Karl's sense of humor can be endearing. Also cheering me up was the woman running the bar, who gave me a secret, slyly ironic smile as we paid up, as if to say, *Yes, El Borracho is quite the toad, isn't he.* And with our mood elevated a little, we four—silent Edmond included here—walked through the black night back to the hotel where, right next door at the Ibra Forest Diamond Merchant's place, was a tiny television set tuned to *Le Coupe du Monde*—the World Cup.

It was Germany versus Spain, and on the tiny glowing screen that contest consisted of a white dot moving erratically back and forth across a bright green washcloth, but the two or three dozen African men in the audience, sitting in plastic chairs and on the concrete floor of the Ibra Diamond office with us, cheered, groaned, gossiped, howled, and laughed uproariously as the dot flitted over the washcloth. I left at halftime, ready to turn in.

I think the diamond merchant must have been associated with the hotel, because a corridor running back from the merchant's office soon turned into the hotel corridor, and, soon after that, I found my own Chambre No. 4. It was the same as the old Chambre No. 2, but without the triangular opening to the outside. Instead, it had a big glass window in the door, which at first was useful, because although the hotel generator was now running, the single lightbulb in my room wouldn't turn on, so I depended on a glow of light from the corridor.

The night manager showed me how to cross certain wires in order to turn the light on, but unfortunately, as I gradually discovered, uncrossing the wires did not turn the light off, and thus I spent the night in a lighted room, with people, as they walked along the corridor, pausing casually to peer through the window into my room. I spent most of the night awake, sweating and suffocating inside the mosquito net while watching the geckos on the walls, the mosquitoes teasing the geckos, the people occasionally peeking into my room, and listening to the hotel generator, the endless thumping of a drum in the farther distance, the diamond merchant's television in the nearer distance, and a long and desultory conversation between a man and a woman next door.

It was not a good night, which will explain why the next day went by so quickly. We checked out of the hotel early. Had a quick breakfast on the patio of the Ten Bullet Hole Bar. Stopped at the small town market to find okapi meat for sale. Hit the road.

The RN4 out of Bafwasende was a lot like the RN4 into Bafwasende, with the occasional man in uniform pathetically trying to extort small bribes, and so on. At one point, a boy walking along the road and carrying a dead monkey with a bright white mustache beneath his nose tried to sell us the meat. The ten dollars he asked for was the price for white people. We passed a red brick mission compound and church, very beautiful—once—and now all in ruins, with trees and vines growing out the side and a big tree growing right up through the middle where the roof used to be. And at the Lindi River (quiet movement of swelling emerald, hanging curtain of vines) a man standing in the middle of a still-being-worked-on bridge waved down our car and told us we had no right to cross the river. Edmond rolled down his window, smiling and self-assured, pulled a card out of his wallet, showed it, and said a few words that magically convinced the man to smile sheepishly and step aside. Edmond later explained that he was "higher ranking," whatever that means.

But mainly the drive that day was a blur, with much of the blur caused by a pair of out-of-control eyelids slowly lowering and slowly lifting. Karl, meanwhile, was wide awake and in fine form, talking away in his usual fashion, working as the tour guide explaining all to his clients, saying things to Dan (and me, when I was listening) like: "A hundred thousand elephants before the war. My estimate is maybe nine thousand left, all south of the Congo River. Wamba. Lomako. There was a campaign where Mobutu sent his army out to poach elephants. That's the same period when the poaching took place in Tsavo in Kenya. Tons and tons of ivory was being sent out on Mobutu's private plane. To Japan and China."

✳

The RN4 eventually led us past the high walls, higher watch towers, and coiled razor wire surrounding a big UN fortress, then past more walls and more razor wire, and into the streets of downtown Kisangani. There were few private cars in the city, the traffic being mostly bicycles and motorbikes, occasional trucks, and once in a while a UN vehicle or some other brand-new SUV with some other doing-good NGO label on the side.

It was hot, intensely humid, the sky chalk-white with humidity.

We drove through a major intersection marked by a large sign showing the rear view of a handcuffed prisoner and the hopeful caption: *Campagne pour la Sensibilisation de Changement de la Mentalité*. Then we turned onto a side street, proceeding into a netherland of garbage, rubble, and crooked passages before finding, at last, a hotel called The Riviera: a stubborn remnant of pre-war prosperity surrounded by a concrete wall and fronted by a steel gate. The door and windows to our suite (which Karl and I shared: one lounge and television, two bedrooms, two baths) were intruder-proofed with heavy grilles made from rebar.

Dan and Edmond took rooms down the open walkway a bit.

I appreciated the security of the barriers and also the luxury of a flush toilet and private bath. Here I was able to stare at myself in the mirror and discover I was covered with red dust in my hair, face, on my glasses, my beard. My clothes were stiff with dust. There was very little water pressure in the bathroom, yet still enough to produce a trickle resembling a shower. Glorious! True, the room was full of mosquitoes, but I went to work on them, and then, having showered and changed clothes, I wandered out to the hotel bar, which was located in a breezeway with the breeze artificially accelerated by slowly spinning ceiling fans. I sat down at a table with Karl, who had already showered and changed and was busy talking to his Azande prince friend, also seated at the table.

I ordered a cold Prius Cinquantenaire, an ordinary beer celebrating Congo's fiftieth anniversary of independence.

The Azande prince was named Isaaka Malamanga Issa. He was young and handsome—chocolate-skinned with bright white teeth, a shaved head, full cheekbones—and wearing a tan short-sleeved shirt with epaulettes and a monogrammed A on the left shoulder. He looked graceful and athletic, and he seemed attentive and alert.

Isaaka was a prince from the Bili area where Karl had tried to set up his conservation operation, saving chimps and elephants in north central Congo with the Elephant Coffee scheme, and now Isaaka was telling Karl that the chiefs wanted him to come back. Karl was seriously reluctant, since to his mind the whole thing had collapsed in an angry chaos of broken promises. In the meantime, though, Isaaka needed spending money and Karl was hiring him to help with a survey of the five meat markets in Kisangani. Isaaka's task was to find elephant and okapi meat and anything else of interest, such as ivory or ape meat, and figure out the normal prices for normal people. Karl handed him one of the pocket pen spy cameras as well, showed him how to use it, and asked him to buy a sample of meat and get some footage with the camera.

But Isaaka wanted to talk to his family back in Bili, and also have Karl talk once more to the chiefs, so the next morning we all went off to dial them up at the Radio Shack.

The Radio Shack was an open pavilion behind a steel gate. The pavilion had a thatched roof, a concrete floor, and a wooden table in the middle with the radio on it surrounded by three plastic chairs, a stack of batteries, and off to one side a yellow backup generator. The radio operator sat in one of the plastic chairs, while the other two were for radio customers. Three wooden benches at the edges of the pavilion supported a small crowd of observers and hangers-on. Scratchy, ghostly voices were coming out of the radio, and after a time Karl paid his fee and handed the receipt over to the radio operator. While we were waiting for the connection, Karl explained why he still might be interested in resurrecting the project at Bili.

"This was one of the last strongholds of elephants in Congo," he said, "and it still is with chimps. I am convinced there are a hundred thousand chimps between Bondo and Garamba, because it's all the same vegetation, and it's all the same human density in that area. So we know there shouldn't be much different density of chimps. There are 1.6 chimps per square hectare. They live on fruit. They cross savanna patches. Ron says he has seen them from the air. . . ."

Pretty soon the radio operator had gotten a response from Bili, and Karl was motioned over to a plastic chair.

He spoke into the mic: "*Bonjour, Chef Selesi. Ça va?*"

There was an extended conversation in French that eventually shifted over to German (Swiss German, as Karl later explained, since he had been talking to Nico the Greek, now married to Isaaka's mother, who used to work in Switzerland) and back to French before Karl turned the radio over to Isaaka.

"*Bonjour, mama,*" Isaaka began, and, as this family conversation went on, Karl moved away from the radio and told me that when he was involved in the Elephant Coffee project, he had a radio at his house in Kenya in order to stay in touch with the folks at Bili. "I can install my radio again," he said now, "but then I talk every day, and all I get is a list: a shopping list. I would fly in tires, but 'Oh, they're the wrong size.' 'But I have it written down.' It took half the airplane to fly them in, but 'OK, I'll take them back.' 'Oh, they're gone. We sold them to someone.' So they just had me fly the tires in for someone else."

Yet still, it seemed, starting up the Bili project once more had at least a passingly wistful appeal: "Even if the elephants are gone," Karl added, "should we look into something for the chimps? That's the big question."

✳

Isaaka went off to do his job at the meat markets, and the rest of us drove to the ivory-for-tourists market: a cluster of booths somewhere in town with ivory and wood carvings for sale. Most of the pieces seemed small and unexciting—bangles, baubles, beads, bracelets, that sort of thing—but at least the vendors in the market were excited, possibly because we looked like the only tourists around.

None of the ivory was legal, but we did our best to resemble potential customers who didn't know and perhaps didn't care, and I finally bought a couple of carved ebony crocodiles. Dan, dressed in T-shirt and shorts, flip-flops on his feet, was busy assessing the ivory, checking prices, taking a mental inventory for his ivory survey. I was pretending to be just another tourist rather than just another spy. And Karl was pretending to be another tourist, too, as he snapped pictures with his camera, enthusiastically shooting me and Dan and the ivory pieces we were examining and talking about. Meanwhile, all the vendors in the market had begun to crowd around us and were, I could see, becoming upset about the photography, so now Karl was grinning obsequiously, shrugging helplessly, and acting confused.

The ivory pieces were, as I said, small—someone was running out of elephants—and the carving unimpressive. "Worst workmanship I've ever seen," Dan scoffed, adding, "There's obviously an ivory shortage here." And he pointed out how to distinguish bone from ivory. Bone has dark spots in it from small blood vessels in the bone. Ivory has a grain to it. There were some pieces of bone being sold as ivory.

As we carried on with this little charade, a strange-looking African man sidled up to us and claimed, speaking in French, that he had bigger and better ivory than what we were seeing in the market, and he could show it to us now if we wished. He was a small man with a gaunt face, shaven head, and a neatly trimmed black beard flecked with gray spirals. What looked strange about him was his outfit. On this hot morning in the middle of tropical Africa he was wearing a red felt sport coat over a cream-colored dress shirt (edged with red at the collar), a red tie, and a brass tie clip. Black slacks and black shoes completed the outfit—and would a normal person dress like that? I had him pegged from the first as a spy, an uncover cop, especially when he said he could get us export permits for all the ivory we wanted, no problem.

He introduced himself as Palambi Kumute Kindo and handed over a business card that identified him further as the Chef de Division Provinciale de la Culture et des Arts. After some discussion about the ivory he was going to show us, Palambi climbed into the front of the car, where, sandwiched awkwardly between Karl and Edmond, he navigated us down one street and up another until, half an hour later, in one of the more depressing sections of a town that already looked very seedy, we found the place. It was a big, two-story building—rusty tin roof, white stucco walls, lower banks of windows and upper window slots—with MINISTÈRE DE LA CULTURE ET DES ARTS DIVISION PROVINCIALE KISANGANI painted in rust red on the side.

He ushered us through a side entry into the downstairs—and so, with no electricity, we entered a large, dark, and chaotic-looking cavern. The second story of the building was unoccupied, so I guessed from looking up through a few sun-brightened holes in the ceiling, but where was the culture and art? There must have been a dozen men hanging around inside the building, downstairs, but it never became clear to me (as Palambi led us stumbling along a warren of dark passages and barren offices, a few desks, an ancient and large-barreled manual typewriter dumped in one corner, a couple of bicycles propped against a wall, and some mote-flecked shafts of yellow light struggling weakly through a few windows), what those silent and conceivably sinister figures normally did with themselves other than sit or stand and stare.

At last we reached the far side of the building, where Palambi had his own office. He unlocked the door, drew it open, let us walk past him and into a musty, murky room with some wooden chairs and a big wooden desk. He drew back some shutters, letting in daylight and a bit of air through a glassless window with protective grille. Pretty soon, two girls and a boy were standing at the grille and peeking curiously in. He shooed them away.

The ceiling of this office had been hung at several slightly different levels, giving it a wandery appearance. The floor was a bare concrete slab. But the walls were indeed covered with *objets de culture et des arts*: a few masks, a tattered and rotting shield, bow and arrow, piles of old ceremonial knives, some carved wooden heads, three bad paintings, a picture of the president on the wall behind the desk. There was also a small heap of minor wood carvings on the floor, an antique clock on the wall, a second ancient large-barreled typewriter in the corner. The bad paintings included a crude one of an okapi in the woods and a more interesting one of a leopard duking it out with a python. The python had wrapped himself in a knot around the leopard who was biting into the neck of the python, who looked very distressed at this unexpected turn of events.

Palambi began rushing around the room trying to sell us things—Paintings? Knives? Antique wood carvings? Bow and arrow? Rotting warrior's shield?—and then he unrolled a smelly and cracking okapi skin and a smellier leopard skin. Negotiations started at $500 for the okapi skin, $300 for the leopard skin, but they didn't get far because Dan was more interested in the ivory Palambi had talked about, while Karl had become preoccupied with the biggest prize of all: a stack of detailed and elaborately signed export documents in the middle of the desk.

While Dan chattered away with Palambi about ivory, how much he had, what were the prices, and so on, Karl had his camera out, working with flash now, and after casually taking pictures of this and that on the walls he zeroed in on the stack of documents on the desk. He stood directly at the desk, his camera a few inches away from the papers, using one hand to leaf through the stack page by page, the other hand holding the camera and snapping picture after picture.

Naturally, our host was upset by this uncivilized behavior. He waved his hands frantically, said "Non! Non! Non! Non!" Karl eventually stopped photographing and began asking him about the permits. Did they really work? Who else was buying ivory? Was he sure there wouldn't be any trouble with customs? And when could we see some actual ivory?

Palambi then rushed over to rip open the door and shout for help, whereupon a half dozen undercover police, guns drawn, raced in and brutally slammed us against the wall, arresting us for planning to buy and export ivory illegally. That's what I imagined might happen, but it didn't. Instead, Chef Palambi soon calmed down, said he was selling quite a bit of ivory to Israelis, and leafed through the stack to find for Karl an official export permit made out for an Israeli. Karl then negotiated to buy the antique warrior's shield—payment in American dollars promised if Palambi would bring it to our hotel with a complete export document—and I bought an old ceremonial knife. The Chef de la Culture et des Arts declared he would meet us tomorrow afternoon at the hotel restaurant with a few nice samples of ivory, and then we could talk about a bigger purchase.

✳

The next day was our last full day in Kisangani, and I slept late and relaxed a little. Dan's motorcycle-riding ivory spies, Richard and André, showed up at the hotel that morning with their field report and interview documents and the camcorder to return.

Isaaka showed up around noon at the hotel restaurant with his report on the Kisangani meat markets. He had seen lots of monkeys, some okapi meat, and fifteen baskets of elephant meat that were about forty to fifty kilos each— altogether one elephant—going for approximately five dollars a kilo. "To me," Karl said, "the evidence is in the footage." We took the spy camera into our suite lounge, downloaded it onto Karl's computer, watched it—and somehow this turned into a discussion of Bili and the Azande, and, as Karl got into his scolding voice, it became a lecture in French directed at Isaaka: "It's not for the blancs. It's for the Azande.

Your heritage, your patrimony, your animals are disappearing. You're losing the elephants, the forests. . . ."

Isaaka, "For me, I understand. . . ."

Karl: "The mentality of the people at Bili is that the whites have millions. They have too much money. 'They come to spend money, and we'll take it whenever we can, however we can. . . .' That mentality cannot work. It's necessary to change. . . . The chiefs respect not the contract!" he declared finally, finishing that declaration with a French puff of air, his arms thrown out.

Then, turning to me, he switched to English: "Their mentality: that they're helping us whites by protecting those animals—and they expect us to pay them something in return. You're got to change that mentality. The first step is for them to accept that conservation is in their interest. If they think it's just in our interest, some crazy whites who want to protect some stupid animals, then they'll just rip you off left, right, and center. It becomes blackmail: 'If you don't pay us, we're going to kill your elephants.'" Referring to Isaaka now: "He's the key. He's a new generation who will have an influence. Give him a chance. He understands. Maybe he has the influence to convince the rest of the population."

In the middle of the afternoon, Palambi Kindo rendezvoused with the three of us—me, Karl, and Dan—at the Riviera Hotel restaurant, as he had promised to do. He hadn't brought Karl's antique shield or the export permit, and he still didn't have the ivory permits, but then we hadn't bought any ivory yet. He did present some nice raffia weavings and a few sample pieces of ivory. I ordered him a beer as he pulled two ivory carvings out of a bag and put them on the table: a pair of small, pointy tusks with pointy heads carved into them. Palamabi said the artist who carved them was a very good artist, very talented. The one carving was entitled "Point Head," the other "Old Wise Man." Dan looked them over and said, quietly, in English, that the tusks were taken from a baby elephant, three to four years old.

When no one got excited about Point Head and Old Wise Man, Palambi then pulled another carved tusk out of his bag, a larger one, and passed it over. Taken from a six- to seven-year-old male, Dan said.

I spent some time considering the raffia-fiber weavings, bought one for twenty dollars, then a second one for less, and we all sat there with the ivory on the table, drinking beer and waiting out the heat of the afternoon. But while Palambi was trying to sell us raffia weavings and ivory, a boy came into the restaurant trying to sell bug-eye sun glasses. He came up to our table, and the Chef de la Culture and des Arts tried on a pair. He looked terrible in them, but they had red frames, which would go with the red jacket, red tie, and the red edge to his cream-colored shirt. He paid the Congolese franc equivalent of a dollar or two for them.

Then Dan bought a pair. He looked like a gangster in them. He paid about three times what Chef Palambi had just paid, shrugging and saying that he had paid the price for white people.

A very fat man at another table in the restaurant tried on a pair. The boy held out a small hand mirror for the fat man to regard himself, to consider the dramatic effect of the shades. They were selling like hot cakes, those bug-eye glasses. The boy was making out like gang busters.

Palambi said he would come back that evening with more and better ivory, along with the warrior's shield Karl had asked for and all the necessary export permits for the knife I had bought, and raffia work, and the shield and any ivory we might finally buy. He said he would meet us at Karl's hotel suite, which was also mine of course, at seven-thirty sharp that evening.

Dan and Karl and I sat in the suite lounge that evening—a noisy air-conditioner over the door turned up high, a cloud of small mosquitoes riding the swirling air currents—waiting for Palambi to show up, and in the meantime reviewing on Karl's computer all the video footage we had of the markets and the elephant meat and ivory for sale. Isaaka had also bought some pieces of elephant meat, which Karl spread out on a towel on top of a table and photographed.

When the Chef hadn't arrived by eight, Dan began to complain: "This is an example of why business doesn't work in Africa. These guys never do what they say."

When he hadn't arrived by eight-thirty, I said I thought he wasn't coming. He had been spooked by all the photos Karl took of his documents yesterday and by now was wise to our game. He wouldn't show, I said. But Karl disagreed: "Don't underestimate the greed of these guys." As it turned out, he was right. Chef Palambi finally knocked on the door two hours late, still dressed in the same red coat, red tie, brass tie clip, and he had brought along the warrior's shield, more ivory to look at, and also the completed export certificates for the shield and the knife and weavings I had bought. He was also ready to write certificates for ivory, he said.

The ivory was no more impressive than anything else he had shown us, however. Two raw (uncarved) tusks, very small. Three small elephants carved into three small ivory pieces. Nine necklaces made out of ivory pieces. In Dan's assessment: "They've obviously got an ivory shortage here."

Of course, we had no intention of buying any ivory in the first place, which meant that we would never have the best kind of hard, journalistic evidence about how easy it was (in spite of all the laws and treaties and promises and posturing and other supposed safeguards against the criminal trade in ivory) to get an official-seeming export permit . . . but we were, at least, getting interestingly identical export permits for the old warrior's shield, the knife, the raffia weavings.

He handed over the export permits but at the same time gave us the additional news that all the export permits also required a tax. It would be thirty dollars on the shield Karl had acquired and a total tax of twenty-five dollars for my purchases. Without thinking deeply about it, I pulled out my wallet and handed over the cash for mine.

Palambi had already begun writing out a receipt when Karl started yelling: "Tax? You want a tax? What a choke! It's always the same goddamned story. It just gets tired. Fuck. Constant!"

And with that, he leaped out of his chair, grabbed the warrior's shield, walked over to the door, opened it, and threw the shield out the door. He slammed the door shut and said, "Come on!" Then he stormed out of the lounge, went to his own room, and slammed that door shut. From the crack beneath the door, I could see that Karl had soon turned out his light.

Dan, I, and Chef Palambi were left momentarily speechless at the drama of this leave-taking. Palambi was shaken, I expect, but he calmly finished writing up my receipt, tore it out of the book, handed it over. I folded it up, put it in my wallet, and stood up. Palambi stood up. Had I been of firmer purpose or stronger fiber, I expect, I might have seen this small, bearded man dressed improbably in a red jacket and red tie as the small-time corrupt official that he most probably was, a parasite, a crook, a professional dealer in the blood-stained remnants of middle Africa's last forest elephants, but what I saw instead was a sad man in a disintegrating world. I said, "I'm sorry," and opened the door to let him out.

17: GIRAFFES IN THE MARA

Nairobi seems like a combination of Boston—crazy drivers and ferocious right-of-way battles—and Dickensian London, with the crowds of seemingly aimless people, the slums, the desperation, and the rare and fortified islands of privilege . . . such as the Muthaiga Country Club, where I (having just taken a hot bath) lie sprawled on clean sheets, naked and fresh as a baby. The Muthaiga: security, privacy, a garden, brass fixtures, mahogany furniture, luxury bathtubs, a parking lot full of Land Rovers, and inside, on the corridor leading to the rooms, the moth-eaten front third of a big male lion now stuck for eternity inside a glass box, his rear two-thirds having been shot off or forgotten one day during a brief and shining paroxysm of colonial stupidity.

At breakfast, the waiter says, "Good morning, suh!" I bite the reflex to respond with *"Bonjour!"* and think: *It wasn't so bad, speaking French.*

Early the next morning, we throw our bags into the back of Karl's nimble little short-wheel-base Land Rover and head south. Karl, confessing something I've never heard before this moment—"I like a little music when I drive"—presses the first of many tapes into the tape player, and so we're driving out of Nairobi listening to favorite hits from the 1950s, songs like "Que Sera Sera" and "I Did It My Way."

We stop for gas, then drive on, listening to "April Love," "Moon River," "Waltzing Matilda," "How Much is that Doggie in the Window?"

Karl: "If it weren't such a hassle at borders, it would have been fun to take this car into the Congo."

We listen to "Summer Time," "Red Sails in the Sunset," "Smoke Gets in Your Eyes" . . . and after maybe two or three hours of driving through a musical time warp, we arrive at the great rift escarpment, with the rift valley over to our left. Karl changes the tape and starts to bemoan the other time warp unwrapping itself in front of us. "We've still got 150 kilometers," he says. "This area used to be covered with game, and now it's all snared out. When I came to Kenya thirty-five years ago, the population was a third of what it is now. It has tripled in thirty-five years. We're still adding over a million people a year. Kenya is a frontline case of overpopulation. The next step is to redistribute land. They've already started buying the large farms and subdividing them. It's all going so fast!"

✶

We finally arrive at the Masai Mara, pay our fees, and drive through the gate and onto an old road. We follow that old road for a long, long time and then just drop off the road and get swallowed by rolling hills of grass and sudden dark thickets of bush, disappearing into a gorgeous landscape of grass and bush and innocent wild animals standing around and looking at us without fear or even curiosity, a landscape that seems to go on forever, or at least a pretty long way. I'm delighted. I have no idea where we are, and I'm disoriented to the point that I never could return to the same place on my own. That's a good thing.

Karl spins the car left, right, left, and runs right into a thicket, no road, no track, no signs, no anything . . . and we're crashing through a web of dark, thorny branches deeper into the thicket and, suddenly, we're lurching over a faint and hidden trail that snakes hither and thither until we come to a small parking spot.

We're soon surrounded by a half dozen Masai warriors, carrying spears and wrapped in red robes, their earlobes pulled open and dangling loosely, who greet us—"*Jambo! Jambo! Jambo!*"—tear the bags out of our hands, then tote all our luggage while walking ahead of us down a little footpath into a clearing and a camp that, I soon learn, is called Simba.

The name is embroidered onto the left shirt pocket of all the green uniforms and onto all the towels right alongside the logo, which is the silhouette of a Masai man with spear standing next to a lion and a bush beneath a small acacia tree. It's complicated to describe, easier to see. The tents are big, and the daily fees (I think Karl got an amazing deal) small enough that having my own tent seems completely reasonable. Inside: a long clothes rack, dresser, two plush beds, two bed tables and lamps, a lunch table, and at the rear a shower with two wash basins and a decent flush toilet. The tent is floored with canvas, of course, but set on flattened earth, with a Hemingway veranda at the front: two chairs, one small table, one spare writing desk for the testosterone-laden author come out to do Big Things while thinking about Truth and Beauty. Black rubber hoses, running on the ground between the tents, help explain where the water in the bathroom comes from. But the best part of all is the quiet and the simplicity of the place. Only a half dozen sleeping tents altogether, as far as I can tell (my view being somewhat limited by the thickety bush around us), along with one kitchen tent, a dining room tent, and a communal lounge tent. The dining room tent has only four tables.

We rendezvous there for a late lunch: really excellent food. And although one side of the camp is entirely obscured by the thicket, in the other direction the land slopes into a clearing and down to the Mara River. We have a splendid view of the glimmering river below, with white birds cruising over the surface, and, beyond that, of pale grasslands rolling off into the distant hills. I relax with an Edenic sense of the world, a feeling of peacefulness, the absence of the human chatter and clutter. No one around, no voices except for the occasional murmurs of two or three Simba staff members and Karl, who seems pretty relaxed himself, saying meditatively, "We lived in tents for two years. Good times. Good times. . . ."

The "we" includes Kathy, and the occasion of living in tents for two years was their marriage twenty-five years ago followed by a long wilderness honeymoon: two years working as volunteers with the Kenya Wildlife Service monitoring cheetahs in the Mara. That happy time was when Karl first took up photography, as I mentioned earlier. As I also mentioned earlier, it was also when Karl started a safari camp called the Intrepids Club, which eventually made him enough money that he could afford to keep on taking pictures.

✳

At mid-afternoon, we head out to look for giraffes. "I normally play music in the afternoon on game drives," Karl says, as he pops in another tape. Out comes: "Love is a Many Splendored Thing."

We emerge from the thicket, bouncing through the yellow grass until we reach a rough track, then turn right, or is it left?—I've already lost my sense of direction, could never in a million years find my way back to camp—then reach a clearing and, like magic: giraffes! Giraffes in the distance, maybe a dozen of them altogether, standing tall and looking at us with apparent curiosity. "That's nice. Quite a group," Karl says, adding, "You tell them to give birth; we'll see the whole thing."

I count eighteen giraffes, one of them lying down, the rest standing and looking at us. They stare. We stare. They stare. We stare. They stare and chew their cuds. We stare and take pictures.

They're Masai giraffes, of course, with flickery ears and tufted tails they switch desultorily back and forth.

Karl (muttering to himself, starting up the car): "See if we get an interesting neck composition over there." He moves us to another spot, different angle.

I see a subtle sort of giraffe democracy at work. One turns. Another turns. A third turns. Soon a half dozen have added their votes and now the entire group is ambling along. Karl: "Try to do once a very wide angle to take them all in."

By luck or very good planning, I'm not sure which, we've come to the Mara during the annual wildebeest migration, when a crazy crowd of about two million feisty beasties, having followed the rains from A to B, are now following the rains back to A once more—and as we're watching the giraffes, we notice a long, long, line of wildebeests on a hill far behind them. And so, having photographed the big group of giraffes, we head out to watch the migration down at the river. All the roads and tracks in this place have disappeared for the moment, and Karl cuts across the grasslands with this amazing machine that seems as tough and determined as a rhino, assuming rhinos are determined. On our way to the river, we listen to more '50s music ("One two three four, tell the people what she wore"), while a group of Thomson's gazelles scatters off, their tails tick-tocking in the style of wind-up toys. . . .

An ostrich runs wildly on, looking like a featherbed racing away from an accident in a plumbing shop: two pipes down, one pipe up.

A family of wart hogs scatters away, single file, daddy in the lead, their tails up straight and short like little antennae.

Then: six giraffes on the other side of a ravine but generally moving in the direction of a riverbed at the bottom of the ravine, the water low and settled into weedy pools and puddles, a slow-flowing current. Karl stops the car: "They will come down to the water next." And (to them): "Oh, go down to the water."

So much with giraffes happens in slow motion. There's a good deal of slow scanning, looking this way, that way, pausing, looking, pausing, looking. But Karl really wants this shot. "Oh, wow, look at the mirror reflection in the water. Yeah, come on. Drink. I need this mirror. Good boy."

When they go down to the water, one by one, we have the advantage of being up high, parked on the other side of the ravine. Karl's camera is out. Click. Click. Click.

An hour later, we arrive at the river to find the wildebeests amassed at the high bank and moving on, tipping and slipping over, racing down the steep bank and splashing-mooing-splashing into the water, swimming through the deeper parts, splashing onto a sandbank and climbing out the other side. A half dozen safari-viewing vehicles are already there, and we settle into our place in the viewing line. . . . And while we're lined up and watching this classic event, hundreds and hundreds of wildebeests are also lined up and about to participate in it: tripping, slipping, racing down the bank, churning through the water. It goes on and on and on until, suddenly, all movement stops, the wildebeests stop, and we see nothing for the moment but a bit of splashy commotion in the water by the far bank.

A look through the glasses confirms: one isolated animal struggling to climb out of the water, tugging, can't make it, or, finally, can almost, and moves far enough out of the water that I can see the head and shoulders of a giant crocodile: armored and shiny with an enormous back and a broad flat head like a big ugly shovel, latched onto the rear leg of the wildebeest. One struggles. The other holds on. But finally, amazingly, the hairy herbivore slips his skinny shank out of the shiny carnivore's toothy grip, steps all the way out of the water and scampers up the bank to the other side. My sympathies are with the mammal, not the reptile, and I feel perhaps irrationally relieved, but in any case, it seems like the two thousand wildebeests gathered on the bank and heretofore thinking about crossing the river have now stopped thinking about it, and that's the end of the crossing for today.

It's astonishing, the sense of open space and eternal peace, as we head back to camp. No traffic. No signs of a human presence. Just rolling hills and grasslands forever. And the grass with green roots but dried pale stalks and flagged yellow heads, so pale, turned brown in the distance, with a touch of ochre or, in the late day sun, brilliant burning gold.

※

Next morning, we head out just before dawn, and soon come upon, lying still beside the road and only faintly visible in the nacreous, pre-dawn light, a lion. When we pull up alongside him, only three yards away at most, he flickers a quick glance in our direction, then yawns, casually showing off a mouthful of yellow daggers. He's a magnificent animal, grass-colored with a great dark mane and massive head, his eyes focused casually in the distance, acting as if he has plenty already to think about and can't be bothered acknowledging the presence of us, mere worms hiding inside a ticking nut with strange noises coming out ("Things are not the same, since you kissed me"—*a-boom, a-boom*—"you kissed me"—*a-boom, a-boom*).

Karl turns off the engine, and the tape player shuts down. After a few minutes of sitting there quietly just admiring the lion, who still refuses to admire us, and taking a few pictures, Karl starts up the car again. We drive on. We're following the dirt track as it curves a bit, this way and that way until, maybe a couple of hundred yards later, we come upon another lion, a female, who is also lying in the grass not far from the edge of the track. As we approach and stop the car, though, she reacts: raises herself up and begins walking slowly away, looking back once or twice over her shoulder, slowly shifting her muscular weight from shoulder to shoulder and haunch to haunch. She proceeds into a denser area of dry grass and settles back down. Karl: "What is she up to? She's smelling something. Might be more lions."

We continue sitting there for a while, looking around, and a few minutes later our patience is rewarded as we catch sight of that male lion we had seen earlier, serenely lying down then and now determinedly up on his feet, working his way slowly in the female's direction. It looks like a romantic rendezvous to me, an assignation, the start of something interesting, and we sit there, engine off, waiting patiently for this drama to advance when. . . .

"Damn!"

Suddenly, from out of nowhere, a safari car pulls up alongside us, filled with a half dozen tourists. The car settles down, engine goes off, and so now we've been joined in the Mara theater, watching the lives of lions unfold. Another safari car then shows up, right behind. "Damn! I used to go *days* without cars in this corner of the park," Karl growls, and he starts up the car and drives off. So much for the lions. . . .

The sun comes up, and pretty soon we've escaped the safari cars and are now driving back into a landscape that, once again, gives the wonderful illusion of real wilderness, of being alone in the world, of having come to the beginning of time . . . or at least the beginning of Africa, or, maybe, the beginning of contemporary Africa before the arrival of the modern catastrophe. Karl, meanwhile, has gotten concerned about the absence of vultures: "The disappearance of vultures here is amazing. I mean thirty years ago you wouldn't go anywhere without seeing them in trees, watching for where the other vultures were headed."

But we're just driving back and forth, restlessly, not seeing any vultures and looking for giraffes or whatever else might turn out to be interesting and photographically engaging. It was chilly last night but now it's beginning to turn hot; and, meanwhile, as we wander across the hills and around the small thickets, onto this track or into that trackless hill and valley, we're listening to a series of ballads on the theme of romantic love, simple tunes with slow rhythms and adolescent emotions, referring to heads on pillows, first kisses, broken hearts, and tears like rain. Then we come across a giant bull elephant, standing next to a tree maybe fifty yards away from us and cogitating away on the matter of his own internal music, it would seem, thinking, thinking, thinking about something serious—but what would that be? His giant, tumescent penis, the size of a fire hose and unrolled, flopped down, the end resting on the ground, suggests one possible answer.

※

At noon, we come in for lunch: dropping back into the mystery thicket, parking our car, and soon landing at our regular table in the dining tent. As we're placing our orders, two big-breasted American women, young and eager and displaying impressive cleavage with tight tank tops beneath open blouses, walk into the dining tent and introduce themselves brightly: "Hello, I'm Nancy." And: "I'm Julia."

And when one of the Masai warriors and the Simba manager arrive to greet them and show them their tent, they say things like, "Hellooo" and "Thank you!" and "Oh, this is so nice."

They're taken to a tent in the trees on the far side, and soon return on their own to the dining tent where they've been assigned one of the other three tables.

Me: "Long flight?"

Julia: "We . . . actually, we stayed in Tsavo. We were doing some volunteer work there. But it was absolutely not . . . I'm in culture shock right now."

They speak with chirpy voices, expressing a subtle kind of social anxiety with regular bursts of formulaic positivity: "Great! We're happy to be here. Yeah, we're great. Just fine. Really nice." And whenever the waiter comes to fill up their glasses and or to bring out or remove something, it continues: "Thank you." "Perfect." "Oh, thank you."

At this point, I scold myself for not appreciating more the ephemeral phenomena of youth and innocence, but unfortunately I'm fading under the combined onslaught of heat and vacuity; and Karl, meanwhile, is eating his salad and talking about CITES, the international treaty supposedly protecting endangered species, including reptiles, that may serve more fully as a trade facilitator. "CITES has granted quotas for Malaysia to export reptiles, but the EU, for some reason"—takes a few bites of his salad—"has not allowed them in from Malaysia, so this woman says they're brought in via Singapore. . . . That's where the official statistics come in handy. . . ."

But I can't recall another word because now I'm just gazing blankly away in a midday daze. A slow breeze passes through the thicket, creating a susurration of gossiping leaves. But from where we sit in the open-sided dining tent, I can watch the bushes opening up, yielding to grassland, and then the grassland sloping down to the river, which is olive and shiny and wrinkled. The gold of the grass turns paler and paler in the distance, rising into hills that, in the haze, are gray green and then, reaching farther and deeper into the haze, pale blue.

※

It's another morning, and we leave before dawn, looking for giraffes, with Karl's tape of '50s hits clicked into the machine and brushing away the cobwebs. Our headlights illuminate a group of Tommies, tiny things with delicate legs and a prancing style; and then, a quarter of an hour later, we come to a dark, open field surrounded by walls of trees and thickety vegetation, like a bedroom. At first, I see three swaying trees with heads on top, and then the trees and heads turn into three giraffes who look as if they're just waking up after a good night's sleep. The sun hasn't yet risen, and the light is still faint—but seething with anticipation.

Karl: "Yeah, it's the nice type of light which says they're just getting up. It's still early in the morning."

Karl stops the car, snaps off a few shots. Then he starts up the car again, circles around for a better view. The giraffes are still waking up, it seems, and maybe they just can't quite rouse themselves enough to move very much. Karl stops the car, turns off the engine, clicks several more pictures, starts it up again, and begins circling some more for an even better shot.

Pretty soon a small welder's torch cuts into the horizon. That initial penetration is quickly wedged open by a bright red ball—and along with that rising orb of intense brightness, a couple of other orbs, dark ones, have also begun rising in the dawn sky. Karl is trying to get a picture of a giraffe with the rising sun artistically situated directly behind, but those dark, drifting globes keep getting into the picture. "You can see," Karl comments, "it's hard to take a fucking picture without getting a fucking balloon in it."

He moves the car, still trying to get a decent position and picture, and then we head off to catch the wildebeest migration. Last time we looked, late yesterday, they had been spooked by the big crocodile in the river and were stalled at the banks, but maybe they'll be moving today. Maybe they'll start crossing again. . . .

We see a couple of hyenas loping along, looking like they have a definite destination in mind, and then we see a big crowd of running wildebeests. We follow them around a corner, discover in a broad open field a family of nine elephants walking in a row, lit up by the rising sun and swaying slowly as they amble up a slope—and pursued from behind by three balloons. "Just makes too much of a circus atmosphere for me. Bloody balloons."

We discover a single wildebeest, wandering by herself and seeming to be lost and bewildered, and then we see a huge racing crowd of them, hundreds of them— thousands, more like—racing downhill and looking like an endless conveyor belt of animals, moving, mooing, moving, bleating. They just keep coming. Along with the wildebeests are some zebras, also on the move. An ostrich races about crazily, preoccupied with his own feathery concerns. A few giraffes are standing still and tall, slowly chewing their cuds and ruminating about all this frantic activity: *Is it really necessary?* And we drive out onto some high grassy plains, dotted with a scattering of lonesome trees. We finally reach the river where, yes, the wildebeests are massing onto the grassy plain above the river, mooing and bleating and considering whether or not to try racing down the bank and jumping into the water, and deciding not to. It's all followers out there, no leaders.

We park by the river and off to one side now, far enough away to avoid bothering the animals, near enough and well placed enough to get a good view of the piece of the river where the crossing might take place, and even a view of a couple of worn pathways down the steep banks, an obvious chute where the wildebeests should, when the time is right, come shooting down into the water—the animals now massing slowly, slowly, five hundred or a thousand of them spread out and massing onto the plains. But the movement is slow. "There is no real pressure building," Karl says, "No one's pushing from behind. This could take hours."

Wildebeests—with big long foreheads, that greasy droopy mop of a mane over the neck, the black face, horns like bicycle handlebars—slowly collect into the grassy plains above the river, bleating and mooing in place at the top of the steep bank above the river.

When we sweep with our glasses down into the river, we see a massive crocodile sprawled in the sun on top of the sandbar, and the wildebeests, maybe a couple thousand of them now, keep milling around the edge, hesitating, backing away, but very gradually being pressed by more and more of their numbers arriving from over the hill and pushing in from behind. Karl: "Funny how the ones in front say, 'Fuck this. I'm not going to be the first one.' They move back, and the next ones say, 'Why should I be the first with crocs waiting?' You could write a PhD dissertation about wildebeest decision-making."

But the wildebeests are just standing around, peering over the edge of the steep bank, walking this way, that way, backing up, inching forward, backing up. Nobody's going anywhere.

$$\ast$$

Next day, we're up early enough to find ourselves an ideal spot at the river, a promising place just at a curve in the river, from where we—parked, I think, perilously close to the edge—can see the gathering herd on the grassy plain and, because of the river's curve, the steep banks and a couple of likely passages, worn chutes, that drop down the banks and into the water. "Oh, yeah," Karl says, hopefully, considering the situation and fussing with his camera, "they will be going down that chute. This time I think it will happen. . . . Ah, the fuckin' cars in the background. . . . The light will be quite nice. . . ."

He's got his digital cameras ready, the bazooka lens out, some actual film ready in case he wants to shoot in film. And while he's fiddling with all the equipment, it starts. Suddenly they're moving, crowding on the plain and funneling into one chute, then a second, then a third, racing down the chutes (a blossoming cloud of dust rising like smoke out of each one), exploding out of the chutes (bawling mooing bleating), leaping free at the last minute and dropping into the water with a white splash. Then they're swimming, braiding through the water, then churning in the middle up to the sandbar, bounding across that and into more water, and at last climbing out and bouncing up the bank on the other side and away.

"No crocodile activity yet."

"This one seems to be stuck."

"Some of them are going back. What are you guys doing?"

"Must be a thousand or two."

"More than that, I guess. See that lineup there?"

We have the perfect spot and excellent light. We can see them leaping out of the dust. Splashing into the river. Bounding through the water. Walking across the shallows of the middle. Splashing through the far channel before climbing out on the other side.

"Pity there was no giraffe with them. But I didn't see any zebras either."

Just then, the phone rings. It's a Swiss German emergency call from Egypt, and Karl's side of the conversation sounds a bit like this: "*Alle gette siergeten. Yeah, yeah, suote derteheiten WWF effescecte esrea alsounteer does Alexandria de ereschalten battleweike dunte weike esknowasken.* OK. OK. *Wunta machte doesn rigen mannafarmech.* OK."

He claps the phone shut, explains the problem: It was a call from his private investigator gone to Egypt to check out the criminal trade in exotic animals there. "We set up a website to show that our man in Cairo had a private zoo. This guy who set it up said I cannot register a fake website on Google. Then our man in Cairo got a call last night: 'We checked you out. You do not exist. You better watch out.' Now the question is, has this guy informed the other animal dealers? Our man gave out his business card, but then they tried to look him up on Google and he wasn't there."

Meanwhile, the light has gone bad: gray and overcast. Karl says: "It's going to burn away in a couple of hours, but then it will be too bright." So he starts up the car, and we leave the river and the running wildebeests, turn around, and head back out to the open grasslands to see what else of this grand and glorious forever African wilderness we can see, listening as we go to "Love Potion Number Nine."

18: INVESTIGATIONS

Karl and I are sitting in camp chairs overlooking the river, drinking our tea and waiting for the afternoon light to become less harsh before going out to photograph giraffes. "When I built the Mara Intrepids camp," Karl says, "I put in twenty sleeping tents in separate units for privacy, with two to three sleeping tents clustered around one mess tent." It was meant to be a "high-end" luxury tented camp, he adds, for people who wanted to experience something like real wilderness. "But then it was sold, and they added more and more tents. And that concentration is idiotic, but you know that's what businessmen do."

I can hear the rushing water from the river below us—so peaceful—as Karl pauses, sips his tea, continues: "That's what you do: When things are going well, you expand and expand. You have a product, which is meant to be wild, exclusive, and then you decide to make more money, so you ruin the wildness. Then you have mass tourism. It's always the same pattern. You create an in-place, and somebody figures, 'Oh, let's build a luxury hotel.' Bali started like this. First there are the backpackers. Then come the jet-setters. Then mass tourists. The backpackers and jetsetters move on, and the mass tourists move in. The Serengeti now has a Four Seasons."

I've heard this idea before, in one version or another, but what I haven't understood until this moment is one tangential fact about the Simba camp where we're staying. It's illegal, as Karl mentions now, a starter camp, a wildcat camp. It's been put up in a hurry. It could be taken down in a hurry. It's hidden in the thicket for a reason. Meanwhile, someone Karl knows is compiling information for a lawsuit against one of the big tour operators who just built a giant illegal lodge in the Mara. Karl offered to take a closer look at the big one and also some of the smaller illegal camps, such as the Simba, which is one of the reasons we're staying there.

Having casually mentioned all this now, Karl weaves it into the cloth of his previous complaint: "This guy"—meaning the guy who started Simba a few months back as a wildcat venture—"is the same thing. If this guy's doing well and he's allowed to stay here, then next year he'll add more tents. Soon there's fifty to a hundred people coming in, then buses, planes rushing in. I hate it. Wait till the Chinese discover safaris! It's just a matter of time!"

"But," I ask, "how did this camp get started in the first place?"

Karl: "He bribed somebody. Probably gave him a piece of paper from the local council. He's just sneaking under the radar. I see no septic tanks. It's all supposed to be inspected. Supposed to be environmental impact assessment. It's a total choke. Looks good on paper, but you just bribe everybody. That's it."

✳

Next day we notice a little red warning light on the car's instrument panel and also a fuel gauge that says we have to tank up sooner rather than later. So we head out to find fuel at one of the bigger lodges, drive through the gates and into the service area. "There's no more diesel," the man at the pump says.

"No more diesel! Come on! What am I supposed to do?" Karl says. He goes into a series of emphatic declarations ending with, "I guess I'll have to speak to your boss: my friend Balou Patel. See what he has to say about this."

A few minutes later, the whole tenor of the conversation has changed: "We do have some diesel."

We get our fuel and soon have fixed the little red light, too, which was probably a complaint about dust in the air filter. "When you come to Kenya," Karl says, as the diesel is being pumped into the car, "it helps to know the big hotel owners' names and then throw them around if anybody gives you a hard time. And, since they're all Indian names, you better have a good memory for Indian names. Maybe throwing tantrums is the answer." Somehow that comment soon slides into another: that the Asians—meaning people of Indian and Pakistani descent—have taken over the travel and tour businesses in Kenya. "There's something about Asian culture, I don't know what, that makes them have no hesitation about paying bribes, and that's the way to get ahead in Kenya, since the African officials are always ready to accept bribes."

I consider that idea for a moment, then say: "That's a bit of a stereotype, don't you think?"

Karl: "Call it 'stereotype' if you like. It's true."

A couple of hours later, we've stopped at another safari camp, a smaller one, for lunch. Karl, meanwhile, has been admiring the furniture and rugs and *objets d'arts et culture* in the dining hall and lounge area, saying that he thinks someone has very good taste. He figures it is probably the owner's wife. "She must have a good eye. I like these oriental rugs. She's chosen well." It's a spontaneous comment and obviously sincere, and soon after that we meet the very person who chose the decor.

The owner of the camp, along with wife and family—a couple of bored and angry-looking sons, two or three daughters and, possibly, some of their young friends—show up right after lunch. He's tall, slightly overweight, a weak chin, a bit bumbling. Najib Chatterjee is his name, and he studies us both from behind bug-eyed sunglasses as he enters into a brief conversation with Karl. It turns out that

Karl is a good friend of the Maharaja Parapututa of some place in India, and the mention of that friendship sparks a positive response: "Oh, we know Pupet! Ah, yes, we've been dear friends of his for a long time. I guess his son was—"

"Yes, he fell off a horse while playing polo. But he's—"

"Recovered now. Yes. Right. He's well again, thank goodness."

That sort of talk goes on for a while, with Karl mentioning that he started his own camp, the Intrepids. Soon, however, Najib gets, or pretends to get, a couple of important messages on his Blackberry and thus has excused and extricated himself, so that his wife—broad face, thin lips, severely plucked eyebrows partially obscured behind her own sunglasses—picks up the conversational rope. She seems more enthusiastic and forthcoming than her husband, and Karl, who has just recently been admiring the decor of the place, soon—and sincerely, I believe—flatters her deeply about her taste and shopping skills.

"Ah," she says, "Nairobi is such a disappointment that way. You really can't get anything there. You have to go to India or South Africa."

Karl mentions a place in Thailand where you can buy container loads of furnishings. It's very convenient. They pack and deliver. She knows about that, the woman replies, but she still prefers South Africa. "Last time we were in South Africa," she continues, "I bought a thousand kilos of lamps and so on, and I was wondering how to get it back to Kenya. But then I saw we were flying Kenya Airways, so I just said to Najib, 'I'll just take this all back with me.' 'How are you going to do that?' 'You wait.' I then brought it all down to the airport, a hundred pieces, and since we were flying Kenya Airways, I knew that all I had to do was pay a bribe. I said to the lady, 'How much of a bribe do I have to pay to get this on the plane?' She said, 'Tell you what: You can pay the maximum for the regular luggage, and then, for the rest, you just pay me and I'll take care of it.'"

✳

Couple of days later, we drive for an hour or three—I've lost track of time here— until we reach the hippo pool. I could never find this myself, so don't ask me how to get there. But we come to a place where the river runs deep and makes a pool, and there we see a single hippo, big and sausage-shaped, pink at the face with small, bulbous eyes, who turns at our arrival and hustles over to the pool, lowers herself in with a slap and a slide. It feels as if we've surprised a naked lady on her way to the bath.

I soon see the many others, already relaxing in the bath. They appear now as round and inverted ceramic bowls, a bit of head here, another bit there, two eye bumps over there. Made shy by our appearance, however, they quickly submerge and disappear . . . but, curious perhaps, they soon appear again, and now I see there must be a dozen of them in the pool, all mostly submerged, slowly rising, slowly sinking, drifting in the cool bliss of a safe and comforting medium.

As we're watching the hippos rising and sinking in the pool, Karl gets another phone call from his Swiss undercover investigator in Egypt—what he calls "Aegypt," which I think sounds a lot better. Things are not looking good in Aegypt. Things have gotten dicey. Karl's side of the conversation sounds like this: "Zoo director *spilles fucking foxes exporten. Zappara aic?* OK. *Dawweign far Huran vizophrentvebast roal Alexandria.* OK. OK. OK. *Yaza. Iberaabouit.* Don't push too hard. *Der abeveitze schaut da wukesert. Voka sernbouheit.* OK. *Ciao.*"

He slaps the phone shut, starts the car. And then, having seen enough of the hippos, we drive away from the pool and river, and follow a track that takes us into a thicket where we soon discover a small, hidden camp—maybe five tents. We act like tourists, try to get some information, but they say they're all filled up, so we get back in the car and continue driving, following another track through the same thicket until we come to a barrier, which is a simple branch stretched between two forked sticks: entry to another hidden camp. Karl stops the car, says: "Let's play the lost-tourist act."

We leave the car at the barrier, walk a few dozen yards down the trail until we're greeted by someone, who says, "*Jambo.*"

"*Jambo.* . . . We're from the Simba Camp. We thought this road would take us back, but I guess it doesn't. Can you tell us?"

Our innocent questions eventually lead to an invitation to check out the camp, and so we're shown around. It's rough compared to what we've seen so far. A single dirt-floored lounge and dining tent. A few sleeping tents. A generator. Eventually we're greeted by Simon, a dodgy-looking sort who claims to be the manager. Simon and Karl trade cell phone numbers. Simon calls his boss to get a price for a night's stay, and it is indeed a reasonable price—if you're a backpacker on a low budget.

After checking out the two wildcat camps, we leave the thicket, drive through some open grasslands, reach an actual road and soon come to a big wire fence and a large metal gate and guardhouse. We stop there, motor running, looking casually expectant, acting as if we belong. A sullen guard comes up. Wants to know our business.

Karl: "Yeah, we're from the Simba Camp. I need to buy some credit for my phone. I was told you have it here."

The gate is opened, and we drive on through, park the car—having entered the grounds of a giant new lodge financed by (as will I read later, in an article in the *The Independent*) a British family, the Sofats, who run tours from the UK under the name Somak Holidays. The newly built lodge is actually leased, though, by Ashnil Hotels, a Kenyan-based business owned by Mr. and Mrs. Suresh Sofat.

It's an impressive place, if you like that sort of thing: huge and brand new, with its structures consisting of canvas, mostly, erected onto concrete and stone foundations with the assistance of various ropes and timbers and so on. I make out about forty sleeping tents, strung out in a couple of long rows, a swimming pool, some walkways. We pass into the heart of the place, a central deck surrounded by dining and drink and lounge structures, concierge and reception areas, gift shop. "When I built Intrepids," Karl mutters under his breath, "it was all tents. I feel either you have a camp or a lodge, but this mixture of camp and lodge doesn't do it for me. I don't want to be in a half-caste."

We reach the concierge desk, where Karl repeats the same need-to-buy-phone-credit line to the woman there. The gift shop is not finished yet, not ready for business, she says, and that would be the place to purchase phone credit . . . but this discouragement yields to a recommendation that we try the check-in desk, which is manned by three people, all pretending to be very busy for a moment before at last looking up to acknowledge our presence. After some preliminary yes-and-noing, the discussion finally settles on a yes. With the right credit card, they should be able to do us a little favor and sell some phone credit, even though we're not guests at the hotel and ordinarily would not be able to make such a purchase. Someone takes Karl's phone and credit cards, walks away; and now Karl, whose camera has been slung by the strap on his shoulder, drifts away from the desk, drifts casually towards the public areas—dining and drinks and lounge structures—and casually starts snapping pictures.

It's quite a fancy place, actually. According to *The Independent*, it's also illegal and built on top of an important piece of habitat for endangered black rhinos. A significant few of those endangered black rhinos can still be found in the Mara, but their habitat is shrinking fast, in part because of new lodges and their protective fencing. Oh, but it's been for a good cause: tourists and money. Grass and bush and trees have been replaced by concrete and canvas, rhinos replaced by rich tourists hoping to see the rhinos—and where are those horny-nosed little bastards when you need them?

The Mara as a whole has in recent years undergone an unprecedented explosion in illegal lodges and camps, so that the entire place, supposedly one important part of East Africa's great wilderness experience, is now offering beds for more than four thousand tourists in well over a hundred different camps and lodges. More than seven out of ten of those camps and lodges are purportedly illegal. Meanwhile, the burgeoning crowds of people coming out to see the wild animals are seeing fewer of them. The giraffe population of the Mara has collapsed—down by ninety-five percent since 1979—while warthog numbers are down by eighty percent and hartebeests by seventy-six percent.

How have things gone so bad so fast? Expanding farms and human settlements all around the Mara. Deliberate poisoning of predators. And now the March of the Tourist. Legally, the Mara is not a Kenyan national park but rather a community-run reserve. Half the reserve is run well by the Trans-Mara regional council. The other half is run as a money-making enterprise by the notoriously corrupt Narok regional council. "Every prominent Masai wants his camp in the Mara," Karl says. "He teams up with an Indian. The Indian gives him a suitcase full of cash and promises of a steady income for the rest of his life, and then you have another illegal camp."

Since this seems to be the day for depressing experiences, after skulking off with a few hasty photos taken of the grand interior of the Somak Holidays' Ashnil Mara Lodge, we drive on until we reach Karl's old Mara Intrepids Club, the luxury tented camp he built twenty years ago. Now it's the Mara New Jersey Shopping Mall complete with its own major airport. On the tarmac sit three giant planes, loading and unloading long lines of tourists tricked out in the latest Ernest Hemingway outfits, come to have their African safari.

"This is mass tourism at its worst. Who wants to be arriving with five hundred other people?" Karl says, through clenched teeth. "Look at that lineup of people ready to travel!" He concludes this brief comment with the sad if unsurprising admission: "I don't want to come here anymore."

19: GIRAFFES AT LAKE NAKURU

Only a few hundred Rothschild's giraffes are left in the known universe, and some minor portion of that final population has in recent years been deposited for safekeeping at Kenya's Lake Nakuru National Park. Thus, after our time at the Masai Mara, Karl and I headed north in the direction of Lake Nakuru, taking the Aitong-Lemek road, although "road" is a serious exaggeration.

By a little after noon, we had grabbed hold of a second-hand strip of macadam, which drew us into a town and landed us at a place serving gas and Cokes. Driving out of town, we passed a few other options, including: Car Wash and Puncture, Rocky Driving School, Famous Butchery, and Ready Made Coffins (Sweet Home for Eternity). Then we climbed up the Mau Escarpment and into an area of big farms followed by scenic beauty on some of the worst ruts I've ever seen or faced down at high noon in a once-in-a-lifetime nightmare.

Eventually, after a long and harrowing drive, we pulled into the dusty town of Nakuru ("*nakuru*" being the Masai word for "dusty place"), which for me was more of a confusing place, with lots of people, heavy traffic, and no obvious signs pointing in the direction of Lake Nakuru. But Karl dead-reckoned our way into town and out the other side, and soon enough we were rattling down a long road that ended at a park office and gate. Admission paid—low for Kenyans, high for non-Kenyans—we drove through the gate in the later afternoon, the sunlight already yellow and beginning its diurnal decline.

Lake Nakuru National Park is a comparatively small piece of land distributed around a shallow and smallish lake in the style of a doughnut around a hole. The lake varies in size from four to forty-five square kilometers, depending on how shallow it happens to be at the moment, and the land around the park is about two-thirds the area of the lake. I'll let you do the math. It's not really that much land, and we took the dusty track that circumnavigates the lake before deciding we had had enough and wanted a place to stay followed by dinner and sleep.

I don't have much good to say about Lake Nakuru National Park, or the lodge we stayed in, or even the guests at the lodge, including Karl and me, so I'll pause here and give you the opportunity to skip on to brighter times in the next chapter. . . .

✳

Still there? OK. The park had a couple of self-catering guest houses and two lodges. I didn't know what "self-catering" meant, precisely, but I imagined it meant "no hot dinner and cold beer." Meanwhile, one of the two lodges was filled up, so that further narrowed the obvious possibilities until they were focused on a single place with a nice sign out front called the Sarova Lion Hill Game Lodge.

We drove up a curving drive, parked in the car park, and, bags in hand, walked up to the reception desk and spoke to the quite pleasant woman there. I asked for a couple of single rooms—with Karl showing his Kenya resident card.

The price of a single room for a Kenya resident, was, as I recall, around two hundred dollars. Very steep, I thought, given what we had so far seen of the place. At the same time, however, we were tired, hungry, thirsty, dusty, and sweaty, and in any case where else would we stay? Alas, the price of a single for me, as a non-resident, was $390.

At this point, Karl took over. How about a double room? He would get a double on his card, and I would be his guest.

No. No. That wasn't possible, she said, and, after a bit more testing and pressing on his part, she disappeared into the back room. A few minutes later, she returned to the desk. They could split the difference, she said, giving us a double and charging half his rate and half mine. Half a double for me would be $250.

At this point, Karl slapped his resident card onto the desk, leaned over, and said: "Come on! I've lived in this country for thirty years! I know how it works! He's my guest. Just give me a room! I guess I'll have to call my friend Ajit Gavaskar," he added, mentioning the name of the big guy who happened to own the place. He pulled out his cell phone and began pressing buttons. I moved away from the desk, found a comfortable chair in the corner from which to sit this one out. But before Karl got very far with the phone call, he gave up—turned away from desk and walked off in my direction. "Let's get out of here," he said. "We'll find someplace else."

"Where?"

Then, as if distracted by the question or a sudden inspiration, he turned around and returned to the desk: "Let me speak to the manager. Where is he?"

"He's not here."

"Come on! You just spoke to him. I heard you."

At that point, I lost track of the negotiations altogether, but the end result was that they gave us, for some not completely impossible price, a single room with a big bed. We would have to share the bed. By then it was dark, and I was hungry and relieved to have some place, any place, to sleep, but I have to say that there was nothing special about the room. No phone. No air conditioning. Not much of a shower. And the bed—big enough, more or less, for the two of us—took up most of the room.

Still, I was looking forward to the dinner, and I read a promising notice in the room that announced the evening's pre-dinner show of authentic African dance and drumming, down by the pool patio. Authentic African dance and drumming sounded ideal, so I changed clothes and hurried on down to the patio and took my seat at a table in the bar overlooking the patio. Ordered a drink. Soon the dancers and musicians began arriving and before long the show began. A half dozen young men and women, wearing old-fashioned bathing suits with fluffy colored bath towels wrapped around their waists, and driven by a good deal of semi-coherent noise made by non-traditional instruments, proceeded through a series of semi-coordinated activities that consisted mainly of whistling, spinning, chanting, and clapping. Karl showed up as this was going on, sat down at the table, and ordered a beer, commenting: "There's nothing at all authentic about it." That hit the nail on the head, although I was trying to be charitable, working on my second beer and anesthetizing myself mentally with a disorganized interior parade of shabby pseudo-analysis, such as: *Like folk music and folk dance anywhere in the world, this is an attempt at nostalgic representation.*

Karl was more direct: "Jesus Christ. This place illustrates everything that's wrong with mass tourism, from the noise level to the dust in the roads. Maybe the Chinese will go for it."

⁂

Karl's comment about the Chinese was probably stimulated by the fact that there happened to be a lot of Chinese people at the lodge that evening. I left the dance show a few minutes after he did, and, with nothing better to do, entered the dining hall about twenty minutes before it was officially open. I took a seat at an empty table, whereupon the glass doors were shut and locked behind me—so that soon people were beginning to assemble outside. Five minutes before the start of dinner, a very large group of lodge guests, including a major contingent of Chinese (Kenya was having some roads built by the Chinese, so perhaps this group was part of that enterprise—or something else), had accumulated outside the glass doors. The Chinese looked thin and hungry, although their children, some of them, looked fat and full. Dinner was buffet-style, and two opposing rows of hot trays, filled with various options for dinner, were now, one by one, uncovered, the steam and all the delicious scents accompanying it blossoming into the air . . . just before the dining hall doors were unlocked and opened.

It was a mad dash, a frantic, crowded, noisy race to the buffet lines, with the Chinese contingent determinedly, doggedly pushing, crowding, cutting ahead, bound to be first at the food. Most of the rest of us rather meekly and weakly filed in behind, but soon an enormous, boiling crowd was carrying trays and dishing up heaping helpings of salads and fruits, steak, veal, pork, turkey, chicken, french fries, mashed potatoes, rice, cassava, peas, beans, and all the rest . . . then settling back into a hundred different social groups at a hundred different tables, digging in with a roaring gusto while being serenaded, one table at a time, by an affable African guitar player wearing a American-style cowboy hat and singing American favorites from the '50s.

"Whenever I want you," he sang, "all I do is dreeaeeaeeeem, dream, dream, dream, dream, dreeaeeaeeeem."

✳

We were up early the next morning, checked out by dawn, and soon were driving around once more to see if we could find the Rothschild's giraffes. Karl was saying hopeful things, such as: "OK. There might be some sun. That would help. Now we have to find a giraffe. I think it would be nice country to have a giraffe in. There can't be very many."

The lake in the middle of the park, now in the early morning sunlight, looked an abnormal bluish-green, which a tourist pamphlet told me was caused by a blooming algae called *Spirulina plantensis*. On top of the bluish-green algae was a strange, shimmering pink froth that, when we moved up closer, then got out of the car to walk even closer, resolved itself into a half million buzzing and sputtering flamingos. I didn't actually count the flamingos, but I'm saying "half million" based on Karl's opinion that there used to be a lot more. "In the old days," he said, "there were millions of these things. Been several die-offs. Nobody seems to exactly know how many are left—but that there are less than there used to be is no doubt."

Back in the car and driving away from the lake now, and the swamps and marshes surrounding it, we passed across some grassland and into some stands of yellow-green acacia and a few major clusters of giant *Euphorbia candelabrum*, which are trees or maybe big bushes that look like giant candelabras built out of angry cucumbers. We looked and looked for the Rothschild's giraffes, at one point seeing a few of their variegated forms in the distance that turned out to be, on closer inspection, variegated trees. We paused to watch and photograph some white rhinos, two-toned with a mud-wallow line, grazing in some high yellow grass. We also saw plenty of baboons, and even some buffalos and cattle egrets on top of the buffalos. The buffalos were monstrous, built like trucks, black with massive curled horns capping their heads, the horns looking like very peculiar hair-dos. But no giraffes.

Meanwhile, the sunlight had shifted from promising to unpromising, the tourists had started waking up and coming out, and we had a long drive ahead. For those reasons and more, and in spite of not seeing any Rothschild's giraffes at Lake Nakuru National Park, we left the place and drove back into town. Looking for money to cover the next leg of our trip, we turned off the main street and into a network of dirt roads, passing a number of sexy businesses: the Eros Hotel, Desirenet Cyber Solutions, the Honey Moon Club. Then, after getting some cash at a bank, we returned to the paved part of town, drove past Ready Made Coffins and into crowds of people people people, and finally, having extricated ourselves from the traffic and the milling crowds, broke out of town at the top end.

20: GIRAFFES AT SAMBURU

We spent most of the day driving north and east from Nakuru to Maralal, a town in the middle of nowhere, more or less, to have a pleasant break, I imagine, and also look at the zebras. There would be thousands of zebras, so Karl was saying as he drove.

We slipped through the town of Marigat—loitering men, laboring women, goats, corrugated-tin shops, ten million tattered plastic bags on the ground—drove past Lake Baringo, then turned right to climb our way onto the Lerochi Plateau, by which time the road was nearly devoid of traffic and the landscape had become scrubby and arid. Then we passed into real desert, where the road crossed through dry river beds. Three goats ambled down the middle of the road, with high cliffs to the left.

The road became a red dirt track, washed out in places, with, occasionally, camels grazing alongside. "This must have something to do with age," Karl said. "I've driven this road many times in the past. It didn't seem long then. Now it seems bloody long."

Then it turned into a complete shambles, barely passable in places. Where it became entirely impassable, we followed the tracks made by people who had carved out their own tentative alternatives. We passed a little place called the Pop-in Hotel For The Hottest Delicious Food South Of The Sahara And That's A Fact, until, at last, we arrived at the southern edge of Maralal, where the zebras were supposed to be. Karl: "There were zebras all around here ten years ago. There were hundreds if not thousands of zebras here. They're gone. The terrifying thing is how fast it happened. It's just so desolate." After a pause, he added, "There's no long-term future for this country."

Maralal was crowded with people when we drove in—crowds there for a big political rally, we were told, the star politicians having that morning flown in by chopper from Nairobi—and gray plastic-bag litter was scattered around everywhere, looking like dirty snow. But we found our way out to the Maralal Safari Lodge before the afternoon was over, and I liked it quite a bit. It was cheap and unpretentious, with rustic, rambling, old-fashioned rooms with big bathtubs (though no hot water to put in them). The dining area and lounge had windows facing a few backyard zebras, who by the time we arrived had started frolicking, squeaking, and snorting at each other. The politicians who had choppered out to Maralal that morning choppered away again near the end of the afternoon. We listened to the roar and clatter of their machines lifting off and passing over. And by dinner time, the Maralal Fire Brigade truck had arrived to pump water into the zebra drinking pool.

One of the regular guests at the Maralal Lodge used to be Sir Wilfred Thesiger, a British explorer and famous author of *Arabian Sands* (1959) and *The Marsh Arabs* (1964), who after exploring and being a famous author retired to the reassuring isolation of this small Kenyan town, enjoying the zebras and looking for something comparable to the hard desert life of the Bedouin where he originally found a freedom unattainable in civilization. Those last few words I stole from the London *Times* obituary of Sir Wilfred, which was kept at the lodge and protected inside a plastic sleeve, so that people with greasy fingers might rudely read and comment on the obituary during dinner, which I had and did.

I thought to stimulate a bit of dinner-time conversation. "So what do you think people will write in your obituary, Karl?"

"Oh, who cares? It's all over by then."

※

Next morning we were chewing good eggs and sipping bad coffee at the breakfast table. Karl had his computer flipped open and, in between bits and sips of breakfast, was working on e-mail, pausing to describe in English the frantic e-mails now coming out of Egypt.

"My guy in Cairo is getting cold feet, and I don't blame him. Once the animal dealers start talking amongst themselves, he's in trouble. So now I have to give him the benefit of my advice: 'Always meet in public places. And give the hidden camera to your driver, have him leave it on the table.' It's a dirty business, all of it. He doesn't feel comfortable about filming the documents, but until you get real evidence, you have nothing."

Karl continued. "At least he's up," he said. "I always like people who are up at seven in the morning. The Aegyptians, they always sleep in. But he's so worried now that he's writing in Swiss German, which I can hardly read. We don't have a written version of Swiss German, so it's all phonetic and made up. When I was there, they broke into my room, stole all my film, read my computer. I told him, 'Take everything with you. Delete messages. Put a password on your computer.' This is a hot potato, especially in Aegypt. You can smuggle wildlife for thirty years, and nothing will happen to you. But dare to expose it with a hidden camera, and they will nail you."

We left after breakfast, following a nice stretch of flat dirt road, then a jumble of tracks across dry creeks and broken bridges. I saw rugged, toothy mountains in the distance, red clay soil up close, a dotting of green and brown vegetation, a stubble of yellow grass, a scattering of trees that seemed hardly bigger than bushes, and enormous boulders appearing out of nowhere. This was Samburu land, Karl said, and still wild. The Samburu want to hold onto their traditional ways, and the area is known for ambushes on cars. But, he added, it was not so much bandit territory as tribal warfare territory.

The country seemed to me more like the wild West. The road dropped down into a valley, a dry gulch, a broken concrete bridge—the remnants of it to one side—and then three Samburu men with spears were racing in the direction of the road ahead, clearly aiming to head off the car. Karl commented dryly: "It's a problem when they drop the spear and pull out an AK-47." But they didn't, and we sped up.

We saw quite a few people wandering by themselves or in clumps of two or three beside the road or across a field, and many were dressed in the traditional Samburu finery: men with feathers fixed in their hair or banded onto their heads and beaded outfits, carrying sticks or, sometimes, spears; the women with elaborate beaded collars and beautifully bright cloths wrapped around them, walking across this barren, dusty land.

The telephone rang. Call from Egypt. Long conversation in Swiss German that included a few comprehensible fragments, such as "Nigerian trickster." The latest news: an Egyptian wildlife smuggler was offering to sell a gorilla. His e-mail, the Cairo investigator told Karl, read: "I'm happy to deal with you. As to gorilla, I offer you one for $300,000." Selling a gorilla like that internationally was illegal, of course, but Karl didn't think the e-mail would suffice as evidence. It's not enough for someone to offer you animals for a certain price. That person could always claim to be a Nigerian trickster or merely a boaster instead of the criminal wildlife thug and kingpin he actually is.

"What really gets me," Karl went on, "is for CITES in Switzerland to send a clerk to interview a few animal dealers in Cairo, and then declare Aegypt totally clean. And for the EU to congratulate Aegypt on cleaning up its act. I mean that's window dressing in its worst form. 'I will send you maps of places to check out in Cairo.' I said that to John Sellars, the head of CITES. And they never took me up on the offer, so they have no interest in really finding out what's going on."

✷

A severe drought had recently killed a lot of animals in the Samburu Reserve. All the buffalos had been wiped out, along with warthogs and zebras. The giraffes? It wasn't clear how many were left. They used to be scattered in lands all around the reserve, twenty years ago, but had lately been exterminated everywhere except inside the reserve, where we were hoping to see and photograph them. Meanwhile, though, the river running through the reserve, the Ewaso Nyiro, had been drying up seasonally, an event that was very unusual—as was last year's devastating flood that wiped out a number of the tourist camps. We had reserved a couple of tents in one of those ill-fated camps, which was recently rebuilt and, this time around, elevated on stilts.

I liked the stilts, which placed all the tents on high platforms. You walked up wooden steps to get to them, and they were roomy, light, and breezy, just the way tents ought to be. The dining and lounging decks were likewise elevated, with big canvas tops stretched overhead and mosquito curtains that could be dropped down and zipped up. There was also an open lunch patio—outdoor tables, umbrellas, and so on—down at the sandy river bank, which was lined with palm and acacia trees. We sat in a couple of director's chairs at one of the tables down there and ordered Cokes and lunch.

The Cokes were brought down right away, whereupon Karl opened up his computer and started poking at it, while I scratched fitfully in my notebook, listened to the wind off the river whistling across the top of my Coke bottle, and admired the table: an octagon made from two-by-fours and two-by-threes of beautiful, naturally finished hardwood, with a wood pole for the umbrella rising out of the center. "One thing," Karl said, looking up from his computer and tapping the table: "Indonesian hardwood. Illegally logged. You find it all over the world. Typically Indonesian, and it just never changes."

As soon as our lunch was brought down, the table was besieged by excited birds with red underneath, dark heads, and bodies and wings feathered in an iridescent blue-green: superb starlings. I looked across the river to see an elephant on the other side, an old male, whitened by the midday sun. But soon the old guy had disappeared, while three others appeared in the shallow water, two of them eating grass along the river's edge, a third in the water. Then there were four. Now five, all dealing with various issues at the river bank: three of them in the water, facing the bank and kicking against the mud with their feet. I heard splashing and a roar, as one elephant pushed against another. They were digging in the mud, causing mighty splashes as they did, then drinking from the mud hole they had just created.

✳

"What's up, guys?"

We were parked at the river bank in the middle of a large troop of baboons, two dozen or more, with an elephant in the thicket behind, waving his ears and eating. "I like baby baboons," Karl said. "You can see the curiosity in these youngsters."

He started talking to them again: "Hi, guys. You're ugly! You're ugly!"

A pleasant, cooling breeze was blowing through the open car windows, as we watched and Karl photographed the baboons. I listened to some twittering, chirping birds, and glanced over occasionally at the river spread wide and shallow, braided and sand-barred before us. After the baboons, we stopped to watch a herd of elephants, with two playing babies. One went off to chase a bird, then bounded back, put a trunk on the other's back. They started bumping against each other, as the more sedate grown-ups solemnly occupied themselves with eating grass: pulling up clumps of grass, twisting and sweeping them around to knock the dirt off the roots, then twisting and sweeping the clumps once again into an open mouth. There were a dozen or so elephants there, plus about twenty white egrets.

Finally, later that afternoon, we found six giraffes in a group down in a little topographical pocket: four younger ones, a bigger female, a darker and even bigger male. These were reticulated giraffes, which is the only kind at Samburu, with liver-colored polygonal plates caught in cream-colored netting. The six animals were spread out but slowly ambling in the same direction. The smallest one tried to suckle, briefly, but mom wasn't very interested. The bigger young ones all seemed about the same age, and they were finely built and delicate-looking. We followed them all, very slowly, as they moved very slowly in a single file out of the pocket: the four youngsters in the middle, the big male taking up the rear, the female in front. . . .

The phone rang. It was another call from Egypt, Karl summarizing the conversation after he clicked the phone shut. "He said the driver is getting scared. The driver is a good guy. I spoke to him this morning. But Bruno says he's getting scared." Bruno was the name of the investigator.

Maybe the giraffes had been alerted by the phone ringing, maybe not, but just about then they all stopped to think about things. They stood still, looking around in several directions and then staring at us in the car—and as they were staring at us, we caught sight of two more giraffes, far behind but slowly catching up. It was a wonderful, timeless moment there, with a dry wind lifting the sweet smell of dried grass and sifting it through the car windows, the sharp late afternoon sun setting into the car, the slow buzzing of a fly too lazy or distracted or stupid to find the open window, and the giraffes looking dazed, sleepy, maybe hypnotized by the yellow afternoon sun. Then the female shook herself awake and went back to eating the green new leaves off an arid thorny acacia.

The two giraffes behind caught up, so now there were eight, and they were all very slowly moving uphill, away from the river below and up towards the hills, and we followed them very slowly as they very slowly continued in that direction, dawdling like distracted school children, pausing opportunistically at each greenish thorn bush they came across. There was a spectacular view in the background, sun-yellowed plains sloping down to the green-lined river, and in the foreground—looking at the giraffes—I was amazed at how thin their necks were: narrow, ribbony even, and intensely flexible.

We came to an area with high acacia trees filled with weaverbird nests dangling like Chinese lanterns, which provided some good photo opportunities: "Look, it's a nice shot: weaverbird nest with giraffe head in it. You're a baby weaverbird looking out of your nest, you might get a heart attack." And pretty soon—I'm not sure how this happened—instead of eight giraffes, there were nine. Then ten. Then eleven. Soon maybe thirteen or fourteen, and we continued following them for another hour, listening to their stripping of leaves from the trees and the sounds of their chewing.

Back at camp that evening, we drank beer sitting in chairs at the edge of the river. Karl had more phone conversations with his investigator in Cairo, which made him more worried. "These guys have an operation in the desert which they guard well," he said—referring to some of the animal smugglers—"and they move it when they choose to. It all goes via Aegypt into private collections in the Middle East. They are a bunch of high profile dealers who are very active. It's gone a little bit underground from before, but nothing has really changed. . . ."

We were sitting beneath a palm tree, the rustling fronds above making a shattering sound like the clashing of knives.

"That's one of the problems of not doing these things myself. I send someone else out, I'm always worried. Aegypt is a very secretive society and a very dirty society. I'd rather do business in the Congo than Aegypt, and that says something. I'll feel better when this guy is out of the country."

"Maybe you should get an Egyptian to do investigations," I said.

"You won't find one. Even if you find someone who is willing, his family won't let him. They're all intimidated," he said, before returning to the subject of his Swiss investigator: "He's got to find someplace to hide his cameras. If they catch him with them, they throw him in chail."

※

At dawn the next day, we were out again searching for giraffes ("Is that tree trunks or giraffes? Yeah, it's tree trunks"), and we eventually found four of them . . . back in the same general area, I think, where we had seen giraffes the day before, away from the river and ambling through a cluster of acacia trees laden with weaverbird nests. Before they had been ambling uphill, and now they were ambling downhill, slowly browsing as they proceeded, gradually, step by step, in a scattered formation downhill towards the river, with the morning sun illuminating the feathery tips of the yellow grass.

Karl was maneuvering the car to get them between his camera and the sunrise, while all four of the animals were quietly feeding in the same tree, sometimes pausing to look our way but intently feeding in the top of the tree. A weaverbird acacia was in the background, the nests looking like Christmas tree balls.

"What's happening to the sun? It looks like it's going behind the clouds."

Then two of the giraffes began neck fighting, swinging their necks and using their heads as clubs as they took turns pounding each other. Maybe it wasn't serious fighting. It could have been play fighting. Karl stopped the car, stepped out, and soon was crawling on the ground underneath the car.

Meanwhile, the other two giraffes had squared off and were banging their heads against each other as well. I could hear the thudding of head against body. The second pair seemed more serious than the first. They were very serious indeed, I thought then, trading great blows that started with a sweep of the neck, a long elegant curving pendulum sweep that ended with a shuddering thump.

Karl: "Sun is already too strong. It goes fast." He had returned to the car, was snapping pictures out the window. "Somehow even the fighting is graceful with these guys."

He started the car, turned and turned to get a better position, as the two males continued trading blows, the thumps audible even from our distance, which then was about forty yards away. They kept on doing that for a quarter of an hour: standing side by side but faced in opposite directions, leaning into each other, pushing, advancing, circling, backing, leaning in, pressing with the shoulders, with the neck, and then the swooping drop and sweep of the neck—the head turned to strike an opponent with those two solid horns.

It was dramatic and, after fifteen minutes, over. The males separated, walked away, started feeding again. Maybe we had just been watching four feisty teenagers, all hanging out together and sparring, like guys in a locker room punching each other on the shoulder or trading blows in a friendly contest that's by no means an all-out fight.

Karl: "This light, this kind of topography, the vegetation and the giraffe: I mean, it's pretty special."

We saw plenty of other animals that morning, such as impalas racing off into the distance, dik-diks close by and scattering, a couple of Grant's gazelles running, some gerunuks standing on tippy-toe like lithe little ballerinas intent on getting good leaves to eat. . . .

✶

I remember being happy at Samburu, feeling very content and peaceful. Down there by the river, Karl and I watched the evening come in and the stars come out, a whole Milky Way of them, and I looked down to the dark whispering glisten of the river and could imagine the same setting fifty or five hundred years ago. I could imagine coming out there, to Samburu, to our quiet spot along the Ewaso Nyiro, but not because it was on the map or because tourist signs pointed to it, but because I knew it was there, a secret and hidden place, and it was Africa, the real thing. An intact ecosystem. The world as it ought to be. *Fifty years or five hundred years*, I thought: *a blink of an eye.*

I was enjoying the cool breeze sweeping off the river, the chorus of frogs by the river, the peace and quiet of the place, the sense of undisturbed remoteness, and the reality that we were, at the moment, the only guests in camp. Later on that evening, during dinner, two other guests did arrive, a couple from Canada, so I deduced from the T-shirt the guy wore that said *Harley Davidson Motorcycles Canada Since 1955*. He was a bit beefy, had an earring in one ear, and his hair was drawn back into a single stringy braid at the back of his head.

But soon it was late, and I climbed the wooden stairs to my elevated tent, unzipped the front netting, zipped it up behind me, dropped down the white side curtains. After the usual inductions and ablutions, I slipped into bed, and for a long time lay there, progressively relaxing, watching and listening to the curtains of the tent rising and falling as the windswept first one way, then the other, the breathing of the wind, the curtains billowing then slackening, snapping then gasping, and the creaking of the ropes—like the lines of an old ship. It was like going to sleep inside a cloud.

When the intruder came, I was asleep, and I only woke up in stages, first feeling the vibrations of his presence as if they were vibrations in a dream. But they were footfalls on the steps leading up to the platform, I thought, as I came half awake. At first I thought it would be one of the camp's night watchmen, the askaris, checking on things, but why walk up the steps? No, I realized, it wasn't someone climbing the steps after all. It was something else, some other kind of perturbation. There were people creeping around the sides of the platform, I thought—but maybe not. I heard a rustling sound, a tearing sound, and another tearing sound. Then I heard a grinding sound, followed by a deep snort. I rolled over, picked up my flashlight, lifted up the side curtain near the bed, shone a beam through the netting to the outside, and saw a huge and impressively tusked male elephant, eating the grass about halfway between my tent and Karl's, a distance of perhaps fifteen or twenty feet. Since my tent was on stilts, the elephant's head was about level with mine.

I expect he smelled and heard me, and he probably saw the little beam of light penetrating the translucent netting of the tent . . . but did he care? The salad was too tender, too delicious right there. He was having an important eating experience right then, chewing noisily and moving slowly as he ate, one steady step at a time.

I shone the flashlight beam over to the side of Karl's tent.

"Hey Karl, there's an elephant outside your tent!"

"Yeah, I see him!"

But he seemed completely unfazed by us, by our voices and smells, by our buzzing commotion, the creaking tents, the stinking camp. He was a very big elephant, and he was single-mindedly eating fresh green grass in the elephant way, a two-part process showing great dexterity—or trunxterity. Part one: Rip up clump and knock off dirt. Part two: Lift clump to mouth and drop in.

Within a few minutes, the elephant had finished his salad from between our tents and was walking away from the far side of Karl's tent: a tip-toeing shadow in slow but steady flight. Then I saw a bright flash. Karl was taking pictures.

21: GIRAFFES IN NAMIBIA

Nine months later I flew to Windhoek, the capital city and geographical center of Namibia. I spent my first couple of nights in Windhoek at the Rivendale Guest House, and if someone could get rid of the barking dogs at night, I might recommend the place. I rented a four-wheel-drive truck complete with camping gear, spare gas tank, spare water can, two spare tires, gas-powered refrigerator, and so on. The spare gas tank meant I could buy about forty gallons at a time, and that expanded capacity combined with an expansive monetary exchange (small stack of US dollars converting into big stack of Namibian dollars) to mean that I had my first experience of paying more than $900 for a gas station fill-up. It was sobering.

Next day, Karl arrived, took a room in the Rivendale, and the morning after that Dr. Julian Fennessy showed up.

Julian is a major giraffe expert, originally from Australia, with small brown eyes, short brown hair, knobby nose and stubbly chin, who acted in a minor manner and wore youngish clothes: flip-flops, cargo pants, red polo shirt with embroidered Tusker beer insignia on the left breast. He usually forgets people's names, Julian confessed over breakfast at a little pub down the way from the Rivendale, but being an Aussie makes it easy. When you've forgotten somebody's name, you just say, "G'day mate."

Unfolding a map of Namibia and spreading it out on the table, he said: "We're headed out heah." He traced a few lines north and then west, over to the Atlantic coast, then continued: "It's desert . . . but, as I told you in my e-mails, we've had a spot of unusual weathah." He got technical on the subject: The average annual rainfall in the northern desert where we were headed would be around fifty millimeters. So far more than seven times that amount had fallen, and the rainy season wasn't over yet. "While people love rain in Namibia," he added, "I do think it's having a negative impact in certain areas and the like, which are not built to sustain that kind of weathah. Recorded history: the biggest rainfall evah. Evah."

We left Windhoek the next day, heading north and watching the traffic and population thin out and the land transform itself from dark green and brown to light green and red. The red was mountain slowly being ground into rock then stone then pebble then grit and finally dust. The light green was the result of the recent rains, which had produced an endless patina of fine grasses and other random vegetation spreading like a sweet frothy fungus over the normal landscape of red dust, red grit, red pebbles, and red stones. The stones were hard, too, like kiln-baked ceramics, so when you stumbled over them, causing one to knock against the other, the result was an unusual musical clink instead of the usual unmusical clunk.

I mention the stones because walking through a deceptively thin layer of grass hiding a surface of clinking red stones the size of golf balls, baseballs, soft balls, and babies' heads constituted the bulk of our outdoor experience, once we got into the desert, and it was laborious and precarious and downright treacherous, walking was. When we saw some of our first giraffes out there, the experience led to an interesting question that I hadn't thought of but Karl did: "How do they walk on this stuff?"

It seemed to me a silly question, the answer obvious. "Well, Karl what do you do when you walk on it?"

Karl: "OK. But I'm not up there looking out. I have to look down in order to know where to put my feet. Does she have to look down in order to know where to put her feet?"

Me: "Karl, if you spent your life walking in this area you wouldn't be looking down every second either."

Karl: "Yeah, but OK. But then tell me, there must be times when they put their foot down on something. Slip, twist an ankle."

Julian: "I'm sure they'll do it and make a mistake a few times and then realize that. . . ."

In other words, Julian didn't know either. And actually, it was a fair question, since a giraffe only needs to slip once and sprain an ankle before becoming vulnerable to predators. A broken leg would be the end. How do the giraffes manage to navigate such an unstable terrain, even run on it, without sooner or later killing themselves?

※

Julian did know how to tell the males from females at a distance, and although I more or less by then knew this also, it was still nice to hear it from an expert: "You look at those horns. The males have the big, thick horns. Like this one over heah. Much thickah. Taller normally. Not much haiah on top."

Me: That's because they've been—

Julian: "Fighting. Rubs off. And the cows' horns are much thinnah. You can see this guy, you know, straightaway, see the really thick horns. Really solid. Two stumps. And then if you look at the one to the left. Much thinnah. With some fluff on top."

But they were beautiful animals, actually, and very different from the East African giraffes we had seen so far. These were Angolan giraffes: a different subspecies or, some would say, species. Their coloring looked to me brighter and lighter than what I had seen with the East African giraffes, though maybe the brightness and lightness were the result of a bright sun. But they looked like chalk and cheese, I thought. *Chalk-and-cheese* was Julian's way of saying apples-to-oranges, but I preferred it as a way of describing their color scheme: the chalk being a whitish or cream-colored network between the plates, the cheese being the yellowish or brownish-yellowy plates.

It was chalk and cheese walking on top of red rocks hidden by a pale green froth. Julian had never seen the desert so green before, he said—and I was already frustrated with it, imagining that Karl's photographs for our book would seem to show giraffes walking on fresh grass instead of the red-rock desert we had traveled all this distance to find. That was one of my two major concerns, the other being how to get those skittish creatures to stand still long enough that Karl could get some good pictures.

Every day we went on a *rekkie*—as Julian liked to say—and our first rekkie took us through a landscape of green-covered hills (and, in the distance, rust-red mountains looking like flat-topped fortresses or, sometimes, round-topped breasts with perfect nipples on top) and then to thirteen giraffes, standing stock still in a state of vigilance, looking like cell phone towers topped by four short antennae: two ears, two horns.

We stopped the car, got out, began walking slowly towards them, giving Karl, with his camera out, the lead. They saw us, of course, so the question was: How close could he get and for how long? As Karl moved in, us behind him, one by one they began to turn, slowly, until all of a sudden, with three or four turning, they had reached a consensus. They took off. But they didn't run too far, and so we tried again. Again we sighted them in the distance, standing still and keeping an eye out, make that twenty-six eyes out, vigilantly watching us with their backs to a steep hill. We were driving on a track maybe a half mile below them, and this time we tried to outsmart them. Julian let Karl off first, saying, "What do you want, Karl? Talk to me."

"Yeah, I can try. But, as I said, with those hills in the background you don't get a silhouette. I can try a few shots just to see."

Karl quietly opened the car door and secretively slipped down into a minor, brush-lined creek bed. The plan was for him to creep forward a little, under the cover of the brush, until he had reached a good position to take pictures. Then Julian drove maybe a quarter of a mile farther, stopped the car. He and I got out of the car and began stumbling slowly but obviously across an open stone field towards the giraffes, staying in their full view, moving in a long curve that would bring us onto higher ground, where we might eventually be above the giraffes and able to press down on them, down the slope and in the direction of where Karl with magic camera was hiding.

Bright idea, maybe, but not bright enough. The giraffes had seen Karl. Not too long after Julian stopped the car, and he and I began proceeding on foot over the rocky field, they turned and ran up and over the hill.

※

Another day, another rekkie. This time it was near sunset when we spotted a small group, maybe a half dozen of them, standing on a hillside and about to be illuminated interestingly by the slanting rays of the setting sun. We had earlier that day tried another one of those you-go-openly-here-while-Karl-sneaks-furtively-there moves to no avail.

But now, this time, and possibly because the light was going and Karl and I were desperate for a good photograph, Julian just drove the truck right off the track and began slowly grinding in four-wheel-drive up the stone field. This maneuver involved a lot of bouncing and banging, and since the stones were only half visible and included a lot of invisible spots where stones were not, a good deal of dropping and crashing as well. The giraffes watched us as we slowly bounced and crashed and ground up the hill in their direction, all the while looking as if they were about to panic and run.

Julian thought they might actually be more anxious about the quiet stalking of a two-legged ape than the cacophonic approach of a four-wheeled box, but just about then, and with a great pneumatic bang, one of the tires blew. Unable to move farther, we all climbed out of the truck, slammed the doors shut. Karl, camera out, started walking towards the giraffes. He was considering, I suppose, the remote chance that the big critters might pause for one or two seconds before fleeing. But Julian and I ignored that problem altogether and turned to the problem at hand: noisily cracking open the rear hatch of the truck and noisily pulling out all the necessary gear for changing a tire.

It was sad, since the giraffes had been so nicely lined up there, and the light had been so nicely angled and lighting them up just so. So sad! Too bad! But we couldn't do much without four functioning tires on the vehicle, so Julian and I just gave up on being quiet altogether and proceeded to pump up the jack, *ahrech ahrech ahrech ahrech ahrech*, and wrench off the lug nuts, *crenk crenk crenk crenk crenk*, then rattle off the wheel, all the while noisily yakking away.

Me: "You still don't know a thing about their social organization, do you."

Julian: "No.... Of course, they're perceived to have a fission-fusion relationship, where they, you know, groups come together and go apart. I think there's stronger bonds than we think. Especially, I think, along the matrilineal line."

Me: "Like elephants?"

Julian: "Like elephants. Maybe not to the same degree. But I've . . . the whole crèche system with babies. You know, is it aunties? It would make more sense than a random. . . ."

Me: "But you don't know."

Julian: "No."

Me: "You don't know anything."

Julian: "No. I'm fucking useless, in all honesty. But if you'd like to fund me, my number is. . . ."

We rattled on the spare, wrenched on the lug nuts, *crenk crenk crenk crenk crenk,* and so on. Meanwhile, the giraffes, instead of running away, were at first standing there and watching us, as they had been, and then slowly, slowly, slowly, they began moving closer, craning their necks to get a better view. I suppose they had never seen people change a tire before.

Karl was all the while moving closer to them and taking pictures as he went. I tried to persuade him to take even more, calling out: "The light looks good. I think that's a good angle over there. Hey, try that one, Karl!"

✳

Julian had done his PhD research on giraffes in this corner of the world, so he knew the area, which helped us avoid getting lost during a rekkie. Julian had also gotten us a good discount at a tourist outpost called the Palmwag Lodge, where we slept in tents at night, ate our breakfasts in the morning, our dinners in the evening, and drank Tuskers at the bar after dinner—chirping and chattering, talking mostly nonsense but sometimes sense and sometimes about giraffes.

Julian: "Part of the research—one of the critical things we used to do was monitor them every single minute over an eight-hour day, and I don't think I've ever done anything more boring in my life. You know these giraffes feed feed feed feed. Then about an hour later, oh, they walk for a minute. Then they feed feed feed feed. So it's quite funny. Earthwatch volunteers, they used to come along, and they used to get really frustrated in the first day, but after the first day, when they actually talked it through together, then they realized, 'Well, what is the life of a giraffe about? And how can we fit that question into the context . . . for the next two weeks when we're studying them?' And then they realize, 'Oh, they actually do things in between the feeding. It's not just sitting there. They go on to chew their cud, and why do they do it at that time of the day, why do they sit with their necks facing away from the sun?' Et cetera, et cetera. And so that's the behavioral part that really gets people interested. But everyone wants to be a game ranger, eh? Everyone wants to come to Africa. They have this sexy idea, and then they come and do research, and after a day, they're like, 'Oh, can we go see lions now?'"

Karl: "The lions just lie in the bush, too, eighteen hours a day."

Julian: "Oh, for crying out loud! They have to be one of the most boring animals, outside of that hour or two when they're, you know, doing something."

Me: "You talking about lions now or giraffes?"

Julian: "Lions."

Me: "Giraffes are up there on the boredom scale."

Julian: "Yeah, but at least they move, rather than just sitting there, or lying there. They stop feeding, and they chew their cud. Energy-related. So they don't lose heat and all of those things. Don't move too much because you're losing energy and heat at the same time. So we're the clever ones. We're the ones rushing around in the middle of the day, the other animals quite happily just munching along."

That might seem a little random. You want bigger random? One morning I showed up for breakfast at the breakfast patio and found Karl, already finished with his morning eggs and coffee, and talking to a pigeon. The pigeon was balled up quietly on a rock just outside the patio, and Karl was seated at a table on the edge of it, where he could keep an eye on the pigeon and the pigeon could keep an eye on him. Karl had his computer open, poking away at it, and every few minutes he would pause to lean over and look at the pigeon, then say things like: "You OK? Coming around? Pretty rough morning start, huh?"

Pigeons don't normally sit still to listen when people talk to them, but this one, Karl explained, had flown headlong into the well-cleaned pane of glass separating the inside dining area from the outdoor patio area, thereby knocking himself down and, momentarily, out. Now he was sitting there, quivering a little, and trying to reassemble his wits. He was not yet ready to try flying again.

This ongoing if one-sided conversation with a pigeon seemed to show a less obvious aspect to Karl's personality, a sensitive part, I thought, that I liked. It wasn't baby-talk. None of that precious falsetto you sometimes have to endure when people act as if their dogs or cats are fur-challenged babies. No, I thought the conversation, or the directed monologue, had a reasonableness about it that I found it strangely appealing. It seemed mature, a man-to-pigeon talk about the world that nevertheless showed a simple kind of empathy or sympathy or—oh, what's the word I'm looking for here?—tenderness.

"Not ready? You take your time. You'll be better soon," Karl would say encouragingly, then go back to stabbing fingers at the computer.

Julian soon showed up, though, and, after he absorbed an abbreviated breakfast, we all left, having planned an all-day rekkie off to the north. As we gathered our things together and got ready to leave the patio, Karl leaned over for one final word with the still not-moving bird. "You're still not flying? We're going to leave you, but you'll be OK, I guess."

✳

The all-day rekkie involved a long drive north that eventually took us past a rough little town called Sesfontein, with sheep and shacks and a little shop filled with Cokes and drinks, and from there we came to a new and advanced form of desert. The dirt track turned into a sand track, and the sand track drew us into the middle of an immense sand valley, flat and surrounded by rounded hills, which looked to be miles away, and mountains beyond the hills. Small green bushes and pale green grasses were growing in the sand valley, and dozens of springboks were racing through the bushes. Six ostriches, one after the other, ran across the road in front of us. The sand track made a left turn at one point and eventually led us, still in the middle of the flat sand valley, to a small lonely mountain looking like a giant's elbow breaking up through the flat sand: a rugged rocky kopje, actually.

We stopped the truck, got out, ran a rekkie up to the rugged rocky kopje's rough and rocky top, which took about ten minutes, and there we saw a few stubby trees and a scattering of bushes, grasses, and white butterflies. It was peaceful, with a long, steady breeze blowing, a clear blue dome of sky overhead, and you could look out across the great flat sand valley for miles in any direction, study it forever. Other than ourselves, there was no one! In fact, aside from two parallel lines of yellow cutting across the valley below, representing the tire tracks through the sand, there was no sign whatsoever that humans had ever been in this valley. No sign anywhere. None. Nothing. Nada. No mark or memory of human civilization or the human endeavor past or present, except for the telephone.

The telephone, an old-style rotary dial device from the '50s, I guess, but looking eternally stylish, as if an angel had spontaneously invented and deposited it there on top of the rocky kopje, was protected from the elements by its own kiosk, which was made of an oil barrel with a curved metal roof bolted on top. Beneath the curved metal roof and next to the telephone were two telephone books and a visitors' book, plus a ballpoint pen for writing in the visitors' book. A small antenna was attached to the oil barrel, and connected by wires to the telephone, making it official: radio telephone from the middle of nowhere to the rest of the world.

From up there, though, the middle of nowhere looked sufficient, and I turned my attention away from the telephone and back to the long-distance view of the sand valley surrounded by a distant rim of hills and mountains. The hills were sprinkled with a touch of pale green, and the pale green spread itself flat and evenly across the sand valley, broken only by the wavering slice of those two parallel tire tracks, going from here to there, snaking north to south, and by the flying saucer landing circles.

Julian said they were fairy circles.

"Aha. And what is the explanation for them, other than fairies?"

"They're termite-related."

"Termite-related?"

"Yeah. The termite colonies release a certain toxin. And the theory, the best theory, is about to be published very, very soon."

"But what a gorgeous, beautiful spot."

"One of God's windows on the world."

The telephone was someone's idea of conceptual art, and I leafed through the visitors' book to find that the last visitors to sign in, George and Alice McCormack, had stopped by while driving from Cape Town to Uganda about a month earlier. I signed in for us:

> April 16, 2011. Karl Ammann, Julian Fennessy,
> and Dale Peterson, looking for giraffes, came to
> this beautiful place and saw white butterflies over
> a valley of pale green grass with fairy circles.

Back on the track and continuing north and west, we eventually left the valley and soon came to a place where the sandy track disappeared. It still wasn't hard to figure out where to drive because by then we were careening down an ancient canyon, with cracked and splintered rocky walls on either side, moving down an ancient riverbed and then, after a while, coming into a wider rocky delta where Julian, at least, knew what he was doing and where we were going.

We followed the ancient river delta until at last we reached a contemporary river, the Hoanib, which was surrounded by grasses and lined with some big trees and much muck with, occasionally, elephant footprints the size of dinner plates. The wet season had ended up there, Julian said, and the river had started drying up. In another month, it would be dry enough that we could follow it west to the coast. We couldn't now. But, he thought, we might try driving east.

Even going east, the river was still completely wet in some places, but it was a very complicated kind of wet, with rocks and roots, islands, long stretches of sand and gravel bars, and mucky banks covered with a cracking layer of dried silt that hid deep-sticky swamp sometimes and shallow-firm swamp other times. It was the deep-sticky kind we hoped to avoid.

Julian slipped into four-wheel drive, and we began churning and spinning our way up the river. Every once in a while we stopped to get out and examine the dried silt up close, to probe its quality and nature with sticks, our feet, our eyes, our brains.

"So, Julian," I said, "what do we do if we get stuck out here."

"I dunno. I lived out here for five years, and it was absolutely fine."

"Ah, I see."

"You need to have an older vehicle, not one of the new ones. An older one that you can look underneath the bonnet and maybe go and fix it. Otherwise, what happens if you do get stuck out here, you just wait. Stay with the car. You know, you give it a little while, and then if there's no luck like at this moment, yup, you have to start walking. And you pick your area you walk to because there's more likely to be traffic back up on the road behind us, at this time, than if you walk along the river. Then you'll probably get taken out by a lion or an elephant. So that's overrated."

"The river?"

"That would be the shortest route to civilization."

"But it's, ah. . . ."

"Maybe a little bit more dangerous. I've done it, and it's not fun. And it makes you think a few times. Yeah, but I mean, the moral of the story is: Let's not get stuck."

✦

Driving up the Hoanib River, we passed a number of huge and ancient-looking trees, with gray and cracked bark: Ana trees, Julian said, otherwise known as *Faidherbia albida*. And we nearly drove right past a large fallen log, which, as Julian pointed out, was actually a large giraffe lying down, muddy and gently splashed with a lace of sunlight and shadow drifting through an overhead sieve of desiccated leaves.

Even after Julian pointed out that the log was a giraffe, I still saw more log than giraffe. I thought some photos might make an interesting display of the camouflage effect, if Karl could ever make the giraffe look like something more than a log. There were cliffs just beyond the river there, high and gray and looking tormented in some places, downright shattered in others, and I thought the right photo ought to have the cliffs in it, too, just to show how rough and tortured the landscape actually was.

We drove as close as we thought we could get without spooking the giraffe, then Karl quietly cracked open his door and discreetly slid down to the mud, crawling towards the giraffe and taking pictures as he went . . . but altogether the scene was too dark, too obscured by the shadows, too confused by the bright clumps of light practicing martial arts with the shadows, and, anyway, I thought (as the giraffe finally, having decided he had had enough of us, stood up and ambled away), this one was too small, too immature to make a very dramatic picture.

"Too small, too young," I said.

"I don't think so," Julian said. "Look at the scars on his neck, his hips, scars on his horns from fighting."

"I just assumed he was young because he's so small."

"Those trees are really tall. So are the cliffs behind the trees."

"Really?"

"The trees are about thirty meters tall."

"So how tall is this guy?"

"He's probably four, four-and-a-half meters tall."

"What's the tallest giraffe on record?"

"Just under five meters, I believe."

So that was that, although I was still sure Karl had just acquired a memory chip full of weak photos that would serve no particular purpose—and with all the wetness around, how were we ever going to get the desert shots Karl and I had come to Namibia for? Julian, meanwhile, was having fun running the rented four-wheel-drive vehicle over the kinds of terrain and in a style a person would never run a vehicle over and in if he owned it. We slipped and slid and sailed across the muddy matrix, taking our chances, always looking for the route forward. Solid sand over there? How do we get from here to there? Can we cross that tongue of silt and not slip into the gullet of quicksand or stomach of despond?

We came across another lying-down giraffe on the river bank. Dead, it turned out, and indeed we had smelled this one before we saw him. "Poor buggah," Julian said.

Giraffes are big animals. Only elephants get bigger. But you need to get up close to one of the big males to appreciate fully the size of a giraffe. This one was lying on his side, collapsed lengthwise like a big tree, the body inflated like a balloon, the end of the tail gone (probably cut off by some enterprising person, since the tail hair is worth money), and the most vulnerable parts of the face starting to decay: the mouth a gaping hole, the eyes two big seething flowers of maggots. There was a deep hole in the sand near his back feet, signs of a frantic struggle to right himself after going down for the last time. But there were no signs of death from violent cause, and Julian believed that the old male had died of old age or illness.

We found cat prints around the body, but they were from a smaller cat of some sort, not a lion. It didn't appear as if the big scavengers, lions and hyenas, had yet arrived.

The scene was not easy to look at, even less pleasant to smell, but I took a moment to examine a foot. Giraffes have cloven hooves, so people commonly say, but biologists sometimes describe them as being artiodactyls. *Artiodactyl*: meaning even-toed, or, in the case of the giraffe, two-toed, rather than, in the case of you and me, for example, five-toed. What's the difference between split-hooved and two-toed? None, you might say. It's merely how you think of it, you might insist. But now, in examining this dead animal's foot, I saw how fitting and accurate the two-toed concept really is. The split hoof, I saw, was actually a pair of enlarged toenails, arranged side by side with a gap between them at the front. And when I examined the bottom of the foot, I actually saw the paired bottoms of two giant toes, each being about the size and texture of a big human's foot bottom.

As I was looking at the foot, I began to notice all the ticks swarming over the animal's body and leg. Then I began to see that several of them were moving in my direction. Soon, I began to see that they were actually leaping off the giraffe, into the sand, and walking towards me. One little tick in particular was racing at the front of the pack, and I tested his determination by keeping a few steps ahead while shifting direction first one way, then the other. When I shifted direction, he did too. This feisty little guy was convinced he had found the next meal and determined not to let it out of his smell.

✷

We drove on, continuing for another half hour or so until we came to the end of the river or, at least, the end of where Julian intended to drive on it.

He parked the truck halfway up a high embankment, and we walked the rest of the way up, discovering at the top a great, flat, sandy plain that seemed to go on for a long time before running into some mountains. At the near side, hardly more than a few yards from the riverbank, was a large and shallow pond constructed from concrete and looking like a giant's birdbath. Julian said it had been built by the Namibian Department of Environment and Tourism as an elephant water hole. Next to the water hole were some concrete barriers protecting pipes and pumps and supporting solar panels. The solar panels were meant to generate enough power to suck water out of the ground and pump it through the pipes and into the pool, which was meant to tempt the elephants away from other places in the desert where people sometimes liked to be, which was supposed to reduce human-elephant conflict and make everyone happy. That was the plan. It wasn't working so well, Julian thought.

Still, aside from the birdbath and the pipes and pumps and solar panels, we had come to a place that looked gorgeously wild and barren, and a whistling wind made it feel even more so.

There was the great sandy plain, stretching on for miles.

There were the high mountains in the distance.

There was, closer, a dramatic wall of rough and wrinkled cliffs, gray and odd-shaped and looking like they had been built out of elephant parts.

The river valley below was tight and muddy, tree-lined and shadowy where we had gone, but where we hadn't gone, it widened out and gave us a long view of the valley ahead, sandy and olive-colored with vegetation.

Most distinctively, however, on our side of the river and farther along the edge of the sandy plain, a long runner of pale dry silvery grass wavered in front of a giant palisade of high sand dunes.

At last, we had found the perfect place to photograph desert giraffes. It looked like a desert. It was a desert in the classical sense, the photographic sense: a desert with tortured rock cliffs here and high sand dunes there. It was the kind of setting that anyone, after seeing a picture of it, would be bound to think, *Aha, this is a desert!* All we needed now were a half dozen or a dozen giraffes.

Since there were none, we chose to have a picnic instead. We walked back down to the car, which had been left in the shade of a river-bank tree and overlooking the mud of the river, and found a shady spot to sit and enjoy some water, oranges, and sandwiches. It was a pleasant respite, and after the picnic was over, we discovered, as if the gods themselves had finally looked down from heaven and decided to come through, eight giraffes in the distance, down in the open valley ahead, and slowly ambling our way. We watched them through binoculars for a while, and then we climbed into the truck and drove down into the valley, first pausing to drop Karl off at a place where he could stealthily climb up the bank and find a hiding spot within sight of the sand dunes and the narrow field of silvery grass in front of the dunes. I stayed with Julian in the truck, as he drove back through the valley and worked our way behind the eight giraffes, so that, applying the nuisance of our noisy, clunky vehicle, we might encourage them to move up the bank and onto the stretch of grassy plain that swept across in front of the dunes, where Karl with his camera would be waiting.

It was a stunning scene. The giraffes gradually cooperated, climbing up the bank and then walking slowly over the silver-grassed plain in front of the dunes. I couldn't see Karl out there, but I knew he was hiding in a good spot and taking pictures.

Julian and I sat in the truck for a long time, watching the giraffes, who by now had congregated in front of the dunes and were not doing very much, although, as Julian noted, there was "a naughty male chasing around a female, trying to take advantage of a stressful situation for them: bloody clevah."

But other than that, the giraffes had more or less settled down, not doing much other than standing there and periodically looking over to a spot in the grass where some big ape with a mustache was trying to hide while doing something strange. After another quarter of an hour passed, Karl gave up on trying to hide. He stood up and began walking slowly in our direction, pausing every once in a while to face the giraffes and take another photo, until he reached the truck.

"How was it? You get any good pictures?"

I thought we had done all we could do, and Karl was in fact pleased with the shots. Sort of. But the afternoon light was harsh and contrasty, he said. The giraffes had gotten boring, he said, just standing there and looking at him. And he had taken a lot of shots through the grass, which might produce some good scenes, with a rough and unfocused border of close-up grass at the bottom—but maybe not. I thought not.

"Well, let's go back then."

He got back in the truck, and we drove farther along, let him out at a place where he would still have a good shot of the dunes, and then we circled back and Julian, very carefully now, began closing in on the giraffes, using the car to herd the giraffes in the style of a sheep dog herding sheep, and the giraffes fell into the routine. Pretty soon they were running in front of the dunes, and Karl was snapping shot after shot after shot. It was a perfect moment, I thought. The grass was bright silver, the dunes a pale gold behind the running giraffes, and Karl was taking it all in, all the color and drama and form unfolding before us: a brilliant splinter of time in a fragile universe.

"I think we have it!" I said. "That's it."

"It's all about the story, isn't it," Julian said, slyly, adding ironically: "You can leave us here to die, but take the camera, please. It's got the pictures in it." Then, less ironically: "Do you think Karl is happy now?"

"I do. I'm sure he is. . . . He ought to be. . . . He'd better be."

⚹ AFTERWORD: THE END OF THE WILD

BY KARL AMMANN

This book is about traveling through a vanishing world, saying good-bye to biodiversity, watching as the human presence mushrooms and pushes the planet's wild animals and wild habitats away and over the edge. It's not the end of the world. It is the end of the wild. The most terrifying aspect of the decline has been its speed—how fast it all happened and is happening—and how this only seems to be appreciated by a few people, mainly those who travel to the same areas regularly and thus are able to compare present with near past. I am one of these people. It has been an unsettling, frustrating experience. And when I project further decline at the same rate I have been observing for the last two decades, it all gets very depressing indeed.

Every now and then I meet a kindred soul and we compare notes and agree on the status quo and the cause and effect. First-time visitors to many of these already devastated areas, however—those who arrive with no sense of what once was— are often still impressed after seeing a few elephants or giraffes with Mt. Kenya in the background. Even Dale for the most part lacked knowledge of what it all looked like ten or twenty years ago, making it challenging to compare past and present, and to imagine what it will look like in the future.

The pattern is the same almost everywhere. Only the details vary from place to place.

⚹

Giraffes and elephants in Samburu. On our last visit to Samburu, Dale and I interviewed one of the guides at the tented camp where we stayed. Julius Lesori is in his thirties and comes from the Wamba area in the foothills of the Matthews Range farther north, in what is considered a very remote corner of Kenya. We talked to him about giraffes. Julius said when he was a boy and used to herd cattle he would see giraffes every day, but his children have never seen a giraffe in their lives. If he wanted them to see a giraffe, he would have to bring them into the reserve. *That's* what it feels like on the ground. Scientific census data for the decade and a half between 1998 and today shows that the total population of Reticulated giraffes has crashed, dropping from twenty-eight thousand to some three or four thousand.

I know from personal experience that the crash in wild animal populations at Samburu is not limited to giraffes. Some ten years ago, I would head out every

February to the Buffalo Springs plains and photograph the very photogenic Grevy's zebras. This would be the time when males were sparring with each other over access to females; it was very challenging trying to capture some of the action. I loved it.

I have been back to the same area in February for the last few years. These days, I find maybe one or two territorial males waiting for some females to come along. Total numbers for the Grevy's subspecies in Samburu are now down below two thousand, having declined some fifty-five percent in the last five years and continuing to collapse. Most likely a female herd will never come along to entertain the lonely male; and cross-breeding with other zebra types, a mark of desperation and the essential end of a species, has now been reported from other parts of the Grevy's range.

The Samburu buffalo just about vanished—supposedly six survived—during a bad drought in 2009. Some of the wildlife living outside the protected area had the good sense to move into the reserve, near to the river. Most of them might have survived the dry spell had it not been for the livestock, brought in from all directions, to compete for what was left in terms of grazing. The invasion of Samburu started with herders coming in at night from all the surrounding villages where the density of people and livestock has increased drastically in recent years. One night I heard a lion roar; within seconds shots were fired, apparently as a warning: *Do not come near my cattle.* A few weeks later no warning was needed: Donkeys, goats, cows were by then roaming into the park without even protective herdsmen, so clearly the threat of lions and other predators was no longer a concern. On game drives during this period, one came across dead cows every few hundred yards. I went to see the warden, pointing out that I had not paid the park entry fee to see livestock. His response was: "These are our people. We cannot prevent them from trying to save their animals, and if that means entering the reserve, so be it." He had no consideration for all the employment the reserve creates for the very same people.

In the end the inevitable happened. The livestock died first, pretty much all of it, and then the wildlife followed. I filmed one dying buffalo who walked right up to the camp with her calf standing nearby. It is not rare for wild creatures in these parts to seek human company to die. They seem to instinctively feel that with humans around they do not have to worry about predators tearing them apart while they succumb. They haven't figured out that humans are the reason for their plight in the first place. Rangers came and pulled the carcass away, so tourists would not see or smell it.

The drought devastated most of the animal populations in the reserve. A lot of the warthogs died. Most of the Grevy's zebras and most of the giraffes have gone. But there are more elephants than ever before at Samburu, so today Samburu is one of the key destinations to watch elephants, to sit in a car right in the middle of them. That must be a good thing, right? Wrong. I am not a scientist with all the latest research at my fingertips, but in talking to Samburu guides like Julius, I have been told that there is much more human pressure around the park today— including poaching for ivory—than ever before. The elephants know that only in the park are they safe. So they move in from the surrounding areas more regularly and stay longer than they used to.

The result has been a serious degradation of the tree cover along the river's edge and even in some areas away from the river. Elephants are hard on trees. The first time traveling to the area with Dale we spent time at a camp that is electrically fenced in but right on the river and shaded by a fantastic stand of trees. Now, just outside the fence there is hardly a tree left that is intact or that has a long-term chance of survival.

The problem is not too many elephants. The problem is too many humans. Human pressure is increasing drastically across Kenya, even in marginal areas where humans have moved in to try farming or grazing livestock. Wildlife used to call these marginal areas home. No longer. The Kenyan population is increasing by more than four percent annually, amounting to around a million new people each year. The United Nations estimates that the current population of about forty million (with many resources already scarce and ethnic groups around Samburu vying over water and grazing land) will reach 160 million by 2100. What hope is there for maintaining wildlife and intact ecosystems? Who is dealing with the human time bomb? Not the "conservationists" who, like the rest of us, passively watch the end of the wild.

The trend of fencing in large private reserves and farms, pioneered in South Africa, is considered one way to protect wildlife populations. But how much longer can this be an option, when arable land is one of the key commodities craved by local populations? The future will bring conflicts at every level between wildlife and farmers and humans over scarce resources. At present, these large and some not-so-large tracts of private land get fenced in to offer tourists a glimpse of what wilderness used to be before the fences went up and created a series of glorified zoos. Human management has taken over from evolution. A ranch manager decides if his area can sustain eighty elephants, and when the number goes over, surplus animals are chased out. The local population on the other side of the fence threatens retaliation, accusing rich landowners of turning their problem into that of their neighbors. Politicians threaten lawsuits on behalf of their constituents. And because animals cannot vote, the losers are wildlife and wild habitat.

In some cases, authorities have embarked on projects involving fertility control to keep the elephant populations down. It is not easy, however, to inject contraceptives into the same females at regular intervals so this does not seem to be the answer either. It would be much easier for NGOs and ranchers to include serious family planning programs in their community-based conservation projects, to educate local communities about the problem of too many humans competing for too few resources. In fact, last year the newspapers reported that a Kenyan politician offered all his female constituents a stipend for each additional child they added to his voting group. There was no outcry.

✶

Dale touched on the subject of ivory in the chapters describing our travel through the Democratic Republic of the Congo (DRC). I would like to give a more analytical assessment of what we saw at the Okapi Breeding Center in Epulu and during the trip to Kisangani, as well as recent developments in the Bili. Dale wrote of the okapis we photographed, stroked, brushed, and fed at Epulu. They are all now dead. The story behind their demise is chilling and instructive.

Early on the morning of June 24, 2012, a group of heavily armed Mai Mai (a local rebel group) attacked and overpowered a small group of park rangers. They reportedly looted and burned RFO facilities, raped dozens of women, abducted scores of people, and murdered six people—two of whom were burned to death. They also killed fourteen of the fifteen captive okapi (the fifteenth later died too). The rebels purportedly have strong links to the Congolese army, which would explain how they acquired their arsenal of heavy arms. Members of the Congolese army's 908th Battalion did some additional looting at Epulu after the Mai Mai withdrew.

This murderous attack was led by an ivory poacher named Morgan who, early in July, reportedly killed some two hundred elephants in the Ituri reserve. At the end of July members of the Simba (yet another Mai Mai group) "arrested" Morgan in North Kivu. They demanded a reward of $10,000 to transfer him into custody. The funds were not paid, and Morgan either "escaped" or paid off his captors.

The attack in Epulu was apparently motivated by Morgan's desire to stop the ICCN rangers stationed there from interfering with his poaching. Two years earlier, during a visit to the same post with a Swiss film team, I had photographed some tusks that had been confiscated at a roadblock further down the route to Nia Nia. The rangers said a group of poachers and their porters had been passing the roadblock at night while carrying the tusks. A guard called out to them, they opened fire, and he fired back. The poachers fled, dropping some of their tusks. Morgan ultimately decided to eliminate the ranger post and get rid of the conservation NGOs financing the reserve and breeding center.

An American NGO set up the Okapi Breeding Center and had been operating it for several decades. They invested around half a million dollars every year to keep it going, including providing an adequate infrastructure for the ranger force, maintaining satellite e-mail and phone links with the outside world, and running the basic tourist facilities that we enjoyed during our stay. They also employed dozens of locals to look after the captive okapis, take care of tourists, and generally maintain the facilities. And they employed all the Pygmies who brought us into the forest as they collected and sorted the okapi leaf rations. So the Okapi Breeding Center defined the economy of Epulu. Now, after the attack and several previous looting sprees and with all the okapis gone, how would anyone be motivated to start anew, especially when the overall security and governance are as bad as ever? So the bad guys win. In a country that is home to the largest United Nations peacekeeping force on the planet, costing international taxpayers over $1 million a day, criminal poachers like Morgan and his group still have free reign to do what they wish. One blogger familiar with the situation wrote, "[Morgan's group's] deliberate and exceptional cruelty against the people and okapi are shocking, but so too is the Congolese government's dereliction of the most basic of its responsibilities."

Dale talked about the drive to Kisangani and our stop at Bafwasende. Kisangani is another hellhole in the Congo. On the trip with Dale and during an earlier trip, I looked into the bush meat and ivory trade while in town. Isaaka, my medical student contact from Bili, played the role of investigator and, with a hidden camera, went into the market each day to document the availability of elephant, chimpanzee, okapi, and gorilla meat. On many days he recorded all of these items for sale. Elephant and chimpanzee were sold every day, okapi most of the time, and gorilla on Friday or Saturday after the arrival of supply trucks coming back from illegal gold mines in the Maiko forest. Isaaka also visited an ivory dealer and filmed half a dozen raw tusks about to be shipped to Kinshasa.

Kinshasa has an open and large ivory market, with raw and carved ivory on display. It's totally illegal under national law and, since practically all buyers are foreigners exporting souvenirs (usually to the Far East), it's also illegal internationally under the terms of CITES (the Convention on International Trade in Endangered Species). The DRC is a party to CITES and as such is supposed to do its share to control the illegal ivory trade. The opposite is true, obviously, and the enforcement officials in Geneva look the other way.

Kisangani is also the base for some western conservation NGOs, and, in cases where they are active in the region, their point of entry and resupply. There is also an ICCN post in town. Having tons and tons of meat from fully protected species on open display, one would expect some complaints from conservation NGOs, and maybe even ultimatums to ICCN to carry out some kind of enforcement action. But the wives of the governor and local officials seem to have no scruples about shopping for choice cuts on a daily basis. Normal law enforcement is not something most people worry about. How can a conservationist hope to stop the hunter from pulling the trigger when the end products of his poaching are on open display every day and the consumers are often the very people who control the law and its enforcement?

※

Chimps, Elephants, and Elephant Coffee at Bili. After the chiefs in Bili asked me to reactivate the Elephant Coffee conservation project, I sent Isaaka back to Epulu to report on the running of the Okapi Wildlife Reserve. I wanted him to understand all the rules and regulations governing protected areas and present the findings to the traditional chiefs, since they are the key to achieving change. Isaaka tried to convince them to sign an agreement regarding their own protected area: promising they will adhere to national laws in the future, in return for assistance and employment through a conservation project to protect elephants and the so-called "Big Chimps" of the Bili area. The negotiations went on for two years, but the main obstacle remained the same as ever: the chiefs are heavily involved in illegal gold mining as well as in trading ivory and elephant meat coming from the protected area. Mining means poachers move in to supply the miners with meat, then ship out any excess for cash. The chiefs would certainly welcome conservation funding, but they still would want to get their returns from a range of illegal activities that completely contradict any conservation objectives.

The sad thing is how promising, how biologically rich this area was until very recently. When I did my initial research on Bili in the DRC and "the lost gorillas of Bondo," I visited the Trevuren Museum in Belgium. There I came across literature going back to colonial times that listed the region as an elephant reserve. One estimate talked about 100,000 elephants living in the forests between the Mbomou and Uélé river systems. There might be a few hundred elephants left today. When I first arrived, heavy elephant poaching was going on, mostly for meat; I interviewed an elderly hunter who was just sending off his three sons with baskets of smoked elephant meat to sell just across the border in the Central African Republic. He let me photograph the meat he kept for home consumption, along with two small tusks, and told me that he had shot one elephant out of a herd of five. Seeing how small the tusks were, I asked, "Why did you shoot the smallest?" His reaction was: "What do you mean? I shot the biggest one." To me, this indicates that ivory poaching has reached a level where few real tuskers are left, which means in turn that the meat may yield a better return than the ivory.

What about law enforcement? Let me give you an example that is, I think, representative of how seriously law enforcement is taken when it comes to cases of poaching. Two hunters based in the Central African Republic crossed into Congo and to hunt an elephant. One fired a shot and injured the animal. He had no high-caliber ammunition left, so he borrowed a cartridge from his colleague and killed the elephant. The hunter who contributed the second bullet wanted half of the meat, a fight ensued, and one killed the other. The case went to court in Zemio in the CAR. The judge passed sentence: The surviving hunter was required to hunt *for the judge* for the next six months.

The nearly complete absence of law enforcement means that small-scale poachers continue killing without ever having to worry about being held accountable. Large-scale poachers such as the Janjaweed or Murahaleen from north of Darfur, who specialize in elephant poaching, work in mobile gangs. They used to come south to the Central African Republic and the Bili area every dry season to hunt. They would take the ivory and leave all the meat to the local population, which was beneficial for all concerned until there were no longer enough elephants left to make the expeditions worthwhile. At that point the poachers moved on to looting Congo's Garamba National Park, and more recently they've moved into Chad and Cameroon. They rely on a good intelligence network to learn where the final concentrations of elephants are. The last slaughter in the north of Cameroon left some 350 elephants dead in a short period of time. There was an international outcry, but not enough to stop the poachers. They boldly traveled from Cameroon back through Chad, and are said to have crossed part of the CAR. They moved completely in the open, but no national security forces felt able to take them on. The Americans, who have about a hundred Special Forces troops a little further south in the CAR, certainly had the capability to gather intelligence (via satellite and fly-overs) on the progress of what must have been a large caravan. But they showed no interest in getting involved. Neither did the French troops based in the CAR. The local security services all are familiar with the Janjaweed and Murahaleen; few are willing to risk their lives to protect elephants.

Recently, a Kenya-based conservation NGO informed me that they would yet again assist with financing another survey of wildlife in the Bili area—especially the Big Chimps and chimp cultures—and that a team of two scientists had already been sent in to begin. I made all the usual noises about the last thing the region needing was another survey and another bunch of field biologists going for some adventure in the bush. I wrote an opinion piece on this, outlining how it was a huge waste of time and resources. I wrote that we know all about elephant poaching, and about how chimps and buffalos and everything else are now targeted regularly. The last thing needed, I said, was more lifestyle artists sitting in the forest with binoculars watching monkeys or cutting more transects to count chimpanzee nests (these transects become convenient pathways into the forests for the local poachers). I suggested, more than half seriously, that the time had come for NGOs to hire eco-psychologists to work with *humans*, the local people, in order to find out what it would take to accept that the remaining few elephants are their heritage and that they might want to keep some of them around. I went on to propose that a new type of eco-missionary should be traveling with backpacks full of condoms, or, alternatively, sitting down with the ICCN and financing an enforcement team that would approach the hard-core elephant poachers with a shoot-to-kill policy.

Advocating such an approach has gotten me into trouble in the past. The notion seems to be that killing humans to protect a bunch of stupid animals is wrong; it's immoral. But when it comes to these parts of Africa, most of the hard-core poachers are little Morgans aspiring to be big Morgans. They loot villages, rape women, force porters to carry out the meat. They are bad news—and a real security problem. Once the elephants, and buffalos, and other big game that produce their big returns are gone, they are not likely to settle down as electricians or carpenters in Bangui or Kinshasa. Instead, they will turn their weapons on the local people. It's only a matter of time.

✳

Orangutans of Southeast Asia. The end of the wild is already here for many parts of Africa and certainly for most of Southeast Asia. Dale and I stopped only briefly in Burma to consider some of the Asian scene; I never took him to Kalimantan (Indonesian Borneo) or Sumatra to fly over the oil palm plantations and the open pit mining areas. Although Dale had gone to that region many years ago, looking for orangutans, a return trip would most probably not have affected him as much as it did me. While producing the photographic book *Orang Utan* (later *Great Ape Odyssey*) with Dr. Birute Galdikas almost twenty years ago, I traveled extensively around those parts. It was a different world then—one might have seen a few plantations while flying over islands of thick forests. Today, however, it is the other way around: all but a few small patches of primary forest remain. Also gone are the orangutans. The same bulldozers that flattened Kalimantan and Sumatra (and turned Indonesia into the third largest emitter of CO_2 in the world, after the United States and China) are now arriving in Africa. The result will be the same, all in the name of "development."

For 50 to 100 million years Kalimantan and Sumatra protected some of the greatest caches of biodiversity on the planet. Even twenty years ago that was true. Today it is not. The government of Indonesia has sold off its planetary heritage to the detriment of every human being on earth. Enormous stretches of rain forests have been turned into chopsticks, construction materials, and luxury items, and in many instances replanted with a monoculture of palm trees. The conservation establishment, having classified those amazing forests as "biodiversity hotspots" of planetary significance, did not manage to stop this depredation. They had (and have) no answers, although in desperation they have tried sleeping with the enemy—by which I mean they have conducted roundtable discussions in Europe and elsewhere on the subject of "sustainable" palm oil cultivation or "sustainable" logging of primary rain forests. Tell me how it can be sustainable when you're cutting down trees that were seedlings when Michelangelo was alive.

Animal welfare groups, meanwhile, try to mop up the mess by moving more and more orphaned orangutans into already overcrowded sanctuaries. They do this while scientists and conservationists argue that these orphans (like the gorilla and chimpanzee orphans in African sanctuaries) are already lost to their species' gene pool and that keeping them going, giving them a second chance, is too expensive; the money spent on the sanctuaries might be better spent helping to protect remaining wild populations. Meanwhile, however, every new orphan coming out of the forest becomes a "feel-good" advertisement for the sanctuaries: it feels good for the ordinary man or woman to give a wretched little orangutan or chimp a second chance in life, so they throw money at the animal welfare groups to keep running the sanctuaries. In the end this may do more to give an ape a second chance in life than throwing more money at the conservationists—who themselves have no track record as far as finding any kind of solution but still need donors to finance their desired lifestyles.

Some three years ago at the Zurich airport and on the tramways I saw a number of large posters showing a baby orangutan sitting in a human hand. The slogan was clever: "His life is in your hands." I soon came across the same campaign posters in Hamburg and Vienna. It was a major media campaign all over Europe. What did that cost? How much came in? How much of that money actually flowed into conservation projects and saved orphaned orangutans? I asked several NGOs those questions, but got no answers to the first two. The third question was answered by the NGO in Indonesia that was expecting to receive the funds. They stated that they had agreed to the campaign based on getting 300,000 Euros (about $327,000) for the various sanctuary operations they were looking after—probably less than one year's operating budget.

This was a typical "feel-good" conservation campaign. Many Swiss, Germans, and Austrians would pull out their wallets or make donations via their mobile phones to accept some responsibility for "the baby orangutans in their hands." They would feel better and get a good night's sleep while imagining that they had done their part. But these sanctuaries do not really play a role in conservation, although they claim they are contributing to creating awareness via education (a claim that has never been tested with any kind of serious survey). At the same time, donors to such campaigns are probably not aware that when they buy outdoor furniture from a local garden store the chance is high that it was made from illegally logged Indonesian timber; and when they buy cookies in the grocery store, the palm oil used in them contributed to orangutan habitat being cut down, animals killed, and CO_2 emissions increased.

Orangutan and other animal sanctuaries provide the settings loved by producers at Animal Planet or the Discovery Channel. The resulting films, with happy endings and human eco-heroes, are very sellable, as are all the contrived "world in order" wildlife tales. The little orangutan with a baby bottle in his hands represents a happy ending. Happy endings represent entertainment. Entertainment keeps viewers tuned in. The harsher reality of what is *really* going on out there— the fact that these sanctuaries are mere band-aids on a patient dying of a terminal cancer—is a story no one has the courage to tell. Really educating the public is not what producers at Animal Planet and the Discovery Channel are interested in. Keeping viewers from grabbing the remote because they already have had their share of bad news for the day is the overall objective.

A recent news story announced that more than four-fifths of the world's rain forests have already been destroyed, while between half and nine-tenths of the illegal logging done in tropical regions in South America, Central Africa, and Southeast Asia is managed by organized crime. Maybe the field biologists getting their PhDs by studying the last of the apes should be out spending their grants and scholarships on investigating and exposing these criminal activities. Maybe they should become conservationists. They could approach editors at National Geographic or Animal Planet or the Discovery Channel to get them to expose some of these realities, do some lobbying and campaigning and see what response they get.

Having said this, I do think that maybe things are changing somewhat. *National Geographic* magazine recently has given up its policy of political correctness (refusing to engage in advocacy); I was very pleasantly surprised to read a recent article that described the out-of-control trade in ivory and ivory products. The article went so far as to do some naming and shaming of countries and individuals. I was surprised their lawyers could be convinced to sign off on the story, having dealt with the magazine on similar proposals. Not surprisingly, the reaction from some of the culprits (in the Philippines) was immediate and strong, indicating that this kind of naming-and-shaming approach might have more potential than the old-fashioned, politically correct "good cop" tactic, which, in my opinion, got us into this mess in the first place. Why not consider a new and different approach after thirty years of failure with the politically correct one?

✸

Mong La and CITES Dale described our experience in Mong La in Myanmar's Special Region 4, right on the Chinese border. Let's put his story in context of the Convention on International Trade in Endangered Species (CITES). Clearly CITES regulations on the trade of things like tiger wine, bear bile products, ivory, and leopard claws and teeth are not being enforced at the Chinese border. At the bear bile farm (the worst case of animal cruelty I have ever seen, with methods of extraction that are no longer allowed even in China) we saw a box packed with bear bile products addressed to a person in southern China, which is as flagrant a CITES infraction as you can find.

I presented photographs of that mailing label to an enforcement official in Geneva. As with previous such evidence, he said he would—and later did—write to the authorities concerned and, predictably, got a response from Yangon that they had no control over the region. It seems he got no response from Beijing.

Since our visit to Mong La, I have visited two more such casino towns in Laos, one located across the border from China and the other bordering Thailand. Both developed along similar lines as Mong La; that is, anything goes, from gambling to prostitution to drugs to the wildlife trade. It's profitable, and profits are why these enclaves are set up; you can break any law you want maybe just a few miles from a border. In one of these enclaves, known as Boten and supposedly owned by the same drug lords as Mong La, there was a minor contretemps recently: It became public knowledge what happens when gamblers are not able to pay their debts. Our guide told us that a party who defaults on gambling debts is locked in a toilet, and a phone call is made to his family stating they have forty-eight to seventy-two hours to deliver the money or they will not see their relative again. Apparently these were not empty threats, as Laos police found and documented body parts in the local garbage pit.

With this level of violation of human rights and, of course, the laundering of money through the casinos from drug trafficking, why would anybody care about pangolins and other endangered animals and animal parts passing through these enclaves? There is no evidence that any CITES officer has ever visited one or expressed interest in doing so.

One of my interests in visiting these casino towns had to do with the trafficking of rhino horn. I recently completed documentary film shoots on the trafficking of horn and tiger products and, most recently, the totally illegal transfer of some 130 chimps and ten gorillas from Guinea to China for the new Chinese safari parks and entertainment centers springing up outside urban areas. These are outrageous violations of CITES regulations, but what can CITES do? Its ultimate enforcement tool is to suspend a member state for non-compliance. To be suspended from a UN convention and subjected to a boycott of trade in all wildlife products could amount to a serious embarrassment, a loss of face at the international level. The problem is it hardly ever happens, and when it does it is usually for failing in administrative obligations (such as filing annual reports) rather than for allowing illegal trade across international borders.

In my opinion, CITES has become part of the problem. In the Third World, officials and ministries compete for appointments to their country's CITES Management Authority, which provides for visas and international travel to attractive places like Switzerland where they can attend meetings. With such posh appointments, nepotism is bound to creep in. The jobs do not go to individuals who are qualified by educational or professional background, but rather to those who have the right connections. Unfortunately, people with the right connections in poorly governed Third World member states are often part of a corrupt elite. How does this corruption move into the CITES administration? Well, selling official export or import permits (for animals and animal products) to traders for personal profit is one way. In the case of Guinea, which exported those 130 chimps and ten gorillas to China (mostly, and some to the United Arab Emirates), the official in charge of the local Management Authority stated that he was ordered to leave blank CITES permits lying around, so various people could help themselves. This same official also alleged that when importing countries decided to check the authenticity of such permits, his e-mails were intercepted and somebody confirmed the permits on his behalf. Guinea has a twenty-year track record of manipulating the CITES system, but nothing was ever as flagrant as the ape sales, with most of these endangered primates not even originating in Guinea. Certainly they were not captive-born animals, which is one precondition for trade in endangered species like chimpanzees and gorillas.

As I already pointed out, China was the major importer of those endangered animals. Of course, China will claim that they had valid export permits, from some obscure, hypothetical company with only a P.O. box address, all officially describing those apes as "captive-born." These were illegal exports and, therefore, illegal imports—but China is not mentioned by the CITES Secretariat in any statement regarding the Guinea apes.

Article 8 of the CITES charter states that illegal importers and exporters should be prosecuted, that animals should be confiscated, and that repatriation in consultation with the country of origin should be the next step. None of this happened, and the Secretary General of CITES made clear in an interview in Geneva that this would never happen. Guinea got a warning and was asked to present another report indicating that they were making progress. (Based on our recent investigation, I would say the opposite is true.) China defended itself in a discussion during the CITES Standing Committee meeting without providing any of the specifics or addressing the evidence in place.

Meanwhile, the Secretary General of CITES flew to Beijing to present the local CITES Management Authorities with a commendation for a job well done. This seems to have been in return for a major public relations exercise by the Chinese authorities: a press release from February 2011 talks about 4,497 personnel and 1,094 vehicles involved in a series of raids trying to curtail the trade in ivory and other wildlife products. In a *National Geographic* article, Bryan Christy pointed out that the total ivory confiscated was 63.5 pounds, or about the weight of an overfed poodle. Lots of people may feel good about this ersatz progress, but the elephant and rhino slaughter continues on larger scale than ever before.

When the *Christian Science Monitor* published an article arguing for the reeducation of the Chinese middle class about elephants and ivory, Iain Douglas-Hamilton of Save the Elephants, whom Dale wrote about, responded that a more appropriate expression would be to promote a "mutual creation of awareness." So CITES and international conservation efforts are largely guided by being politically correct, not by rocking the boat. This is the route of least resistance. It has been followed for several decades, and the results are there for all to see. Is it not about time to try a different approach? The sixth extinction is upon us. It is man-made, and if anything or anybody is going to make a difference it will have to be us: Man.

In the meantime, local CITES Management Authorities based in places like Guinea, Egypt, China, or Congo, order another beer and have a good laugh about how easy, how much fun, and how lucrative it is to beat the system. It's a total choke.